HONEY AND
VINEGAR

HONEY AND VINEGAR

Incentives, Sanctions, and Foreign Policy

RICHARD N. HAASS AND
MEGHAN L. O'SULLIVAN
Editors

BROOKINGS INSTITUTION PRESS
Washington, D.C.

Copyright © 2000
THE BROOKINGS INSTITUTION
1775 Massachusetts Avenue, N.W., Washington, D.C. 20036
www.brookings.edu

Library of Congress Cataloging-in-Publication data

Honey and vinegar : incentives, sanctions, and foreign policy /
Richard N. Haass and Meghan L. O'Sullivan, editors.
   p.   cm.
   Includes bibliographical references and index.
   ISBN 0-8157-3356-4 (cloth) — ISBN 0-8157-3355-0 (paper)
   1. United States—Foreign relations—1970– 2. Economic sanctions,
American. 3. Diplomacy. I. Haass, Richard. II. O'Sullivan, Meghan L.
   JZ1480.H66 2000   00-008815
   327.73—dc21   CIP

Digital Printing

The paper used in this publication meets minimum requirements of the
American National Standard for Information Sciences—Permanence of Paper
for Printed Library Materials: ANSI Z39.48-1984.

Typeset in Minion

Composition by Cynthia Stock
Silver Spring, Maryland

ℬ THE BROOKINGS INSTITUTION

The Brookings Institution is an independent organization devoted to nonpartisan research, education, and publication in economics, government, foreign policy, and the social sciences generally. Its principal purposes are to aid in the development of sound public policies and to promote public understanding of issues of national importance.

The Institution was founded on December 8, 1927, to merge the activities of the Institute for Government Research, founded in 1916, the Institute of Economics, founded in 1922, and the Robert Brookings Graduate School of Economics and Government, founded in 1924.

The general administration of the Institution is the responsibility of a Board of Trustees charged with safeguarding the independence of the staff and fostering the most favorable conditions for scientific research and publication. The immediate direction of the policies, program, and staff is vested in the president, assisted by an advisory committee of the officers and staff.

In publishing a study, the Institution presents it as a competent treatment of a subject worthy of public consideration. The interpretations or conclusions in such publications are those of the author or authors and do not necessarily reflect the views of the other staff members, officers, or trustees of the Brookings Institution.

Foreword

American enthusiasm for using economic sanctions to advance U.S. foreign policy interests reached its peak with the passage of the Iran-Libya Sanctions Act in 1996. Since that time, many individuals in both the legislative and executive branches, as well as business representatives and academics, have come to view that propensity as misplaced. In recent years, sanctions have come under increasing scrutiny, with many credible studies calling for their more selective use. Yet, despite widespread agreement about the need to consider sanctions in a larger context that includes other policy tools, little research has been done that seriously explores alternatives to punitive policies. This book, in its examination of the strategy of engagement and the use of incentives, provides one of the first in-depth appraisals of using inducements for foreign policy purposes. In this sense, it is both a welcome extension of the debate about sanctions and an important contribution to our overall understanding of the options open to the makers of foreign policy.

Richard Haass and Meghan O'Sullivan make no pretensions about the ability of incentives to replace penalties in the repertoire of U.S. foreign policy tools. However, aided by seven experts on the cases explored in this volume, they provide an honest assessment of the strategy of engagement and highlight the need for policymakers to accord it at least as much attention as the more conventional options of military force, sanctions, covert action, and diplomacy. As demonstrated by some of the cases explored in this book, engagement—although a difficult strategy to manage—has a record of delivering success where more punitive options have failed or not been tenable. In their conclusion, Haass and O'Sullivan offer insights into where and when engagement might be most usefully employed and provide guidelines to policymakers who do adopt such strategies. Together, the cogently written case studies and the astutely argued conclusions convince the reader that, at the very least, strategies of engagement and the use of incentives deserve the greater attention of scholars and policymakers.

This book has its origins in an April 1999 conference that was hosted by the Robert R. McCormick Tribune Foundation on the wonderful premises of the Cantigny Estate outside of Chicago. It was in this setting that the authors of the case studies included in this book presented the first versions of their papers. Since that time, the authors have shaped and re-shaped their contributions, so that in the final versions included here, each chapter presents unique insights into its own case while coming together with the others to make a compelling collective argument for the greater consideration of engagement strategies. For the efforts, expertise, and enthusiasm of these authors, the editors of this volume are deeply indebted.

At the April conference, which was adroitly managed by the National Strategy Forum, participants held spirited discussions about past episodes of engagement and sought to tease out themes common to the cases at hand. Appreciation for their time and ideas is owed to all those who took part in the conference, including the authors of those case studies that became chapters in this book (Pauline H. Baker, Frederick Z. Brown, James Goldgeier, Kenneth I. Juster, Johannes Reissner, Leon Sigal, and Robert Suettinger) as well as Shaul Bakhash, Richard Behrenhausen, Neal Creighton, Catharin E. Dalpino, Richard Falkenrath, John M. Flanagin, Chas W. Freeman, Constance Freeman, Richard E. Friedman, Robert L. Gallucci, Adam Garfinkle, Jeffrey Herbst, Merle Lipton, William Long, Rodney V. MacAlister, Richard Nuccio, Marina Ottaway, Dianne E. Rennack, Gideon Rose, Sam Sarkesian, David Tarr, Earl Tilford, John Allen Williams, and Endy Zemenides. The content of this book was also influenced by many people who read the manuscript and reflected on it. To David Cortright, William Long, Scott Lasensky, Thomas Christensen, Steven Hurst, Robert S. Litwak, Udo Steinbach, and others, the editors of this book are grateful.

A large number of people were integral to the production of this book, to whom the editors would like to give special recognition. Susan Jackson and Eric Longnecker verified the manuscript, doing a thorough job despite considerable time pressures. Candice Geouge ably handled administrative concerns, as well as lent her keen eye to proofread the book. Diane Hammond did a fine job of copyediting the nine chapters of this volume, while the work of Charles Dibble in proofreading the text was greatly appreciated. For the fastidiousness of Robert Elwood in generating the index to the book, and for the creative talents of Susan Woollen and Beth Schlenoff in coordinating and designing the book cover, the editors are thankful. Finally, Becky Clark deserves acknowledgment for her ongoing efforts to market the volume.

Lastly, Brookings owes great thanks to the Robert R. McCormick Tribune Foundation for generously supporting all aspects of this project and the production of this book. Conoco, the Daimler-Chrysler Corporation Fund, the GE Fund, the John M. Olin Foundation, Inc., and the Arthur Ross Foundation also kindly provided funding which made this volume possible.

The views expressed in this book are those of the authors and editors and should not be ascribed to the organizations whose assistance is acknowledged above or to the trustees, officers, or other staff members of the Brookings Institution.

MICHAEL H. ARMACOST
President

Washington, D.C.
June 2000

Contents

1

Introduction

RICHARD N. HAASS AND
MEGHAN L. O'SULLIVAN

The strategy of engagement, or the use of incentives alongside other foreign policy tools to persuade governments to change one or more aspects of their behavior, has received relatively little scrutiny. Instead, the attention of scholars, policymakers, and pundits has generally focused on those instruments of foreign policy—in particular military force or economic sanctions—that seek to attack, harm, or otherwise diminish the capacities of the target country.[1] Thanks to a vast and ever-growing body of literature on these tools, policymakers have a better sense of the best circumstances for using these "negative" instruments as well as the ideal means of managing their use. However, with a few notable exceptions, far less effort has been devoted to discerning the most favorable circumstances and strategies for employing incentives or rewards, rather than penalties or punishments, to shape the conduct of problem regimes.[2]

The term *engagement* was popularized amid the controversial policy of constructive engagement pursued by the United States toward South Africa during the first term of the Reagan administration. However, the term itself remains a source of confusion. To the Chinese, the word appears to mean simply the conduct of normal relations. In German, no comparable translation exists. Even to native English speakers, the concept behind the word is unclear. Except in the few instances in which the United States has sought to isolate a regime or country, America arguably "engages" states and actors all the time in one capacity or another simply by interacting with them. This book, however, employs the term *engagement* in a much more specific way, one that involves much more than a policy of nonisolation. In our usage, engagement refers to a foreign policy strategy that depends to a significant degree on positive incentives to achieve its objectives. Certainly, engagement does not preclude the simultaneous use of other foreign policy instruments such as sanctions or military force. In practice, there is often considerable overlap of strategies, particularly when the termination or lifting of sanctions is used as a positive inducement. Yet the distinguishing feature of engagement strategies is their reliance on the extension or provision of incentives to shape the behavior of countries with which the United States has important disagreements.

During the cold war, the United States overlooked the egregious behavior of many regimes or leaders in the interest of securing their support against communism.[3] Post–cold war American foreign policy, however, has the luxury and the need to be more discriminating, thereby justifying further consideration of engagement strategies. The ongoing sanctions debate has exposed the drawbacks of relying on economic coercion, particularly when exerted unilaterally, as the primary instrument of foreign policy. Although there is still a range of opinion about the efficacy of sanctions and the frequency with which they should be used, some broad areas of consensus have emerged.[4] Sanctions almost always result in some economic hardship, but this impact is often insufficient or unable to force the desired political change in the target country. Moreover, sanctions can be costly for innocent bystanders, particularly the poorest in the target country and American businesses and commercial interests.[5] In addition, sanctions often evoke unintended consequences, such as the strengthening of obnoxious regimes. Given these findings, there is increasing recognition that reliance solely on punitive tools like sanctions rarely constitutes an effective foreign policy strategy. This growing awareness has been behind calls to explore more nuanced foreign policy strategies that, while possibly having a sanctions component, are not entirely dependent upon it for achieving U.S. objectives.

Moreover, just as the efficacy of sanctions has been questioned, the limits of military force have been exposed. Although military action will remain an essential foreign policy tool, its application is expensive and by no means certain of achieving its goals. Even in the face of overwhelming American military and technological superiority, recalcitrant regimes such as Iraq's Saddam Hussein have displayed the capacity to withstand military attack for surprisingly long periods of time. The more recent case of Kosovo demonstates how even the most carefully orchestrated military campaigns can result in serious collateral damage to civilians and risk creating further conflicts by straining diplomatic relationships. The bombing of Serbia also poignantly reveals that even when military force is successful in achieving most of its original objectives, the costs associated with these achievements often suggest that alternative tools may have been preferable to the use of military force.

In addition, the changing nature of post–cold war world threats makes them increasingly ill suited to being managed by strategies based on punishment alone. Threats from proliferation of weapons of mass destruction, terrorism, and ethnic conflict increasingly occupy the attention of those concerned with national security and global stability.[6] One may argue that the United States can address these issues by using sanctions to isolate and weaken regimes that sponsor and support offensive behavior as it has done in the past. However, quite possibly, insecure regimes are more likely to pose these sorts of threats to America and the international system; if so, then policies that destabilize and ostracize countries can be expected to exacerbate problems, not mitigate them.

Although these developments signal the need to consider other foreign policy strategies, the dissolution of cold war alignments has both opened new opportunities for engagement strategies and created new rationales for them. Even nations that have demonstrated little enthusiasm for adopting American ideals and norms—North Korea, Libya, and to a lesser extent, Vietnam—are today more receptive to American initiatives. Their heightened economic vulnerability and strategic insecurity in the post-Soviet era have opened new possibilities for American foreign policy strategies that involve incentives. Conversely, just as former Soviet allies are no longer bound to follow certain policies due to cold war cohesion, so too are America's allies freer to shape their foreign policy agendas subject to their own desires. If America hopes to enlist the support of its allies to deal with problem regimes, it needs policies whose appeal extends beyond rigid American preferences. Within the last decade, many of America's closest allies in Europe have revealed a preference for using incentives, rather than punitive actions, to achieve foreign policy goals.[7] Finally, because the use of certain incentives can incorporate countries into world markets while at the same time promoting American exports, engagement strategies can be consistent with U.S. economic interests and positive trends toward liberalization and global integration.

In short, the changing parameters of the post–cold war era suggest that policymakers seriously consider engagement as a foreign policy option, not only because of the need to supplement old foreign policy tools, but also because of new circumstances that may make incentives-oriented strategies particularly potent. However, it is worth highlighting that eagerness for policymakers to *contemplate* engagement strategies alongside more common foreign policy approaches is not to be confused with advocacy of the greater *use* of engagement in all situations. In part, our reluctance to promote engagement per se is based on the realization that all policies—like sanctions and military force—are applicable and useful only in specified circumstances. In addition, unlike other foreign policy tools, engagement is open to charges of not only appeasement but also moral hazard. Arguably, the provision of incentives to curtail offensive behavior could encourage others to engage in similar activities in the hopes of extracting benefits. Finally, engagement is likely to involve even higher risks and uncertainties than other foreign policy strategies given that it is a strategy that often depends on reciprocal actions between the United States and the target country.

As is evident from the fairly small existing literature on the use of incentives in foreign policy, many different engagement strategies exist, depending on such variables as the actors engaged, the incentives employed, and the objectives pursued. The first important distinction to be made in any typology of engagement is whether the strategy is conditional or unconditional. A strategy of *unconditional engagement* would offer certain changes in U.S. policy toward the country without the explicit agreement that a reciprocal act would follow. Depending on the intention behind these unconditional initiatives—and, of course, the reaction of the target country—this form of engagement may be short-lived. Charles Osgood, in his GRIT (graduated and reciprocated initiatives in tension reduction) theory offers a model of cooperation that stems from an uninvited, opening initiative by one country.[8] Although the act in itself is unconditional, the failure of the target country to reciprocate with meaningful gestures soon leads to the abandonment of the strategy; alternatively, if the initial accommodating steps are met with positive moves, cooperation ensues. President George Bush's 1991 nuclear reduction initiative, which was reciprocated by Soviet President Mikhail Gorbachev, is one instance of a GRIT approach spurring cooperation. Conciliatory gestures made by the United States to Iran in March 2000 may be another.

Another form of unconditional engagement takes a broader perspective, by regarding inducements offered to civil society and the private sector over time as playing an important role in creating openings for cooperation further down the road. In these unconditional strategies, certain initiatives or changes in U.S. policy toward the country are made without necessarily expecting, or even soliciting, reciprocal acts from the regime. This form of engagement may be implemented by nongovernmental actors, such as the programs sponsored by the National Endowment for Democracy that promote democracy and the development of institutions in many authoritarian regimes. Alternatively, this engagement may entail explicit modifications to U.S. policy, as occurred with Cuba in March 1998 and January 1999. By allowing licensed sales of food and agricultural inputs to independent entities in Cuba, by easing travel and financial restrictions, and by promoting communication between America and the island, the United States sought to buttress the development of civil society and the private sector in Cuba.[9] In doing so, the United States hoped to build momentum leading to greater political changes, which would facilitate U.S.-Cuban cooperation in the future, perhaps many years down the road.

In contrast, the expectations surrounding *conditional* engagement strategies are more contractual; in its most narrow form of the tit-for-tat process explored by Robert Axelrod, cooperation is based on a strict cycle of reciprocity.[10] However, conditional engagement can also refer to a much less tightly orchestrated series of exchanges in which the United States extends inducements for changes undertaken by the target country. These desired alterations in the behavior of the target country may be particular, well-defined policy stances, or as in the case of Alexander George's conditional reciprocity, they may refer to more vague changes in attitudes and the overall orientation of regimes.[11] While recognizing the subtle differences among the various concepts of conditional engagement, this book uses the term largely to refer to strategies of reciprocity with focused, policy objectives in mind. The Agreed Framework struck between the United States and North Korea in 1994 is one such example. In a specific effort to curtail nuclear proliferation, America linked the provision of economic incentives to the fulfillment of North Korean commitments to halt Pyongyang's development of nuclear weapons.

Architects of engagement strategies have a wide variety of incentives from which to choose. Economic engagement might offer tangible incentives such as export credits, investment insurance or promotion, access to technology, loans, and economic aid.[12] Other equally useful economic incentives involve the removal of penalties, whether they be trade embargoes, investment bans, or high tariffs that have impeded economic relations between the United States and the target country. In addition, facilitated entry into the global economic arena and the institutions that govern it rank among the most potent incentives in today's global market.[13]

Similarly, political engagement can involve the lure of diplomatic recognition, access to regional or international institutions, or the scheduling of summits between leaders—or the termination of these benefits. Military engagement could involve the extension of International Military Educational Training (IMET) both to strengthen respect for civilian authority and human rights among a country's armed forces and, more feasibly, to establish relationships between Americans and young foreign military officers.[14] These areas of engagement are likely to involve working with state institutions, while cultural or civil society engagement is likely to entail building people-to-people contacts. Funding nongovernmental organizations, facilitating the flow of remittances, establishing postal and telephone links between the United States and the target country, and promoting the exchange of students, tourists, and other nongovernmental people between the countries are some of the incentives that might be offered under a policy of cultural engagement.

This brief overview of the various forms of engagement illuminates the choices open to policymakers. The plethora of options signals the flexibility of engagement as a foreign policy strategy and, in doing so, reveals one of the real strengths of engagement. At the same time, it also suggests the urgent need for considered analysis of this strategy. The purpose of this book is to address this need by deriving insights and lessons from past episodes of engagement and proposing guidelines for the future use of engagement strategies. Throughout the book, two critical questions are entertained. First, when should policymakers consider engagement? A strategy of engagement may serve certain foreign policy objectives better than others. Specific characteristics of a target country may make it more receptive to a strategy of engagement and the incentives offered under it; in other cases, a country's domestic politics may effectively exclude the use of engagement strategies. Second, how should engagement strategies be managed to maximize the chances of success? Shedding light on how policymakers achieved, or failed, in these efforts in the past is critical in an evaluation of engagement strategies. By focusing our analysis, these questions and concerns help produce a framework to guide the use of engagement strategies in the upcoming decades.

Seven cases provide the basis for analyzing engagement strategies and formulating recommendations for their future use. In selecting these cases, we were interested in the use of incentives not with allies, or even "friendly tyrants," but with "rogues," adversaries, or other problem regimes.[15] As policymakers have preferred to use largely punitive policies to deal with these countries, the range of engagement efforts available for analysis is small. Within this grouping, we chose the most prominent examples of the use of incentives to pursue foreign policy objectives. Six of the cases examine a period of engagement between the United States and a country with which

America has had a turbulent relationship; one of the cases involves European efforts to engage a problematic regime. Although many of these cases involved economic coercion, in each instance the dominant tool employed was the extension of incentives. As a result, the success or failure in each case must be evaluated as a product of a broader engagement effort.

China is an essential component of any study of the strategy of engagement, in part because it remains one of the largest ongoing challenges to U.S. policy. Under the umbrella of a somewhat ambiguous policy toward China, the United States has pursued a range of objectives, including the security of Taiwan, human rights, nuclear nonproliferation, the stability of the Korean peninsula, democratization, trade issues, and intellectual property rights. The results of this strategy are the subject of great controversy. Some argue that engagement with the United States has influenced China to be more democratic, more market oriented, and more cognizant of international norms than it was even two decades ago.[16] However, others point to Chinese theft of U.S. nuclear technology, America's burgeoning trade deficit with China, continuing threats of force against Taiwan, and a stagnating human rights agenda as evidence that U.S. engagement with China has failed miserably.[17] In this volume, Robert Suettinger moves beyond the advocacy of such positions to examine both the difficulties and the benefits of using engagement to manage a complex relationship with a major emerging power.

Iran has posed a challenge to both European and American policymakers since its revolution in 1979. Until recently, the United States mostly lobbied for the international isolation of Iran, but Europe has sought moderation of Iranian behavior through much less extreme measures. These differences in strategy—epitomized by American legislation mandating secondary sanctions on foreign firms investing in the Iranian petroleum industry—have fueled significant friction between the transatlantic powers.[18] Nevertheless, despite American pressure, the provision of incentives has continued to be the centerpiece of European policy toward Iran. As explored by Johannes Reissner, the European Union's "critical dialogue" with Iran is an example of a particularly conciliatory engagement strategy in which Europe sought to translate its economic ties with Iran into effective pressure to advance human rights, nuclear nonproliferation, and peace in the Persian Gulf.

Iraq, while now an object of U.S. animosity, was not too long ago the subject of an American policy of engagement. From 1988 to 1990, the Bush administration sought to moderate Saddam Hussein's regime in Iraq by extending credit guarantees for trade and other selected economic incentives to the country. Kenneth Juster's chapter, in delving into this episode of American diplomacy, augments knowledge about the benefits and drawbacks of using economic engagement to accomplish strategic goals. Particularly when assessed in the wake of Iraq's 1990 invasion of Kuwait, this engagement effort raises important questions about the evaluation of such strategies and highlights some of the domestic risks of carrying them out.

North Korea and the Agreed Framework—an accord in which North Korea consented to abandon its nuclear ambitions in exchange for certain economic and diplomatic concessions from the United States, Japan, and South Korea—is perhaps the best example of the use of incentives to promote foreign policy objectives. As such, a close consideration and the extraction of accurate lessons from this case is essential for the management of similar situations bound to arise elsewhere in the near future. However, as revealed by Leon Sigal in this book, the North Korean experience is also of great utility in what it exposes about engagement efforts with extremely closed, totalitarian regimes with long histories of hostility to the United States. Moreover, U.S. endeavors to engage North Korea bring to light important issues concerning the role that American allies should and could play in U.S. engagement strategies.

South Africa is an interesting case in its own right; its inclusion in this volume is essential as the concept of constructive engagement first gained prominence in relation to the policies pursued under President Ronald Reagan. The many seemingly mutually exclusive lessons that have been drawn from this case attest to the need to reexamine this episode.[19] Moreover, the South African experience reveals the many faces of engagement. During the first term of the Reagan administration, the United States followed a policy of offering political and economic incentives in the hope of achieving strategic objectives. However, in Reagan's second term, the sequence of priorities reversed and the instruments of engagement changed; seeking improvement in the human rights situation in South Africa above anything else, the United States sought to promote civil society while imposing economic penalties. As examined in the chapter by Pauline Baker, these two periods of engagement attest to the importance of various U.S. actors and constituencies in formulating and implementing engagement strategies.

The Soviet Union and the United States were arguably intertwined in some form of engagement throughout most of the cold war. Even when America sought to contain Soviet influence most strictly, U.S. policy was formulated with the hope that it would eventually lead, in the words of George Kennan, to the mellowing of the regime and society.[20] However, the détente period of the late sixties and early seventies examined in this book most clearly meets our criteria as an episode of engagement. Soviet and American leaders made arms control pacts and commitments in other realms in anticipation of more extensive economic ties and strategic agreements. As demonstrated by James Goldgeier in this volume, although the fruits of détente ultimately fell far short of the expectations of both sides, this episode remains an important example of how America used engagement to manage a vital relationship with a major global rival.

Vietnam is an instructive case in part because it offers vivid comparisons and contrasts. The Carter administration attempted an unconditional normalization of relations with Vietnam without success; more than a decade later the Bush and Clinton administrations achieved many of Carter's goals under terms more favorable to the United States. Frederick Brown explains how such a contrast not only highlights the importance of the changing geopolitical context to engagement strategies undertaken in the wake of the cold war, but also explores important lessons the Vietnamese case offers about managing the domestic politics of engagement in the Unites States.

The concluding chapter brings together the lessons from the individual cases and synthesizes them into general guidelines for when and how to use engagement strategies. In addition, the conclusion considers the current relationships between the United States and China, Cuba, Iran, Libya, North Korea, Russia, and Syria, asking whether incentives might be better incorporated into U.S. policy. Using the general lessons extracted from the historical cases examined in this volume, the conclusion assesses the suitability of engagement and, where appropriate, suggests steps that policymakers could undertake to better advance U.S. interests in the process of moving away from the strategies of isolation currently in place.

Notes

1. Some of this scholarship has called for an in-depth consideration of incentives alongside these other tools. See Alexander L. George and Richard Smoke, *Deterrence in American Foreign Policy: Theory and Practice* (Columbia University Press, 1974), pp. 606–07.

2. Alexander L. George, *Bridging the Gap: Theory and Practice in Foreign Policy* (Washington, D.C.: United States Institute of Peace Press, 1993); David Cortright, *The Price of Peace: Incentives and International Conflict Prevention* (Lanham, Md.: Rowman and Littlefield, 1997); David Baldwin, *Economic Statecraft* (Princeton University Press, 1985); David Baldwin, "The Power of Positive Sanctions," *World Politics*, vol. 24 (October 1971), pp. 19–38. Also see William J. Long, *Economic Incentives and Bilateral Cooperation* (University of Michigan Press, 1996); Eileen Crumm, "The Value of Economic Incentives in International Politics," *Journal of Peace Research*, vol. 32 (August 1995), pp. 313–30.

3. See Daniel Pipes and Adam Garfinkle, eds., *Friendly Tyrants: An American Dilemma* (St. Martin's Press, 1991).

4. The literature on sanctions has grown tremendously in the past two years. For a range of recent opinions, see George E. Shambaugh, *States, Firms, and Power: Successful Sanctions in United States Foreign Policy* (SUNY Press, 1999); Daniel W. Drezner, *The Sanctions Paradox: Economic Statecraft and International Relations* (Cambridge University Press, 1999); Ernest H. Preeg, *Feeling Good or Doing Good with Sanctions: Unilateral Economic Sanctions and the U.S. National Interest* (Washington, D.C.: Center for Strategic and International Studies, 1999); Congressional Budget Office, *The Domestic Costs of Sanctions on Foreign Commerce* (Government Printing Office, 1999); Jesse Helms, "What Sanctions Epidemic? U.S. Business' Curious Crusade," *Foreign Affairs*, vol. 78 (January/February 1999), pp. 2–8; Richard N. Haass, ed., *Economic Sanctions and American Diplomacy* (New York: Council on Foreign Relations Press, 1998); Margaret P. Doxey, *International Sanctions in Contemporary Perspective*, 2d ed. (St. Martin's Press, 1996); David Cortright and George A. Lopez, eds., *Economic Sanctions: Panacea or Peacebuilding in a Post–Cold War World?* (Boulder, Colo.: Westview Press, 1995); Gary Hufbauer, Jeffrey J. Schott, and Kimberly Ann Elliott, *Economic Sanctions Reconsidered*, 2d ed. (Washington, D.C.: Institute for International Economics, 1990).

5. American commercial interests generally suffer disproportionately to European and other businesses because U.S. sanctions often do not command the support of other nations. As exemplified by the rise of USA*Engage, a coalition of American businesses opposing the imposition of unilateral sanctions, these interests seek—often quite effectively—to influence the formulation and implementation of American sanctions policy.

6. For example, a 1997 National Security Council document identifies ethnic conflict, weapons of mass destruction, terrorism, organized crime, and environmental damage as the major areas of global concerns today. Executive Office of the President, *A National Security Strategy for a New Century* (May 1997) (www.white house.gov/WH/EOP/NSC/html/documents/nssr-1299.pdf [January 2000]).

7. See Richard N. Haass, ed., *Transatlantic Tensions: The United States, Europe, and Problem Countries* (Brookings, 1999).

8. Charles E. Osgood, *An Alternative to War or Surrender* (University of Illinois Press, 1962).

9. See William J. Clinton, "Statement on United States Policy toward Cuba," *Weekly Compilation of Presidential Documents* (White House, January 11, 1999), pp. 7–8.

10. Robert Axelrod, *The Evolution of Cooperation* (Basic Books, 1984). Alexander George points out that tit-for-tat is most relevant in symmetrical relationships in which there is not a great imbalance of power. See George, *Bridging the Gap*, pp. 53–54.

11. George, *Bridging the Gap*, pp. 50–57.

12. Of the various inducements possible, economic ones have received the most attention. See Long, *Economic Incentives and Bilateral Cooperation*; Crumm, "The Value of Economic Incentives"; Klaus Knorr, "International Economic Leverage and Its Uses," in Klaus Knorr and Frank Trager, eds., *Economic Issues and National Security* (University Press of Kansas, 1977), pp. 99–126. In addition, the scholarship on aid, although it has tended to be more related to the literature concerning development,

is of direct relevance to studies like ours. See William J. Long, "Nonproliferation as a Goal of Japanese Foreign Assistance," *Asian Survey*, vol. 39 (March-April 1999), pp. 328–47; Carol Graham and Michael O'Hanlon, "Making Foreign Aid Work," *Foreign Affairs*, vol. 76 (July-August 1997), pp. 96–104; Steven Hook, *National Interest and Foreign Aid* (Boulder, Colo.: Lynne Rienner, 1995); Congressional Budget Office, *Enhancing U.S. Security through Foreign Aid* (CBO, 1994); Nicole Ball, *Pressing for Peace: Can Aid Induce Reform?* (Washington, D.C.: Overseas Development Council, 1992); James A. Blessing, "Suspension of Foreign Aid: A Macro-Analysis," *Polity*, vol. 13 (Spring 1981), pp. 524–35; Hans Morgenthau, "A Political Theory of Foreign Aid," *American Political Science Review*, vol. 56 (June 1962), pp. 301–09.

13. David Cortright and George Lopez identify entry into international economic (and political) institutions as the most powerful of all inducements. See Cortright, *Price of Peace*; David Cortright and George Lopez, "Carrots, Sticks, and Cooperation: Economic Tools of Statecraft," in Barnett R. Rubin, ed., *Cases and Strategies for Preventive Action* (New York: Century Foundation Press, 1998), pp. 113–34.

14. Given the prominence of the military in many regimes around the world, these relationships are important windows to key institutions during times of both peace and crisis. For instance, America's termination of IMET in Pakistan in 1990 meant that the United States had far fewer levers with which to exert influence on the Pakistani army during the coup in 1999.

15. See Pipes and Garfinkle, *Friendly Tyrants*.

16. See Bates Gill, "Limited Engagement," *Foreign Affairs*, vol. 78 (July-August 1999), pp. 65–76.

17. For just a few of the recent criticisms of the Clinton administration's current engagement policy toward China, see William Kristol and Robert Kagan, "Call Off the Engagement," *Weekly Standard*, May 24, 1999, pp. 9–10; Peter D. Feaver, "I Love Zhu, Zhu Love Me: Clinton's China Policy," *Weekly Standard*, April 26, 1999, pp. 27–29; "Broken Engagement," *New Republic*, June 14, 1999, pp. 11–12.

18. See Geoffrey Kemp, "The Challenge of Iran for U.S. and European Policy," in Haass, *Transatlantic Tensions*, pp. 48–70.

19. For instance, Robert Massie argues that international economic pressure directly contributed to South Africa's decision to democratize. Robert K. Massie, *Loosing the Bonds: The United States and South Africa in the Apartheid Years* (New York: Nan A. Talese/Doubleday, 1997); in contrast, Philip Levy argues that it is unlikely that economic pressure played a significant and positive role in these changes. Philip I. Levy, "Sanctions on South Africa: What Did They Do?" *American Economic Review*, vol. 89 (May 1999), pp. 415–20. Also see Merle Lipton, "The Challenge of Sanctions," *South African Journal of Economics*, vol. 57 (December 1989), pp. 336–61; Anton D. Lowenberg, "Why South Africa's Apartheid Economy Failed," *Contemporary Economic Policy*, vol. 15 (July 1997), pp. 62–72; Bronwen Manby, "South Africa: The Impact of Sanctions," *Journal of International Affairs*, vol. 46 (Summer 1992), pp. 193–217.

20. Kennan argued that "a long-term, patient but firm and vigilant containment of Russian expansive tendencies" would lead to "either the breakup or mellowing of Soviet power." X, [George F. Kennan], "The Sources of Soviet Conduct," *Foreign Affairs*, vol. 25 (July 1947), pp. 566–82.

2

The United States and China: Tough Engagement

ROBERT L. SUETTINGER

R elations between the United States and the People's Republic of China—since their inception in the minds of President Richard Nixon and his national security adviser, Henry Kissinger—have had a kind of vagueness and intellectual artificiality about them. Founded as they were on a mutually convenient and tactically necessary convergence of perceived interests in confronting the then-growing menace of Soviet military expansion, U.S.-Chinese relations always have been defined in the language of grand strategy and global politics. In the early stages of the relationship, this characterization of relations permitted the development of a working relationship between two governments that were divided by vast differences in history, ideology, regional perspectives, values, attitudes, culture, and economic conditions.

In 1972, when Nixon made his celebrated visit, China was an enormous, backward, politically unstable regime in the terminal stages of decay. The sweeping purge of the military leadership in the wake of Defense Minister Lin Biao's attempted coup in 1971, followed by the decapitation of the left wing of the Chinese Communist Party after the death of Mao in 1976, created significant turmoil and political uncertainty. The return of Deng Xiaoping and other party elders in the late 1970s put strategic considerations on the back burner, while the party and government focused on restoring domestic control and legitimacy.

Under Deng's guidance, China began a tortuous and controversial movement away from doctrinaire Maoism, totalitarian controls, and mass mobilization and toward economic modernization and international respect. The U.S. role in this process was essential for China not only from an economic perspective, but also as a factor in domestic Chinese politics. The successful handling of relations with the United States—very popular among the Chinese—was a source of strength for Deng in his struggle for primacy within the still divided Chinese leadership.

For the United States, China's strategic significance faded as tensions with the Soviet Union eased and détente became a practicable reality and as the war with Vietnam came to its unhappy close. Nixon's disgrace and resignation, followed by the deaths in 1976 of China's Premier Zhou Enlai and Chairman Mao Zedong, removed the key strategic thinkers who had formulated and developed the bilateral relationship. Nonetheless, the relationship continued to flourish because it brought tangible benefits to both sides in the form of increased trade and economic cooperation as well as educational, cultural, and other exchanges. The relationship also maintained its strategic guise, as it continued to provide a certain sense of strategic leverage against a still formidable, if more tractable, Soviet Union.

Strategic solidarity also provided both sides with a larger justification for sustaining and expanding the relationship. Full diplomatic normalization was accomplished on January 1, 1979, and by 1986 the United States was considering the sale of aeronautical equipment to upgrade the Chinese air force. Deng Xiaoping's early 1979 visit to the United States, in fact, began a period of amicability and cooperation in the bilateral relationship that contributed both to China's economic development and to the Reagan administration's growing confidence in dealing with Asian issues. Talk of friendship and cooperation, however, only barely disguised growing divergences between the two countries on matters pertaining to Taiwan and its relationship with the United States, China's trade policy and its growing surplus with the United States, and China's approach to the proliferation of weapons of mass destruction.

The suppression of democracy activists by the Chinese People's Liberation Army (PLA) on June 4, 1989, fundamentally changed the parameters of the bilateral relationship. Support in the United States for a cordial relationship evaporated nearly overnight as the public and the Congress looked to punish China for its actions. The following year, when the dissolution of the Soviet Union began to be more evident, the strategic rationale for maintaining a cooperative relationship was badly damaged. Although President Bush tried to maintain a minimal level of cooperation, Tiananmen and its aftermath left him little option but to go along with public and congressional opinion. The brutality of the June 4 repression and the continuing perceived resistance of China to U.S. policy initiatives in a number of areas created a profound sense of distrust among legislators and administration leaders alike, resulting in sanctions becoming the policy tool of choice for dealing with the People's Republic.

In the wake of Tiananmen, unilateral economic sanctions were imposed in several areas (some remaining in place until today):

—Military aid and weapons trade were banned in 1989 (a further embargo was placed on the import of light arms and ammunition into the United States in 1994).

—Nuclear trade and cooperation agreements were suspended.

—Support for new Multilateral Development Bank loans for China was revoked in 1990, unless the loans were for the purpose of satisfying basic human needs.

—Activities of the Overseas Private Investment Corporation and the Trade and Development Agency were canceled starting in 1990.

—Export of U.S. satellites and items on the munitions control list was prohibited (although waiver clauses enabled this trade to continue under both the Bush and Clinton administrations).

—Import of items produced by prison labor was proscribed.

—Export licenses for crime control and detection equipment were prohibited.[1]

China had already been under certain sanctions restrictions since before June 1989. For example, China has been in a specially restricted group for U.S. exports, particularly high-tech materials. Moreover, it is ineligible for the generalized system of preferences (GSP) because it is ruled by the Communist Party.[2] China has also been denied permanent most-favored-nation (MFN) trade status since 1951 (modified by the Jackson-Vanik Amendment to the Trade Act of 1974), although Congress may approve permanent normal trade relations for China in 2000.

In addition to the sanctions imposed after Tiananmen, the Bush administration froze high-level contact with Beijing, breaking off military-to-military ties and limiting official civilian meetings to the assistant secretary level. These latter restrictions were not adhered to in July 1989, when National Security Adviser Brent Scowcroft and Deputy Secretary of State Lawrence Eagleburger visited Beijing to clarify the new parameters of the relationship.

Disregarding both public opinion polls and congressional anger after Tiananmen, President Bush worked to ensure that the basic nature of the relationship was not significantly changed. He made full use of waiver authority for permitting American satellites to be launched on Chinese rockets and worked to include China in UN actions pertinent to the growing crisis in the Persian Gulf. He also vetoed congressional efforts to deny MFN trade status to China.[3]

In the presidential election campaign of 1992, Democratic candidate William Clinton criticized Bush's China policy on several occasions, hinting that he would take a tougher approach in support of the U.S. goals of human rights, trade, and nuclear nonproliferation. After his election, President Clinton took steps to follow through on his campaign rhetoric, the most important of which was to link the extension of China's MFN privileges to the achievement of an "overall significant improvement" in human rights.

On May 28, 1993, President Clinton signed an executive order extending China's MFN status for an additional year and established conditions for the continuation of MFN in 1994. Those conditions included requiring the secretary of state to certify that "overall, significant progress" had been made in several areas related to human rights: liberalizing emigration policy, ending exports of prison labor goods, releasing political prisoners, permitting international monitoring of prison conditions, protecting Tibet's "distinctive religious and cultural heritage," and improving access to international radio and television broadcasts.[4] President Clinton also warned that sanctions would be imposed if it were proven that China had violated the Missile Technology Control Regime (MTCR) guidelines banning the export of certain classes of ballistic missiles.[5] Thus the stage was set for a significantly more confrontational approach toward China than that pursued under the Bush administration.

From Sanctions to Engagement

As a matter of record, China has long opposed in principle the threat or imposition of economic sanctions, particularly in circumstances in which their use was unilateral in nature. China has been somewhat more pragmatic in cases of multilateral sanctions directed at another country, such as UN-approved sanctions on Libya and Iraq, voting in the United Nations with the majority when it perceived such a move to be in its interest. In response to sanctions directed against itself, however, Beijing has been generally much more obstinate, describing sanctions-related legislation being considered by the U.S. Congress as a "gross interference" in Chinese internal affairs.

But as Robert Ross points out, China has responded to unilateral U.S. sanctions aimed at influencing its own behavior with caution and shrewd calculation.[6] Ross judges, for example, that China's reactions to various U.S. sanctions reflect a calculus that includes the importance of the behavior being sanctioned, the domestic political flexibility of the regime, the likelihood of the United States actually imposing sanctions, and the American domestic political costs involved in the issue. He concludes that limited sanctions, when applied in a context that holds out prospect for improvement in overall relations, can be effective with China.[7] He also notes that when U.S. sanctions policy is clear and unambiguous, or when the president's flexibility is limited by partisan dispute, China is more likely to choose an accommodationist approach.[8] He draws these conclusions based on studies of China's response to U.S. human rights sanctions as examples of failed sanctions, while observing that Beijing's reaction to American actions and threats on nonproliferation issues has been more responsive.[9] Another critical distinction for Chinese leaders is between efforts to change China's external behavior and attempts to force change in its domestic policies. Given China's history of foreign encroachment, its leaders—and general populace—are particularly sensitive to anything that might be construed as interference in its internal affairs.

China's reaction to the Clinton administration's approach, therefore, could best be described as a pragmatic effort to get the sanctions withdrawn with the least possible domestic political and economic costs. Following the executive order linking MFN and human rights, China expressed "strong opposition" to the move but did not make clear whether it would cooperate with the approach in detail. Although some China experts in the United States doubted the wisdom of the linkage, other analysts at the time believed China would cooperate, mainly because the changes called for were not onerous and the vague standard of judgment appeared easy to meet.[10]

However, the approach did not really get tested early, as the overall relationship continued to drift downward in other areas during the summer of 1993. In July, both chambers of the U.S. Congress considered resolutions opposing Beijing's high-profile bid to host the year 2000 summer Olympics, moves that, while inconsequential to the actual selection process (the International Olympic Committee chose Sydney over Beijing), nonetheless incensed both the Chinese government and public opinion in China.[11] In August, based on intelligence evidence, Washington imposed limited sanctions on China for violating restrictions of the MTCR on sales of ballistic missile equipment.[12] Although China had long been suspected of having shipped M-11 missiles and launchers to Pakistan, no conclusive evidence of the transfer had yet emerged, and the Clinton administration chose the less punitive sanctions as a means of warning Beijing (and reassuring the Congress) of its serious intent to enforce its policies on nonproliferation. The low point probably was reached in early September, when a U.S. challenge inspection of the Chinese freighter *Yin He*—on suspicion it was carrying restricted chemical weapons compounds to the Middle East—turned up nothing. China demanded, but did not receive, an apology, compensation for economic losses, and an assurance that the incident would not be repeated.

At the same time as it was criticizing Chinese human rights abuses and imposing sanctions on its nonproliferation behavior, the administration appeared to view China in a somewhat positive light. Particularly after Deng Xiaoping reinvigorated economic and commercial reform in 1992, both the American business community and U.S. officials recognized there were trends operating in China that were in America's interests to promote. All saw the Chinese government's acceptance of private enterprise and entrepreneurship, encouragement of foreign investment, development of commercial law, and increased freedom of movement for citizens as leading ultimately toward a more pluralistic society and internationally cooperative regime.

Crafting a policy that discouraged China from pursuing goals and taking actions the United States did not like, while at the same time encouraging behavior that was perceived to be consistent with U.S. interests and ideals, would have been a daunting task for any administration. For the Clinton administration, it was particularly challenging, given its own domestic policy focus, the distraction of smaller international problems gone awry, such as Bosnia, Haiti, and Somalia, and the occasional lack of full accord among the principal spokespersons for the administration's foreign policy. At the outset of the administration, there seemed to be clarity about the goals of the U.S.-China relationship—to change China's behavior in a variety of areas, particularly human rights—but not about the means to be used to attain them. The first inclination of President Clinton, as noted, was to punish China into compliance with vague American norms of behavior. When that did not succeed, a more pragmatic approach was sought. Ultimately, all agreed upon the general use of the term *engagement*, but not on a definition of what that term meant.[13]

The term *engagement* can be used and understood in a number of ways, depending upon the context of the relationship being described. With respect to China, the Clinton administration has used the term in three ways. This conceptual confusion has resulted from the fact that the word itself has been overused and poorly defined by a variety of policymakers and speech writers. This ambiguity has contributed to domestic and international bewilderment about both the meaning of the term and the various policies and attitudes that engagement has been intended to portray.

First, in its broadest and most general sense, the Clinton administration used the term *engagement* to signify a policy that implied involvement and interaction as opposed to isolationism. Such a formulation was largely intended for the domestic American audience. This usage entailed a willingness to continue to be involved actively in international affairs, and especially to provide international leadership, rather than retreating from international responsibilities and paying more attention to American domestic issues. In a post–cold war world, with a president known to be more interested in domestic issues, the Clinton administration felt obligated to defend its actions in Haiti, Somalia, Bosnia, and the Middle East as constituting positive engagement, consistent with American interests. Secretary of State Warren Christopher gave voice to this philosophy in September 1993, in a speech at Columbia University. "The United States chooses engagement. . . . We must reject isolationism for the dangerous argument that it is. . . . We must remain engaged not out of altruism . . . but because there are real American interests that will suffer if we are seduced by the isolationist myth."[14]

The second way in which engagement was used by the Clinton administration in reference to China was to connote a strategic agenda involving the carefully considered extension of incentives and penalties to influence Beijing's behavior. This strategy was conceived as an alternative to a punishment-or-sanctions-only means of dealing with recalcitrant or hostile states. Its rhetorical opposite appears to be containment, the policy applied to the Soviet Union and China from the 1940s to the early 1970s. In this sense, engagement implies a willingness to use positive incentives as a means of rewarding good behavior and, to a certain degree, linking these incentives to other areas of behavior. National Security Adviser Anthony Lake, in a speech delivered the day after the Christopher speech cited above, appeared to be reflecting both this somewhat more strategic understanding of the term *engagement* and the ambivalence about China that had characterized the administration from its outset. Lake called for the United States to pursue a "strategy of enlargement—enlargement of the world's free community of market democracies."[15] China, however, did not fit into a neat category, and Lake's description of the administration's China policy did not provide much clarity. China was not lumped in with hostile "backlash" or "rogue" states like Iran or Iraq, but neither was it a new democracy, like Russia, and certainly it was not included among the friendly or cooperative nations with which the United States would work together in a multilateral context to achieve common goals. Advocating engagement in this strategic sense, Lake declared:

> We cannot impose democracy on regimes that appear to be opting for lib-eralization, but we may be able to help steer some of them down that path while providing penalties that raise the costs of repression and aggressive behavior. These efforts have special meaning for our relations with China. ... It is in the interest of both our nations for China to continue its eco-nomic liberalization while respecting the human rights of its people and international norms regarding weapons sales. That is why we condition-ally extended China's trading advantages, sanctioned its missile exports and proposed creation of Radio Free Asia. We seek a stronger relationship with China that reflects both our values and our interests.[16]

On balance, Lake's position on China appeared to focus on the negative and to place the onus for improving bilateral relations on Beijing. His advo-cacy of "enlarging" democracy throughout the world must have had a chill-ing effect on Beijing, reinforcing the growing negative perspective of hard-liners in the regime about the future of bilateral ties. Unlike engage-ment, enlargement (*kuoda*) was clearly understood and was synonymous with expansionism.

The third manner in which the term *engagement* has been used is in the sense of a general dialogue between high-level U.S. and Chinese officials. This usage of the term is not entirely distinct from the second usage; origi-nally, *engagement* in the second, or strategic, sense of the word was believed to encompass dialogue as an incentive to be offered to the Chinese. How-ever, as U.S.-Chinese relations progressed, this dialogue came to represent the engagement itself. The prominence of dialogue on its own is in large part a reflection of dissatisfaction that developed within the U.S. govern-ment—particularly among senior officials in the Departments of State and Defense—over the general direction of U.S. policy toward China, which they saw as being in a potentially dangerous downward spiral. These officials, who included Assistant Secretary of State for East Asian and Pacific Affairs Winston Lord, believed that the restrictions placed on high-level contacts and dialogue between the United States and China after Tiananmen posed both a practical and a psychological burden on the relationship. Engaging with senior policy officials in China meant seeking to communicate more effectively with them so as to promote better understanding of U.S. policies and positions. Proponents believed that enhanced communication also would enable the United States to bring more effective pressure on Beijing to adjust some of its troubling policies, particularly in nonproliferation. The opposite of this concept of engagement could best be described as shunning, or sinophobia, which had prevented substantive high-level meetings from taking place since 1989. Implicit in this notion of engagement was the premise that linkages should *not* be made between issue areas (such as human rights and trade). Specific issue areas should be dealt with on their own merits, and problems in one area should not impede progress in other areas.

This third and final usage of *engagement*—as a dialogue between U.S. and Chinese officials—ultimately became known as *comprehensive engagement* and, as a policy, began to be put in place in September-October 1993. There was still confusion about the goals and outlines of the new policy and how it fit with the administration's enlargement approach being articulated at the same time. Although the policy was approved at a senior-level Principals Committee interagency meeting in September, its implementation was not publicly discernible until November, when Assistant Secretary of Defense Charles W. Freeman traveled to Beijing, breaking the four-year ban on high-level defense-military visits to capitals.[17] Freeman and other administration officials touted the new approach as a means of improving communication with the Chinese government, and particularly with senior PLA officials, in hopes that more regular contacts would eliminate misunderstandings and enable better resolution of nuclear nonproliferation issues.

The policy change was also intended to facilitate a meeting between President Clinton and China's President Jiang Zemin at the planned "leaders meeting" at the first expanded session of the Asia Pacific Economic Cooperation (APEC) forum at Blake Island, Washington, in November 1993.[18] China, of course, had long sought to bring about more high-level meetings, as they would serve as a symbolic emergence from the political isolation into which China had been cast since Tiananmen. Members of Congress, however, were determined to ensure that Beijing did not see the new approach as an easing of pressure. Representative Nancy Pelosi of California, one of the strongest critics of China in the Congress, gave the approach qualified approval, saying "There is no problem as long as we continue to put pressure on China where it's needed."[19]

Practicing Engagement: Wins and Losses

Following the summit meeting at Blake Island, cabinet-level visits to China picked up sharply in 1994, with both Agriculture Secretary Mike Espy and

Treasury Secretary Lloyd Bentsen visiting in January. Bentsen's practice of engagement was quite fruitful: not only did he revive the Joint Economic Commission consultations, but he also signed a memorandum of understanding for implementing the bilateral agreement on preventing the export to the United States of products made by Chinese prison labor. Given that this was one of the areas in which "overall significant progress" was required for the extension of MFN in 1994, the Chinese were clearly signaling their approval of the new approach.

China had reason to be satisfied with the approach. It moved Washington away from a sanctions-based policy, brought senior American officials to Beijing in ways that helped restore the regime's still tattered legitimacy and prestige, and provided opportunities to pit U.S. government agencies against one another. Once President Clinton decided to break the linkage between human rights and China's most-favored-nation trade status in May 1994, China's position eased even further, as it was by then clear that the United States was not prepared to invoke sanctions that would damage important sectors of the American economy. The warm reception accorded to Commerce Secretary Ron Brown by Chinese officials in August 1994 was both a reward for business pressure on the White House to extend MFN trade status and a response to Brown's expressed desire to build a more healthy relationship with China through "commercial diplomacy."

The experience of the State Department was more mixed, however, and in some ways the interaction between State Department and Chinese officials amounted to a setback for engagement. Although Secretary of State Warren Christopher had met with China's Foreign Minister Qian Qichen on several occasions, Christopher's first visit to China in March 1994—months before the delinking of human rights and MFN trade status for China—was a debacle. Christopher's agenda was dominated by demands for progress on the human rights criteria set down by the executive order of May 1993, to which the Chinese had responded negatively. Consistent with that policy, Christopher had made several public statements in which he indicated that China's MFN status was at risk unless the Chinese were more forthcoming in addressing the human rights concerns of the United States. Moreover, just one month earlier, the Department of State had issued its annual report on China's human rights practices, which was harshly critical of Beijing's record. The State Department's other key concern, nuclear nonproliferation, remained in sharp dispute, as China refused to discuss the issue until the United States lifted the MTCR-related sanctions it had imposed on China in August 1993.

The atmospherics for Christopher's visit were further marred by the arrests by Beijing authorities of several prominent dissidents just before his arrival. That action probably was triggered by fear that Christopher would try to meet—either publicly or clandestinely—with dissidents, as Assistant Secretary of State John Shattuck had done in February 1994. Public pressure grew for Christopher to cancel his visit to protest the arrests. Although he completed the trip, the talks were icily formal and did not contribute to an overall improvement of the relationship. Christopher himself declined to attend a number of ceremonial events of the sort the Chinese consider an important part of engagement. These refusals—as Christopher's trip took place during a plenary meeting of China's National People's Congress during which considerations of respect and "face" are especially sensitive—probably smarted even more than was intended. Neither did the trip achieve significant progress in altering China's approach to human rights issues. Although Christopher made some progress on the president's human rights conditions for MFN extension, it was nowhere close to enough.

The Washington meeting between Christopher and Qian in October 1994, several months after the delinking of human rights and trade status, proved somewhat more successful. In that situation, the United States had a clear agenda: improving China's acceptance of the provisions of the MTCR as relevant to its missile exports. It had a specific incentive to offer, namely the lifting of the sanctions it imposed in 1993 for M-11-related technology transfers to Pakistan and the easing of restrictions on U.S. commercial satellites being launched on Chinese carrier rockets. And it held out the possibility of another Clinton-Jiang summit meeting at the APEC forum as another incentive for China's cooperation. Although China continued to refuse formally to join the twenty-three-member MTCR, it did promise to ban sales or transfers of missiles that exceeded MTCR parameters (300-kilometer range, 500-kilogram payload).[20]

One of the most successful examples of active engagement to solve specific problems was the experience of the Office of the United States Trade Representative in resolving serious disputes over China's illegal piracy of American intellectual property.[21] On the face of it, U.S. efforts to force China to address its concerns on intellectual property rights might be used as a case study for sanctions that worked. The illegal piracy of copyrighted music, film, and computer software programs by Chinese criminals, combined with lax enforcement by Chinese authorities of their own laws and regulations, had led to U.S. industry losses estimated at $800 million by 1993.[22] After lengthy negotiations and efforts to get Chinese authorities to resolve the problem, the Office of the Trade Representative, under statutory authority of Section 301 of the Trade Act of 1974 and the Omnibus Trade Act of 1988, threatened to impose 100 percent tariffs on a specified range of

Chinese imports to the United States. Each time, the Chinese government backed down, making significant changes in both its trade and legal systems to accommodate U.S. demands.

However, the process by which officials of the Office of the Trade Representative educated, persuaded, and assisted Chinese officials—from customs inspectors to judges—to bring about important changes in China's trade practices, legal system, and structure of political responsibility is better understood in the context of engagement rather than sanctions. Without those efforts, it is unlikely the sanctions (or rather, the threat of sanctions, since they were never actually imposed) would have achieved such positive results. Although extremely time-consuming and intense, the efforts of the Office of the Trade Representative showed that engagement, carefully planned and expertly executed, could bring about significant change in China's behavior, even inside its own borders.[23]

From Engagement to Management to Strategic Partnership

Although there were successes and disappointments in U.S. efforts to engage Chinese leaders in resolving problems through dialogue and cooperation, the relationship as a whole continued to flounder through 1996. Critics in the United States continued to assail shortcomings in the key issue areas in which the United States had been the *demandeur*—especially of human rights and nuclear nonproliferation—and had achieved the least results. As partisan divisions within the Congress and between the Republican Congress and the Democratic executive branch grew more rancorous after the 1996 elections, China policy became even more controversial.

However, in terms of bilateral relations, the principal problem was the one that had dogged every administration since Nixon: Taiwan. While it is beyond the scope of this chapter to detail the history of the Taiwan issue or present its nuances in a comprehensive manner, suffice to say that, from Beijing's perspective, the handling of the question of Taiwan's status and relationship to China is the sine qua non of healthy U.S.-Chinese relations. In mid-1995, the Clinton administration's comprehensive engagement strategy with China was beginning to show some positive results, particularly in international property rights and other trade issues, and the relationship appeared to be generally on the mend. However, President Clinton's May 1995 decision—under heavy pressure from Congress—to permit Taiwan President Lee Teng-hui to visit Cornell University to receive an honorary degree (and in effect, to kick off Lee's presidential election campaign) sent U.S.-Chinese relations into another sharp tailspin.

China's reaction to the Lee visit was extreme but indicated clearly the domestic sensitivity of the issue in Beijing. After warning for months of serious consequences if Lee were permitted to make the visit, and being reassured by Secretary Christopher that such a visit was not consistent with the "unofficial" relationship between Taiwan and the United States, Beijing leaders evidently believed they had no alternative but to take serious steps in response. Beginning in mid-June, Beijing broke off all bilateral dialogues with Washington, withdrew its ambassador, and initiated a series of military exercises, including missile launches into the Taiwan Strait, which eventually drew a military response from the United States. From slow mend and engagement, the relationship had suddenly deteriorated into crisis and confrontation.

Interestingly, it was the administration's engagement-as-dialogue approach that helped move the relationship out of the doldrums and into a more productive phase. In January 1996, as part of a review of policy toward China (with which this author was involved), it was decided that efforts needed to be made to manage better the bilateral relationship, anticipating problems and looking for solutions in advance of the headlines. Doing so required a more sustained and detailed communication process—at a high level—to avoid misunderstandings and misperceptions on both sides.

National Security Adviser Lake chose to play a more active role in this process than he had in the past. He invited vice foreign minister and head of the Foreign Affairs Office of the State Council, Liu Huaqiu (the closest counterpart to Lake) to an off-site meeting in rural Virginia on March 8, 1996, for an in-depth (it turned out to be nearly seven hours) discussion of the entire range of issues in the U.S.-Chinese relationship. Taking place as it did while China was launching M-9 missiles into the Taiwan Strait, the Taiwan issue dominated the discussion, but other issues were also raised, including trade and international property rights, human rights, nuclear nonproliferation, and Korea. Lake's approach was one of laying out U.S. strategic goals in the Asia-Pacific region, making certain China understood what the United States planned to do and why, making clear what the United States wanted China to do, and listening carefully to China's corresponding presentation.[24] Even though the Taiwan Straits crisis actually came to a head following the meeting, with the United States dispatching two aircraft carrier battle groups to the vicinity, the Lake-Liu meeting established a precedent, a larger context for managing the relationship jointly, and a point of contact for senior Chinese policymakers. These developments enabled the Taiwan crisis to be surmounted more readily, and with less mutual ill will, than might otherwise have been the case.

In a follow-on trip to Beijing in July 1996, Lake took the step of attempting to put the bilateral relationship into a strategic framework. Although his own depiction of his presentation as a "strat rap" (strategic rap)[25] suggests that he did not take it all that seriously at the outset, Lake developed his ideas carefully and coherently. In broad strokes, he sketched out a worldview in which the established big powers worked cooperatively (rather than competitively, as implied in the current Chinese "multipolar world" thesis) to extend peace and economic development throughout the world, and he indicated China had a key role to play as one of the global powers. He also, for the first time, conveyed to China the president's willingness to exchange state visits with China's President Jiang Zemin.[26] Following the Lake visit, and especially in Clinton's second term, when Samuel R. Berger replaced Lake as national security adviser, administration officials began justifying engagement in somewhat different terms—as a process of "integrating" China into the international community so that it would voluntarily observe and contribute to the growth of international norms in nuclear nonproliferation, trade, human rights, and environmental protection.[27]

The exchange of summits—Jiang's visit to the United States in October 1997 and Clinton's trip to China in June-July 1998—gave the appearance that the bilateral relationship had achieved breakthrough success and that a new plateau of cooperation had been reached. The administration pointed out that it had achieved important agreements on nuclear nonproliferation (China signed the Comprehensive Test Ban Treaty, cut off assistance to the Iranian nuclear program, and tightened export controls on nuclear-related materials in 1997), human rights (China signed two UN human rights conventions and released several high-profile political prisoners, including Wei Jingsheng in 1997 and Wang Dan in 1998), and other issues. The two presidents had reached such a level of comfort with each other that they could engage in spirited debates on each other's national television about controversial issues. They agreed publicly to describe U.S.-Chinese relations as moving toward a "constructive strategic partnership" in the twenty-first century.

Ironically, however, the bilateral relationship is still in very fragile condition. In the United States, support for the administration's China policy reached an all-time low in 1999 after lengthy congressional investigations into alleged illegal campaign contributions by China to the Democratic National Committee and successful espionage activities by China against American nuclear research laboratories. Reports of expanded Chinese missile deployments opposite Taiwan elicited calls for more active defense cooperation between Taiwan and the United States, including possible joint development of a ballistic missile defense system. Crackdowns against democratic activists in late 1998 renewed calls for a tougher approach on human rights, while critics of trade relations with China cited the $60 billion surplus in 1998 as a reason for reassessing the entire relationship. Numerous commentators observed that China and the United States were not strategic partners, but strategic adversaries. Others went further, accusing the Clinton administration of appeasement, kowtowing, and treason.[28]

In China, hopes likewise have been disappointed for a significant turnaround in the relationship. President Clinton's unwillingness—evidently for domestic political reasons—to accept China's sweeping concessions on market access issues and agree to its accession to the World Trade Organization (WTO) during Premier Zhu Rongji's April 1999 visit to Washington left Zhu and other economic reformers angered and vulnerable to criticism at home. However, the most shocking event for Beijing was the accidental bombing—by U.S. and NATO forces attacking Serbia—of China's embassy in Belgrade on May 7, 1999, which killed three Chinese journalists and wounded twenty embassy staffers. China responded with a paroxysm of rage and anti-Americanism and a week of government-organized protests in front of U.S. embassies and consulates in China, which did significant property damage. The Chinese media denounced American "hegemonism," cultural imperialism, racism, and anti-Chinese bias. Similar to what happened in past critical disputes, various "dialogues" were temporarily suspended. As in the United States after Tiananmen, senior political leaders, opinion makers, and ordinary Chinese citizens began to ask questions about why China should seek friendship with the United States or try to establish a strategic partnership.

However, despite the surfeit of ill will and suspicion on each side, U.S.-Chinese relations have recently again shown their resilience. Since the November 1999 signing of an agreement to facilitate China's entry into the WTO, some analysts have noted a gradual warming of relations between America and China. While this is a welcome development, the coming year—with U.S. presidential elections, ongoing friction between China and Taiwan, and a possible U.S. embrace of missile defense—will continue to provide challenges to the relationship.

Observations and Conclusions

The twists and turns of the U.S. policy of engagement with China suggests several problems and lessons. The first is that it is essential to provide more conceptual and substantive clarity to the use of the term *engagement*. The expression has become shopworn to the point that there is little agreement on what it actually means. Most recently, it has come to symbolize Republican dissatisfaction with both the content and the conduct of the Clinton administration's China policy.

Similarly, engagement in the second usage of the term laid out earlier in this chapter—that is, as a grand strategy of managing a strategic relationship through the explicit offering of incentives and the threat of sanctions—has not been particularly successful as a strategy for changing the Chinese government's internal political behavior, at least not in ways visible to critics in the United States. Efforts to link MFN trade status with Chinese human rights failed abjectly, only delivering the Clinton administration a painful retreat and a huge amount of U.S. domestic criticism. China's modern history is in many ways focused on recovering from and preventing foreign interference in its domestic affairs. Linkage that seeks to force change in China's management of its internal security is resented and resisted. Even were this not the case, linkage of one or more issue areas to progress in another puts the entire relationship at risk.

Neither has this form of strategic engagement influenced China to adopt new policies on international issues, mainly because there were few explicit incentives the United States could offer that China did not already have. Although China occasionally complained that the United States sought to isolate and contain it, China is a member in good standing of the international community. It will expand or contract its interaction with the international community, contribute or detract from consensus on international norms as its leadership sees fit, not in response to American incentives.

China is too large, complex, and interdependent with the United States for Washington to try to manipulate the entire relationship toward a particular strategic, economic, or other goal. Complicating any such efforts is the reality that the creation of a web of overlapping relationships between China and the United States has drawbacks as well as benefits. While such a web might induce China to alter its behavior on one front, it would also constrain the United States by inhibiting American policy flexibility in a similar way. One need only take note of the annual ritual congressional voting on China's normal-trade-relations (formerly most-favored-nation) status to see the web process operating in reverse. The intense lobbying of Congress and the executive branch taken up every year by well-organized and well-financed business organizations attests to the fact that engagement creates reverse dependencies as well, making the reversal of American policy a costly proposition.

Finally, the U.S. government (including both executive and legislative branches) is too cumbersome, disaggregated, and diverse to enforce the kind of rigid discipline that such a carefully managed strategic engagement process entails. Particularly when the presidency and Congress are controlled by different parties, managing a foreign relations process that does not involve the most urgent matters of national security has become extraordinarily difficult.

In contrast, engagement in the third sense of a dialogue, as a process of communication and management of relations or as a means to an end, should be not only maintained, but also strengthened and reaffirmed. Engagement in this most modest sense of the word is indispensable to the achievement of any American foreign policy goals with China and, when clearly understood and effectively practiced, can achieve significant results in changing Chinese behavior. It should not be seen as an alternative to sanctions, nor should it be regarded as relying principally on incentives (or in the overused metaphor, the "carrot") rather than disincentives (the "stick"). Successful engagement does not necessarily preclude the use or threat of sanctions.

This realistic sort of engagement involves carefully identifying U.S. goals, developing the most effective and appropriate means of achieving them, and working intensively with the existing government of the target state to progress toward those goals. That entails developing a thorough understanding of the domestic political context of the target country and working with the government bureaucracy, the legal system, and the press of the target country to build support for U.S. positions. It requires patience and persistence—as quick results are unlikely—and recognition of circumstances in which compromise may be appropriate. Obviously, such engagement is not going to be successful in all cases, and there should be a clear identification of which policy objectives may not be amenable to an engagement approach. The benefits and drawbacks of this form of engagement should be understood before the process is embarked upon. Most notably, successful engagement involves:

—*A labor-intensive process.* Engagement with China requires U.S. negotiators to work extremely hard in cooperation with Chinese authorities to bring about changes. On occasion, different bureaucracies must be sought out for help in making the American case.

—*Giving and getting.* U.S. negotiators must bring more than demands to the table. Chinese officials expect to negotiate and must see a tangible benefit to China before they will change policies. "Integration into the international community" in the abstract is not an incentive.

—*According respect.* Engagement requires a willingness to treat others with respect, even if they sometimes do not deserve it. Chinese leaders put great store in symbolic actions and monitor very carefully the degree to which foreign countries treat China, and the leaders themselves, with dignity and esteem. Given China's history of subjugation by foreign powers in the last two centuries and the importance of "face" in Chinese culture, it is difficult to overstate the importance of this factor. U.S. negotiators should keep in mind that sometimes the form of communication with China is as important as, or even more important than, the substance.

—*Involving the leadership.* Whether the issue is intellectual property rights, nuclear equipment sales, human rights covenants, or WTO protocols, senior Chinese leaders, including President Jiang Zemin and Premier Zhu Rongji, will need to be brought into the decisionmaking process at some point. Personal engagement by their American counterparts is an important element in completing the process.

—*Defining clear goals.* U.S. negotiators need to ensure that Chinese officials understand clearly what the United States wants. Demands must be specific, focused, achievable, and consistent. "Moving the goalposts" should be avoided, particularly in late stages of negotiations.

—*Maintaining domestic support.* Communicating U.S. goals and approaches in specific issues to members of Congress, nongovernmental organizations, industry groups, and other constituencies can have a positive impact on the outcome of long negotiations with the Chinese. They can provide not only political support, but also information and communication through their own channels.

—*Keeping alternative policy tools handy.* Engagement does not have to equate to being nice. Sanctions and other disincentives will be necessary in dealing with the Chinese. There should be no illusions about friendship or partnership when important interests are at stake. Used sparingly and carefully, sanctions have proven effective in some instances.

There are, in sum, no real alternatives to a policy of engagement—at least in the sense of maintaining a dialogue—with China. Its economy is too large to be susceptible to economic sanctions or a trade embargo, unless the United States is prepared to inflict significant damage on its own and other Asian economies in the process. China's military, while no match for U.S. armed forces, will not be intimidated by threats. Its political system, while unpopular and overly reliant on repression, does not appear to be in danger of collapse.

Moreover, accusations that engagement has failed are more a reflection of domestic American politics than an accurate assessment of the record of Washington's China policy. While many problems remain to be resolved, the changes that have taken place in China—from economic prosperity and open markets to village elections and the growth of nongovernmental organizations to the explosive growth of mobile telecommunications and the Internet—are inextricably related to the American policy of engagement. Engagement should not be discarded without careful evaluation of its full record and without a balanced assessment of the prospects for alternative approaches.

Notes

1. Dianne E. Rennack, "China: U.S. Economic Sanctions," Report 96-272 F (Congressional Research Service, October 1, 1997), p. 1; see also Kerry Dumbaugh, "China: Current U.S. Sanctions," Report 94-92 F (Congressional Research Service, April 14, 1995), p. 1.

2. Rennack, "China," pp. 8–9.

3. See George Bush and Brent Scowcroft, *A World Transformed* (Alfred A. Knopf, 1998), pp. 89, 105–11, 159.

4. Thomas Lippman, "U.S. Gives China Renewal of Favored Status in Trade," *Washington Post,* May 29, 1993, p. A21.

5. Although China is not a member of the MTCR, it has agreed not to sell missiles that exceed MTCR guidelines.

6. See Robert S. Ross, "China," in Richard N. Haass, ed., *Economic Sanctions and American Diplomacy* (New York: Council on Foreign Relations, 1998), pp. 10–34.

7. Ibid., pp. 28–29.

8. Ibid., pp. 29–30.

9. Ibid., p. 21.

10. Harry Harding, then a China specialist at the Brookings Institution, is quoted as saying, "Basically, what the Chinese have concluded is that they will keep MFN unless they do something particularly outrageous or provocative" in Lena H. Sun, "U.S. Warns China That Renewal of Trade Status Depends on Several Conditions," *Washington Post,* May 13, 1993, p. A19; Lena H. Sun, "China Protests Trade Decision, Issues Warning," *Washington Post,* May 29, 1993, p. A21.

11. In July 1993, the House of Representatives passed a resolution to this effect by a vote of 287 to 99.

12. Although the MTCR does not mandate sanctions, U.S. law does. In 1993, the Clinton administration invoked Section 73(a) of the Arms Export Control Act and Section 11B(b)(1) of the Export Administration Act, pertaining to the export of missile-related technology, not entire missiles (Category 2 of the MTCR Equipment and Technology Annex). The sanctions blocked the export of high technology that can be used in military applications as well as electronics, military aircraft, and space systems and equipment. The restrictions fell most heavily on the United States, particularly the American satellite industry, which had increasingly been using Chinese commercial carrier rockets to launch U.S.-made communications satellites. Similar

restrictions had been imposed by the Bush administration in 1991; see Shirley Kan, "Chinese Proliferation of Weapons of Mass Destruction: Current Policy Issues," Issue Brief 92056 (Congressional Research Service, January 6, 1997), p. 6; also Steven Greenhouse, "$1 Billion in Sales of Hi-Tech Items to China Blocked," *New York Times*, August 26, 1993, p. A1.

13. Beijing's difficulties with the new American policy were probably confounded by linguistic confusion. There is no precise counterpart for the word *engagement* in Chinese and certainly not one that carries the positive nuance of the English-language term. The Chinese generally translate the term as *jiaowang*, which literally means to "exchange visits and contacts."

14. Warren Christopher, "Building Peace in the Middle East," speech delivered at Columbia University, September 20, 1993, pp. 5–6. Text provided by Office of the Spokesman, Department of State.

15. Anthony Lake, "From Containment to Enlargement," speech delivered at Johns Hopkins University School of Advanced International Affairs, September 21, 1993, p. 4.

16. Ibid., p. 8.

17. Daniel Williams and R. Jeffrey Smith, "U.S. to Renew Contact with Chinese Military," *Washington Post*, November 1, 1993, p. A1. The ban was more strictly implemented by the Clinton administration than it had been by the Bush administration.

18. Don Oberdorfer, "Replaying the China Card: How Washington and Beijing Avoided Diplomatic Disaster," *Washington Post*, November 7, 1993, p. C3.

19. Williams and Smith, "U.S. to Renew Contact with Chinese Military."

20. Elaine Sciolino, "U.S. and Chinese Resolve Dispute on Missile Sales," *New York Times*, October 5, 1994, p. A1.

21. Douglas Jehl, "Warning to China on Trade," *New York Times*, April 30, 1994, p. 39.

22. Thomas A. Moga, "A Journey into China—Notes from over the Wall, Part 2," in *Intellectual Property Today* (May 1997) (www.lawworks-iptoday.com/05-97/moga.htm [April 2000]).

23. According to Charlene Barshefsky, in testimony on July 9, 1998, before the U.S. Senate Committee on Finance, sixty-four illegal CD and CD-ROM production lines in China have been destroyed, more than 800 people have been arrested for international property rights infringement, 15 million illegal CDs have been seized by the U.S. Customs Service, 3,000 Chinese judges have received training in international property rights issues, and China has issued more than 100,000 new patents and registered more than 120,000 trademarks per year, many to American corporations. Of course, China's improved compliance with international copyright practice was in its own interest, but the Office of the Trade Representative's persistent pressure and advocacy clearly played a role both in China's adoption of tough legal codes, such as its trademark and patent laws, and more important, in their enforcement. Charlene Barshefsky, "Renewal of Normal Trade Relations with China," Senate Committee on Finance, 105 Cong. 2 sess. (July 9, 1998) (www.ustr.gov/treasury/barshefsky_20.pdf [April 2000]).

24. The author was present at the meeting as note taker. A credible account of the

meeting, and the entire Taiwan Straits crisis of 1996, can be found in Barton Gellman, "U.S. and China Nearly Came to Blows in '96: Tension over Taiwan Prompted Repair of Ties," *Washington Post*, June 21, 1998, p. A1.

25. Barton Gellman, "Reappraisal Led to New China Policy: Skeptics Abound, but U.S. 'Strategic Partnership' Yielding Results," *Washington Post*, June 22, 1998, p. A1; James Mann, *About Face: A History of America's Curious Relationship with China, from Nixon to Clinton* (Alfred A. Knopf, 1999), p. 343.

26. This paragraph is derived from the author's participation in the meetings. See also Gellman, "Reappraisal Led to New China Policy"; Mann, *About Face.*

27. See, for example, Berger's speeches to the Center for Strategic and International Studies on March 27, 1997, and the Council on Foreign Relations on June 6, 1997; also President Clinton's speech of April 7, 1999, at the United States Institute of Peace.

28. See, for example, Robert Kagan and William Kristol, "Stop Playing by China's Rules," *New York Times*, June 22, 1998, p. A19; Gary Bauer, testimony in *China and Economic Engagement: Success or Failure?* Hearing before the Subcommittee on International Economic Policy and Trade of the House Committee on International Relations, 105 Cong. 2 sess. (Government Printing Office, 1998), p. 35; William Safire, "U.S. Security for Sale," *New York Times*, May 18, 1998, p. A19.

3

Europe and Iran: Critical Dialogue

JOHANNES REISSNER

Critical dialogue, a European policy crafted to maintain contact with Iran and to influence its regime, was endorsed by the European Council at the European Union (EU) summit in Edinburgh on December 11–12, 1992. The backdrop to the formulation of this policy was a number of events, some of which suggested the need for caution in dealing with Iran. For example, Ayatollah Khomeini's death edict against British writer Salman Rushdie had been reconfirmed by his successor, Ayatollah Khamenei, in February 1992, and in September of the same year, three Kurdish opposition figures were killed in the Greek restaurant Mykonos in Berlin.[1] However, other developments suggested that great opportunities would arise from increased interaction with Iran. European-Iranian trade had just reached its highest level since the revolution of 1979. At the same time, popular opinion in Iran appeared to have shifted toward a mood of reform and reconstruction under President Hashemi Rafsanjani, suggesting that the regime itself would move toward moderation. Moreover, the American policy of isolating Iran had not yet found its full expression; it was not until the spring of 1993 that the policy of dual containment toward Iraq and Iran was announced.

Nevertheless, over the following years, the EU policy of critical dialogue lost its momentum as a viable mechanism with which

Europe could influence change in Iran. The policy came under serious attack, not only from the United States and Israel but also from the European public. It became regarded as an immoral cover for maintaining lucrative commercial relations with Iran that ignored Iranian behavior concerning human rights, terrorism, the Arab-Israeli peace process, and weapons of mass destruction. In addition, the internal power struggle in Iran prevented the regime from cooperating in these fields, and Europeans were not willing to use their economic relations with Iran as leverage for achieving their policy goals. European countries tried to follow their own bilateral agendas with Iran, causing the regular meetings between the EU troika (a representative body encompassing the current, former, and future presidencies of the European Council) and Iran to become empty rituals.

While all these factors hampered the critical dialogue policy, the conclusion of the Mykonos trial in the spring of 1997 forced the immediate end to the policy. On April 10, German courts found the highest Iranian authorities—including the leader of the revolution—responsible for killing members of the Kurdish opposition in Berlin. Critical dialogue was thereby suspended, and all European ambassadors were withdrawn from Tehran for seven months in a demonstration of unprecedented solidarity within the European Union.

Only after the landslide election of President Mohammad Khatami a month later did the situation improve. With his softening of official rhetoric and his talk of "dialogue between civilizations," Khatami changed the political climate and paved the way to reforms that promised a more balanced foreign policy and even improvements in U.S.-Iranian relations.[2] In this improved atmosphere, the meetings between the EU troika and Iran resumed. Efforts to label these new meetings "constructive dialogue" or "comprehensive dialogue" were ephemeral; it seems that no one wanted to be reminded of critical dialogue.

Whether these latest meetings will form the basis of a new EU engagement policy that works in conjunction with U.S. policy toward Iran is yet to be seen. Even as one looks to the future, it is instrumental to elicit the lessons of past European efforts to engage Iran under the critical dialogue policy. This chapter reveals how Europe's particular global perspective, its interpretation of Iranian domestic developments, and its significant economic interests in Iran resulted in the largely ineffective use of incentives to change behavior.

The Goals of Critical Dialogue

The critical dialogue policy was adopted to pursue a range of goals, some of them explicit, others implicit. The official goals were expressly articulated by the European Council of Ministers:

Given Iran's importance in the region, the European Council reaffirms its belief that a dialogue should be maintained with the Iranian Government. This should be a critical dialogue which reflects concern about Iranian behavior and calls for improvement in a number of areas, particularly human rights, the death sentence pronounced by a Fatwa of Ayatollah Khomeini against the author Salman Rushdie, which is contrary to international law, and terrorism. Improvement in these areas will be important in determining the extent to which closer relations and confidence can be developed.[3]

Of these areas of explicit concern, the issues of greatest urgency to the European Union were those surrounding human rights and terrorism. The Arab-Israeli peace process, arms procurement, and arms proliferation were also deemed important, but they figured less prominently in Europe's calculations. Notably, weapons of mass destruction were mentioned only in the paragraphs following the above-quoted passage from the European Council's declaration.[4]

Interestingly, the United States held the same concerns but accorded them different priority, reflecting the varying political circumstances and contrasting worldviews of these powers. To the United States, as the only superpower, global security was paramount. In contrast, the European Union, despite its worldwide economic power, was in a process of becoming a world player and espousing more global concerns.[5] The emergence of the European Union's critical dialogue policy coincided with this process. Only on May 17, 1998, when the United States waived the sanctions against the French company Total, did any convergence of priorities between America and Europe concerning Iran become evident; in return for this waiver, the Europeans promised better cooperation with the United States in respect to the question of stemming the spread of weapons of mass destruction.

Equally important were the unstated goals of the critical dialogue policy. In particular, a powerful motive behind the policy was to maintain contact with Iran not simply as a means to change Iranian behavior, but also as a way to sustain EU-Iranian commercial relations, which were highly lucrative at the time of the formation of the dialogue. Despite the unspoken nature of this objective, its importance was widely recognized. In fact, as the critical dialogue policy progressed, the perception arose in the international community that maintaining commercial relations was the primary goal of Europe's policy toward Iran. This view was widely discussed and, as is considered further in this chapter, had an impact on the Iranian attitude toward critical dialogue as well.

Factors Shaping the Critical Dialogue Policy

To fully appreciate how and why the critical dialogue policy developed as it did, it is necessary to understand several factors that framed the environment in which the policy was crafted. First, at the time that the critical dialogue was adopted, European trade relations with Iran not only were considerable but also held promise of further development, as Iran was in the process of reconstruction after its eight-year war with Iraq. In 1991, Iranian oil exports to Europe peaked; in the following year, European exports to Iran reached their highest level for the decade 1986–96.[6] Whereas Great Britain, France, and Italy were primarily oil importers, by 1990 Germany had become the most significant importer of Iran's nonoil exports (34.4 percent).[7] In 1992 German-Iranian trade relations reached a volume of more than U.S. $6.8 billion,[8] the highest since the Iranian revolution, and Iranian shares in German stocks were worth more than DM 600 million.[9] In this economic climate, the mood of German exhibitors at the Tehran fair in October 1992 was aptly described as one of euphoria.[10]

The prominent role that Germany played in shaping the dialogue not only was due to its commercial relations with Iran, but also stemmed from the special historical relationship between Iran and Germany that began in the nineteenth century and had continued to unfold until the time of the Shah. In particular, the Islamic Republic had appreciated Foreign Minister Hans-Dietrich Genscher's attribution of aggression to Iraq during his visit to Tehran in 1984. During Genscher's second visit in May 1991 (followed by the visit of the German minister for economics, Jürgen Möllemann, in the summer of 1992), he subsequently promised German assistance for the reconstruction of Iran and supported Tehran in its wish to be recognized as a participant in the Persian Gulf region.[11] Moreover, President Rafsanjani accepted the invitation of German Chancellor Helmut Kohl to visit Germany, although in actuality, it was Iranian Foreign Minister Ali Akbar Velayati who went to Germany in the summer of 1992. The early 1990s was also a time of rising hopes that Germany could be an intermediary between Iran and the United States.[12]

Second, the European assumption that Iran was moving toward moderation and compliance with internationally recognized norms was essential for the formation of the dialogue. Several factors contributed to the impression that this move was occurring. Most notably, Rafsanjani's accession to the presidency after Khomeini's death in 1989 and his new policy of opening Iran for reconstruction were widely perceived as the end of the revolutionary period in Iran. As later analysis has shown, during his first years in office Rafsanjani in many respects laid the groundwork for Khatami's policy of today, although his efforts were hampered by a faction of Iranian conservatives, especially after the parliamentary elections of 1992.[13] Iran's neutral stance in the 1990–91 Gulf War also underscored the perception of growing Iranian moderation. In response to Iran's position during the Kuwait conflict, in October 1990, the European Union lifted the economic boycott measures imposed at the time of the Iran-Iraq War. Finally, the last Western hostages in Lebanon were freed with Iranian help in December 1991, thereby removing a major impediment to rapprochement. These developments cultivated an optimistic attitude toward Iran, and the European Commission argued in favor of the political and economic integration of Iran into the international community to "assist its economic reconstruction" and "strengthen the hand of the pragmatic wing of the regime."[14]

The final factor shaping the formulation of the dialogue was Europe's newly established common foreign and security policy. The new policy reflected the commitment of the European Union to promote human rights as "a core element" of its foreign policy, particularly in light of several events involving human rights in Iran.[15] Shortly before the policy of critical dialogue was proclaimed in December 1992, negotiations for a European-Iranian trade agreement had faltered over the issue of incorporating human rights concerns into the agreement. As mentioned, only three months before the declaration of critical dialogue, Kurdish opposition leaders had been killed in Berlin; less than a month before the policy was enacted, the reward for killing Salman Rushdie was raised to over U.S. $2 million.[16] These infractions stirred up widespread indignation in Germany and spurred a special debate in the German Bundestag. Some members pressed for sanctions against Iran, but the only concrete step taken was to suspend efforts to ratify the recently negotiated cultural agreements between Germany and Iran.[17]

In retrospect, these occurrences foreshadowed one of the greatest criticisms to be made of critical dialogue: the inability of the policy to secure progress in the area of human rights.[18] The European Parliament, which had promoted the incorporation of human rights into its common foreign and security policy, became one of the most ardent critics of the Iran policy of the European Council because of this failure.

The Failure of the Critical Dialogue Policy

The policy of critical dialogue failed insofar as it could not influence the behavior of the Iranian government not only in human rights, but also in other areas of concern. This failure is not attributable to one overriding factor, but to a confluence of factors, which include the intensive power struggle within Iran, Europe's unwillingness to use its economic ties to exert leverage, and discord with the United States over the dialogue. Each of these factors reinforced the others.

While the European Union's assumption that the Iranian government was moderating was not unreasonable, Europe failed to appreciate the importance of the inner Iranian power struggle that surfaced in 1992 and essentially continued to block political reform from that time onward. The Islamic left and Iranian modernists (who became today's "reformers") suffered a serious defeat in the parliamentary elections of February 1992. Subsequently, the leader of the revolution, Ali Khamenei, began a campaign against the "cultural aggression of the West" and stunted Rafsanjani's economic program for "structural adjustment."[19] Although a June 1993 election returned President Rafsanjani to office, the fact that the turnout was low and that he received 53 percent of the vote (down from his overwhelming victory in 1989) signaled the declining power base of the president. The parliamentary elections in spring 1996 led to the rift between right-wing modernists-technocrats (the pro-Rafsanjani "workers for construction") and the right-wing conservatives, who nevertheless consolidated their power in the Majles (parliament).[20]

Circumstances surrounding these political developments within the revolutionary regime minimized the potential influence of any external actors on internal Iranian politics. Critical dialogue thus became mere symbolic diplomacy. The regular meetings between the EU troika and Iran turned into inconsequential rituals involving tiresome discussions about the principal issues of concern. The Iranians—much like many skeptical members of the international community—regarded these meetings as necessary if Europe were to justify its continued relations with Iran. With regard to the normative aspects of the core issues of concern, particularly in the area of human rights, the Iranians saw these talks as a forum for theoretical deliberations; actual changes in political behavior were regarded as objects of bargaining for further concessions. Like the German-Iranian seminars on human rights (begun in Hamburg and Tehran in 1984), the futility of these discussions became obvious once it was evident that only philosophical debate was involved.[21]

Economic changes and their impact on European attitudes also played into the failure of the critical dialogue policy. From 1993 onward, largely due to an internal economic crisis in Iran rather than political reasons, European-Iranian trade saw a steady decline. German-Iranian trade reached its lowest levels in 1998 with a volume of only DM 3,295 million.[22] In this context, the focus of EU-Iranian relations shifted from trade volumes to that of credits and the rescheduling of debts. In 1989, when Rafsanjani took power, Iran had held little foreign debt despite the eight-year war with Iraq; however, at the end of 1993, Iran had amassed U.S. $28 billion in foreign debt.[23] The looming debt crisis first appeared in the fall of 1992; at that time, the mood of German investors was still described as one of euphoria, and Germany happily rescheduled the debt. This rescheduling began as early as October 1993, even while the much-criticized meetings were occurring between the Iranian intelligence minister Ali Fallahian and the German minister of state and coordinator of German intelligence services Bernd Schmidbauer.[24]

Confronted with declining trade and growing Iranian debts, the Europeans became even less willing to use their economic ties as political leverage against Iran. In the German administration, largely due to historical, cultural, and psychological reasons, thinking in terms of "carrots or sticks" was discouraged.[25] Neither sanctions nor the creation of a step-by-step strategic plan were seriously considered as tools for changing Iranian postures on issues of concern.[26] In March 1996, when the German high court issued a warrant for the arrest of Iranian Intelligence Minister Ali Fallahian, accusing him of being responsible for the Mykonos killings, Tehran saw this step as a retributive measure. Nevertheless, the German government, overlooking the anti-Iranian and anti-mullah climate in Germany, did its best to dispel these perceptions, insisting that it was a purely judicial step having nothing to do with politics.

While the European Union was reluctant to threaten the use of an economic stick, it also had no real incentives to entice behavioral changes with an economic carrot. The rescheduling of debts was hardly a favor to promote Iran's development, but was done as a means of getting European money back. As such, it was too obviously in the interest of the European side to be considered by Iran as an incentive. Tehran saw it more as the price Europeans paid for maintaining business with Iran. Whereas this reality limited the leverage that could be wielded with economic incentives, the use of political incentives was also constrained by European public opinion. No favorable political climate existed in which whatever Europe was to offer would be interpreted as an incentive. Instead, European public opinion treated Iran as a rogue state, held it up to moral scrutiny, and did nothing to satisfy the Iranian desire for basic recognition and respect.

The Iranian side had no reason to believe that the Europeans would use their economic ties as political leverage and increasingly saw European demands with respect to the critical issues of concern as rhetorical gestures reflecting the goals of the United States and Israel. The growing transatlantic difficulties that surfaced as a result of critical dialogue made the European Union appear powerless to enforce its aims. Iran's initial hopes of using the Europeans as partners against Washington faltered. Instead, Tehran began to search intensively for new partners in the East. Russia and China were treated as strategic partners, and the Asian industrial countries were seen as a substitute for Europe.

The critical dialogue policy also faltered because, beneath the level of a common foreign policy and the ritual meetings between the EU troika and Iran, many European countries pursued their own agendas with Iran. Because of this, overall European political relations with Iran were hampered by bilateral problems as each country sought to push the issues of greatest concern to it. For example, to the British, the case of Salman Rushdie was most urgent. France, on the other hand, became increasingly interested in the oil business with Iran and was eager to prevent the United States from imposing even stricter sanctions. In 1995, Iran offered the French firm Total the contract to develop gas fields in the Persian Gulf after the plans of the American firm Conoco had been blocked by President Clinton. Germany had its own bilateral troubles with Iran. The case of Helmut Szimkus, arrested in Iran and accused of spying, was rather spectacular. After being freed in the summer of 1994, Szimkus admitted that, contrary to previous statements, he had worked as a spy for the United States and Iraq.[27] The most controversial element of this case was the contact between the German minister of state and the coordinator of the German intelligence services with the Iranian Intelligence Minister Fallahian. The Iranian minister's first visit to Bonn was in October 1993, shortly before the Mykonos trial—in which he was ultimately implicated—began in Berlin.[28]

In 1996, Germany became troubled when Iran was accused of being at least indirectly responsible for the terrorist bombings in Jerusalem in February of that same year. After the German court issued a warrant against Iranian Intelligence Minister Fallahian in March, German-Iranian relations became more tense. When the EU troika visited Tehran again in April 1996, the Iranian side distanced itself from international terrorism but showed its "understanding" for the Palestinian fight against Israel. Such a posture, however moderated, was still not acceptable to the EU emissaries. Many in the German media advocated ending, or at least revising, the critical dialogue. However, German Foreign Minister Klaus Kinkel declared that the "policy of nonisolation" (*Nichtausgrenzung*), along with the goal of "active influence," had the strong support of all fifteen foreign ministers of the European Union.[29] However, despite this declared unity in principle, European countries continued to deal with Iran according to their respective bilateral agendas, undermining the joint policy.

Finally, the policy of critical dialogue lost enormous political influence due to the significant difference of opinion between the European Union and the United States over how best to treat Iran. U.S. disapproval of the dialogue policy surfaced in the spring of 1993 after the Clinton administration entered office.[30] In March 1993, the new secretary of state, Warren Christopher, branded the Tehran government an "international outlaw,"[31] demonstrating the new administration's willingness to adopt a more confrontational approach toward Iran than that taken during the Bush administration. From then on, the promotion of American global security interests involved the well-known policy of dual containment of the two "rogue" states, Iran and Iraq, and culminated in the passage of the Iran and Libya Sanctions Act by the American Congress in the summer of 1996.[32] This legislation, which essentially mandates secondary American sanctions on any foreign firms that invest in the Iranian or Libyan petroleum industries over a certain threshold limit, became a source of serious friction between the United States and its European allies.

Besides the U.S. complaint that a dialogue with Iran, "combined with extensive trading ties and favorable financial treatment, may encourage Iran to think that it can improve relations with the West without changing its behavior,"[33] a principal difference in approach existed. In contrast to the European Union, which worried primarily about the internal behavior of the Iranian regime, the United States perceived Iran foremost as a security threat. Not only was the United States concerned with security in the Persian Gulf and for Israel, but it worried about prospects for global security as well. Given the U.S. desire to limit Iranian influence in order to promote regional and global stability, the United States frowned upon the boom in European and Japanese exports to Iran. Of even greater concern to America was Germany's introduction of a new system of export controls that America thought was negligent in curbing Iran's access to dual-use items.[34]

Overall, the United States considered the dialogue to be a political as well as a moral mistake. This perception not only heightened U.S.-EU discord, but it stoked disapproval of the policy in Europe, particularly within Germany. Abundant criticism in the media portrayed critical dialogue as selling out human rights to the devil; American rhetoric calling Iran a pariah and "rogue" state was highly welcomed. German politicians of the Social Democrat and Green parties, at that time in the opposition, sometimes voiced criticism even harsher than that of the Americans and the Israelis. Such criticism contravened the official policy of these parties to keep contact with

Iran despite their opposition to critical dialogue. Certainly, this discrepancy between rhetoric and official policy must have confused the Iranians, leaving them uncertain about the foundations of the European policy.

The transatlantic discord over the policy toward Iran also stemmed from the different priorities held by the United States and Europe. Although a difference of emphasis unquestionably existed between the United States and the European Union regarding the issues of concern in Iran, no definite priorities were articulated on either side. This ambiguity and unspoken dissension between the United States and Europe encouraged Iranians to believe that the Europeans were more or less acting on behalf of the United States. In particular, the moral criticism voiced in Europe led to the perception in Iran that Europeans were as interested in the retributive aspect of policy—wanting "to seek retribution, or punitive action without regard for behavioral change"[35]—as were the Americans. This impression of the Europeans, reinforced by the "Down with the mullah regime" battle cry of some of the German media, made it easy for the Iranian regime to portray critical dialogue as just another effort to change the Iranian system altogether.

Evaluation of the Critical Dialogue Policy

Critical dialogue was more a political reaction and a name for a common political stance than it was a political strategy. It was one component of Europe's efforts to develop a common foreign policy, at a time when such an outlook was in its infancy. Despite the desire to function as a unified entity on a global level, European policy continued to be bedeviled by frictions between states and the various subdivisions and interest groups within states. Formulating the joint policy of critical dialogue was challenging enough; implementing it seemed beyond Europe's institutional capability at the time. This was particularly the case in the wake of the demise of the Soviet Union when Europe was mostly concerned with European dilemmas, and compared to those problems, Iran seemed to be a remote and relatively unimportant country.

However, the dialogue had two important aspects: it was an effort to change Iranian behavior and it maintained contact with Iran. Furthermore, critical dialogue was significant because it was a European policy that involved the provision of rewards as a motivation for change in a target country. The European Union had chosen a policy that made "closer relations and confidence" with Europe ostensibly contingent upon change in Iranian behavior.

Yet the provision of closer relations and confidence was too general to be regarded by the Iranians as an incentive. What power this vague incentive held was diluted by the Iranian perception that Europe needed Iran as much as Iran needed Europe and the belief that Iran could easily diversify its economic relations to the newly industrialized countries of Asia if Europe were to curtail economic contacts with it.[36]

Was the policy launched at the appropriate time? It can be argued that when the dialogue was adopted, the Iranian government under Rafsanjani was plausibly assumed to have begun its way toward moderation and compliance with international norms. However, on closer inspection, it seems likely that critical dialogue was poorly timed. After the conclusion of the war with Iraq in 1988 and the death of Khomeini one year later, great enthusiasm for reconstructing, opening up to the West, and gaining international recognition initially existed in Iran. Yet by 1992, this enthusiasm was already in decline. The climax in European-Iranian trade relations of that year may have led the Europeans to overlook the fact that the Iranian people already sensed that their expectations would go unfulfilled. To have maximum influence on Iran and its trends toward embourgeoisement,[37] the critical dialogue policy came too late. The actual timing of the policy was more a reaction to the positive trade balance, the Rushdie case, and the Mykonos killings than to favorable circumstances within Iran.

Did the critical dialogue policy address the right actors in Iran? The policy was almost entirely a government-to-government affair. Hopes for moderation were pinned to the government, while basic movements toward moderation within the society were overlooked. In fact, the German parliament froze cultural agreements with Iran and neglected human rights seminars. Thus the chance to develop a real dialogue with elements of Iranian civil society was missed. The mentality behind such behavior was that business contacts were necessary, but that cultural contacts with "rogue" regimes should be curtailed.

Furthermore, the critical dialogue policy, as formulated by the European Union, was too vague and implicit to be effective. While Europe warned that there would be "no closer relations if there was no change in behavior," more explicit goals and penalties were not laid out. The lack of specific guidelines to evaluate the behavior of the Iranian regime hindered the policy, particularly because there was never an objective basis to call for the imposition of sanctions or other lesser penalties. In this environment, the fact that Iran was reluctant to change its behavior while Europe was reluctant to use its economic weight as political leverage resulted in a stagnating policy.

Finally, the failure of the critical dialogue policy can also be attributed to Europe's inability to mobilize support for the policy, either internationally or domestically. Particularly in Germany, the strategic aspects of foreign policy toward Iran were considered and crafted inside the government with little discussion beyond a small inner circle of policymakers. Only the moral aspects of the policy stirred any sort of public debate. The almost complete lack of public debate surrounding the strategic justification of this policy meant that there was no broad understanding of Iran's importance to Germany in strategic terms, regardless of the (even diminishing) benefits in trade. As a result, when the policy came under attack from the public, the debate was polarized into two, somewhat artificial camps: those who were "for business" and those who were "for human rights." Without efforts to convince certain constituencies that the policy was worth continuing, even in the face of disappointing results, critical dialogue became a victim of the original expectations set for it. Originally heralded as a means for effecting change in the human rights situation in Iran, critical dialogue faltered when these expectations appeared ungrounded. When this occurred, critical dialogue lost its comparative advantage to the U.S. strategy, which put the fulfillment of conditions ahead of talks.[38]

It would be incomplete to evaluate critical dialogue only in the context of bilateral EU-Iranian relations. Rather, the policy needs to be examined in the triangle of U.S.-EU-Iranian relations. At least superficially, the respective positions of the European Union and the United States resembled the "good cop, bad cop" paradigm; however, such a coordinated philosophy found no echo within the European Union.[39] As a result, Iran tried to exploit the divisions between Europe and the United States by accusing Europe of being unable to chart a foreign policy independent of the United States and Israel. This allegation resonated in a Europe torn between defending its cooperation with America as a product of its own free will and resisting American unilateralism.

However, defenders of critical dialogue claimed the policy was a necessary means of preventing the total isolation of Iran and of keeping communications open with Iran. Whatever the drawbacks and failures of the policy, these two goals were achieved, and their importance should not be underplayed. Effective global isolation, which might very well have happened if it were not for European policy, could have made Iran even more unpredictable. Such isolation, in combination with a rapidly deteriorating economic situation and the absence of a viable alternative to the governing elite, could have made Iran even more volatile and, therefore, an even greater threat to the entire region and to Western interests there. Nevertheless, maintaining open communications with Iran should not be confused with the effective functioning of critical dialogue. Iran's inclusion into the Six plus Two Committee for Afghanistan, in which Iran came to sit at one table with the United States, had nothing to do with the Europeans, but certainly was a key forum for Iran to express its opinions.[40]

It is difficult to assess whether critical dialogue had a positive impact on Iran and, more specifically, whether President Khatami's election can partly be attributed to this policy. On the one hand, it would be rash to attribute internal change in Iranian domestic politics solely to external pressure. On the other hand, at the very least, some indirect impact can be deduced. As mentioned, critical dialogue was suspended in April 1997 after the conclusion of the Mykonos trial, just one month before the presidential elections occurred in Iran. The withdrawal of European ambassadors from Tehran demonstrated to Iranians, perhaps for the first time, that Europeans might be willing to base their policies on principles rather than economics. If true, the real isolation of Iran was feasible. This realization may have contributed to the overall desire to usher in a new government, one that would be more likely to meet the approval of the international community. Ironically, the critical dialogue policy may have been most influential in its demise rather than in its continuation.

Lessons of the Critical Dialogue Policy

Despite the failure of the EU's critical dialogue, the policy and its implementation offer some useful lessons to those formulating future engagement strategies, either with Iran or with other countries. First, a detailed understanding of the internal situation of the target country is imperative to the formulation of a successful engagement strategy. To craft an effective package of incentives and penalties, policymakers need accurate information about what motivates various actors in a society, as well as which actors hold the reins of change in areas of problematic behavior. When critical dialogue was initiated, the Europeans paid insufficient attention to the internal power struggle occurring inside Iran. Had they focused on these dynamics, they might have recognized the importance of crafting a specific package of incentives to bolster the influence of the elements of Iranian society in favor of greater contact with the West. As it was, Europe discounted internal Iranian political circumstances and instead formulated a policy that relied upon incentives—such as debt rescheduling and export credits—more reflective of European economic interests in Iran.

The case of critical dialogue also reveals the importance of carefully considering the level and kind of engagement (whether conditional or unconditional) and the issue of whom to address when crafting an engagement strategy. Critical dialogue, from its beginning, was more or less restricted to government-to-government contacts. Particularly because critical dialogue sought to address human rights questions, the government-to-government dialogue should have been accompanied by an unconditional dialogue with burgeoning elements of Iran's civil society. Instead, rather than simultaneously promoting contacts with civil society, Germany suspended its cultural agreements with Iran shortly before the proclamation of critical dialogue.

The emphasis on government-to-government relations was particularly inappropriate given the hostility much of the European public felt for the Iranian regime. This apathy among Europeans dismayed the Iranian side, which hoped the policy would generate some "reciprocity" and "mutual respect."[41] The absence of these sentiments limited the progress that could be made in government-to-government talks, given that "one of the potential benefits of an engagement strategy is in the recognition it gives to the other state, thus diminishing the sense of insecurity and propensity to resort to tactics associated with weaker nations."[42]

The European attitude toward Iran has changed since Khatami's election. The wider public in Europe has become aware of a sprouting civil society in Iran and its struggle for more freedom and rights. These developments are rightly perceived to provide opportunities to engage the emancipating heterogeneous urban middle class, which has proven to be a strong impetus for liberalizing political trends in Iran, even before Khatami came to power.[43] Together with the women's movement, this group is struggling to promote a civil society and the rule of law against the power of the more conservative clerico-bureaucratic classes. The future of Iran and of its relations with the West will, to a high degree, depend on whether this middle class will be able to develop viable centrist political institutions vis-à-vis the political factions still dominated by clerics.[44]

This case also argues that sanctions should not be excluded from any engagement strategy, and, if endorsed, their role should be explicitly stated in policy pronouncements. Critical dialogue is an example of how engagement that threatens no penalties in conjunction with the incentives it offers is likely to be ineffective. However, the circumstances under which sanctions will be employed should be specific, targeted, and well articulated. In retrospect, promising closer relations—or threatening to withhold them—in the hope of eliciting behavioral changes in four areas of concern was not a valid political strategy. Moreover, because one of the policy's underlying premises was to maintain contact with Iran, the threat that Europe would resort to punitive action in the form of disengagement was far from credible. As a result, the leverage Europe wielded through its substantial economic ties was significantly undermined. Although Iran may have felt a need to present its policies in a better international light or to temper them in response to internal politico-ideological necessities, it was unlikely to alter its behavior in any significant way as a response to European threats. For instance, the Iranian phrase "We are against the peace process but do not act against it" is one example of the cosmetic changes that occurred over the course of critical dialogue.

Finally, the most obvious lesson from critical dialogue is that every kind of engagement needs support internationally and at home. The failure of the proponents of critical dialogue to build a domestic constituency that endorsed the continuation of the policy would have led to the policy's downfall, even had the other precipitous ingredients been absent. In Germany and other countries, proponents of the policy were unable to convince the average European that their country had important interests in continuing its engagement with Iran. Eventually, the realpolitik position became viewed as simply a cover for business. With this impression gaining ground, the credibility of advocates of critical dialogue arguing that the Iranian regime was capable of change was undermined.

These lessons, while pertinent to any attempts to fashion an effective engagement strategy, are particularly relevant for policymakers on both sides of the ocean looking to engage Iran in the near future. Certainly, the chances for a comprehensive dialogue with various segments of Iranian society are better today than they have been in some time. Iran is prepared for a dialogue at the civil society level (as well as other levels) with all of the West, including the United States. However the "dialogue between civilizations" that Khatami has advocated is realized, this dialogue has become official policy and is even accepted in conservative circles opposing the president. The United States, for its part, has softened its position toward Iran and its opposition to the European-Iranian political dialogue. Whether the issues of concern can be tackled fruitfully will depend on developments in Iran. While there are grounds for optimism, Europeans and Americans alike should recognize that Iran is a country in motion. As sympathetic as the reformers may look to Western eyes, and as important as the movement headed by President Khatami is, the old politico-economic structures are still functioning and may inhibit future engagement efforts.

Notes

1. The Mykonos killings occurred on September 17, 1992.

2. Khatami's rhetoric contrasted with that of the Iranian conservatives who spoke of the "clash of civilizations" and the "fight against the cultural aggression of the West."

3. European Council, "Conclusions of the Presidency," Edinburgh, December 1992, quoted in V. Matthias Struwe, *The Policy of Critical Dialogue: An Analysis of European Human Rights Policy towards Iran from 1992 to 1997*, Durham Middle East Paper 60 (Durham [U.K.], 1998), pp. 25–26.

4. Ibid., p. 26.

5. Also note the differentiation between the United States as a "national security state" and the European nations as "trading states" in Peter Rudolf, "Rogue Regime or Regional Power? Transatlantic Conflict over Policy towards Iran," in Matthias Dembinski and Kinka Gerke, eds., *Cooperation or Conflict? Transatlantic Relations in Transition* (New York: St. Martin's Press, 1998), pp. 144 f.; Peter Rudolf, "Critical Engagement: The European Union and Iran," in Richard N. Haass, ed., *Transatlantic Tensions: The United States, Europe, and Problem Countries* (Brookings, 1999), pp. 71–101.

6. Eurostat, *Jahrbuch '97* (Luxembourg: Eurostat, 1997), p. 478.

7. Farrokh Moini, ed., *Iran Yearbook '93* (Bonn: MB Medien and Bücher Verlagsgesellschaft mbH, 1993), p. 317.

8. The trade volume dropped to DM 1,969 million in 1998. International Monetary Fund, *Direction of Trade Statistics Yearbook, 1999* (Washington, D.C., 1999), p. 260.

9. Thomas Dreger, "Einige Absonderlichkeiten," *Die Tageszeitung*, March 2, 1993, p. 13.

10. "Noch sorgt Teheran bei den Exporteuren für Euphorie," *Handelsblatt*, October 8, 1992, p. 15.

11. As important as Genscher's visit to Tehran in 1984 was for German-Iranian and European-Iranian relations, the claim that Genscher "founded" critical dialogue is an exaggeration. Hans Krech, "Was der 'kritische Dialog' gebracht hat," *Das Parlament*, February 12, 1999, p. 14.

12. Klaus-Dieter Frankenberger, "Genscher: Iran wünscht besseres Verhältnis zu Amerika," *Frankfurter Allgemeine Zeitung*, May 8, 1991, pp. 1–2; Udo Bergdoll, "Zu Reparaturarbeiten nach Teheran," *Süddeutsche Zeitung*, May 6, 1991, p. 4.

13. Anoushiravan Ehteshami, *After Khomeini: The Iranian Second Republic* (New York: Routledge, 1995), pp. xiv f.; Shaul Bakhash, "Iran since the Gulf War," in Robert O. Freedman, ed., *The Middle East and the Peace Process: The Impact of the Oslo Accords* (University Press of Florida, 1998), pp. 241–64.

14. Struwe, *The Policy of Critical Dialogue*, p. 22.

15. Ibid., p. 17.

16. "Iran Offers a Higher Reward for Assassination of Rushdie," *New York Times*, November 3, 1992, p. A9.

17. "Bonn: Keine Sanktionen wegen Rushdie," *Die Tageszeitung*, November 6, 1992, p. 1.

18. The common accusations against the ineffectiveness of the critical dialogue in the field of human rights are reflected in *Große Anfrage der Fraktion Bündnis90/Die Grünen, Iran-Politik der Bundesregierung*, Drucksache 13/1973, 13. Wahlperiode (Bonn: Deutscher Bundestag, July 6, 1995). For a pronounced and typical German critique of the critical dialogue, see Arthur Heinrich, "Zur Kritik des 'Kritischen Dialogs': Der Sonderweg Bonn-Teheran," *Blätter für deutsche und internationale Politik*, no. 5 (May 1996), pp. 532–43.

19. Rainer Hermann, "Von der Wirtschafts- zur Legitimationskrise," *Orient*, vol. 35 (1994), pp. 541–64, p. 548f.

20. Wilfried Buchta, "Irans fraktionierte Führungselite und die fünften iranischen Parlamentswahlen," in *KAS-Auslandsinformationen*, vol. 12 (Sankt Augustin: Konrad-Adenauer-Stiftung, 1996), pp. 50–78.

21. Johannes Vandenrath, "Menschenrechte in Islam und Christentum: 'Deutsch-iranisches Kolloquium, 3.–6. Oktober 1990 in Teheran,'" *Orient*, vol. 32 (1991), pp. 515–20.

22. This number is actually for January to November, rather than for the entire year. Deutsch-Iranische Industrie- und Handelskammer, *Deutsch./Iranischer Wirtschaftsspiegel*, no. 16 (December 1999), p. 17.

23. Hermann, "Von der Wirtschafts- zur Legitimationskrise," p. 553.

24. "Deutsch-Iranische Kontakte im Zwielicht," *Neue Zürcher Zeitung*, October 16, 1993, p. 1.

25. Moreover, not having suffered the traumatic ordeal that the Americans underwent after the revolution, Germany was more hesitant to think about shaping its relationship with Iran with punitive measures.

26. To my knowledge, a calibrated agenda akin to the "road map" idea expressed later by U.S. Secretary of State Madeleine Albright in her June 17, 1998, speech was never considered by Europe during the period of critical dialogue. See Geoffrey Kemp, *America and Iran: Road Maps and Realism* (Washington, D.C.: Nixon Center, 1998).

27. "Bonns intensive Beziehungen zu Iran," *Neue Zürcher Zeitung*, August 7, 1994, p. 3.

28. These contacts prompted British Foreign Minister Douglas Hurd to remind his German counterpart that the critical dialogue had made the improvement of the human rights situation in Iran a condition for any improvement in European-Iranian relations. "Schmidbauer: Iran-Connection ganz human," *Die Tageszeitung*, October 18, 1993, p. 2. For later contacts between Schmidbauer and Fallahian, see "Geheimdiplomatic Enge Bande," *Der Spiegel*, March 6, 1995, p. 28.

29. "Kinkel zufrieden über EU-Entscheidung," *Frankfurter Allgemeine Zeitung*, April 24, 1996, p. 4.

30. The U.S. presidential election happened to coincide roughly with the declaration of critical dialogue.

31. Elaine Sciolino, "Christopher Signals a Tougher U.S. Line toward Iran," *New York Times*, March 31, 1993, p. A3.

32. Rudolf, "Rogue Regime or Regional Power?" p. 138.

33. State Department spokesman Mike McCurry, quoted in Steve Vogel, "Allies Oppose Bonn's Iran Links," *Washington Post*, November 6, 1993, p. A18.

34. See Steve Coll, "German Exports Helping Iran Rebuild, Rearm," *Washington Post*, December 6, 1992, pp. A33.

35. Raymond Tanter, "Rogue Regimes," in Bassma Kodmani-Darwish, ed., *The United States, Iran, and Iraq: Containment or Engagement?* (Paris: Institut français des relations internationales, 1998) (les notes de l'IFRI, no. 7), pp. 21–30, p. 28.

36. Some diversification in that direction did occur during the 1990s.

37. For this term see Val Moghadam, "Islamic Populism, Class, and Gender in Postrevolutionary Iran," in John Foran, ed., *A Century of Revolution: Social Movements in Iran* (University of Minnesota Press, 1994), pp. 189–222, p. 189.

38. It should be noted that the United States has been open to an authoritative dialogue, but this offer has not been accepted by Iran.

39. See Johannes Reissner, "Europe, the United States, and the Persian Gulf," in Robert D. Blackwill and Michael Stürmer, eds., *Allies Divided: Transatlantic Policies for the Greater Middle East* (MIT Press, 1997), pp. 123–42, p. 140.

40. The committee consists of the six neighbors of Afghanistan plus the United States and Russia; it first met in New York in October 1997.

41. This sentiment was expressed by the *Iran Daily* on the first EU troika visit after the break in relations caused by the Mykonos trial, quoted in "Dailies Comment on Iran-EU Rapprochement," Islamic Republic News Agency, July 20, 1998 (www.irna.com [February 2000]).

42. Shahram Chubin and Jerrold D. Green, "Engaging Iran: A US Strategy," *Survival*, vol. 40 (Autumn 1998), pp. 153–69, p. 158.

43. Here the term *middle class* is used in its social and politico-ideological sense and refers to intellectuals as well as bureaucrats and parts of the Bazaaris. For an interesting analysis of the term *middle class* in the context of today's Iranian political factions, see Sa'îd Barzîn, *Jenâhbandî-ye siyâsî dar îrân* (Political Factions in Iran) (Tehran: Nashr-e Markaz Publishing, 1998). The Bazaaris should not automatically be considered to belong to the conservative faction, particularly not the so-called neo-Bazaaris. Their "passion is not policy, but profit. For their partners in the leadership, the overarching goal is not ideological rigor but power." Jahangir Amuzegar, "Adjusting to Sanctions," *Foreign Affairs*, vol. 76 (May-June 1997), pp. 31–41, p. 39.

44. Shaul Bakhash, "Iran's Remarkable Election," *Journal of Democracy*, vol. 9 (January 1998), pp. 80–94, pp. 93 f.

4

The United States and Iraq: Perils of Engagement

KENNETH I. JUSTER[1]

The debate about the relative merits of an engagement policy or a sanctions policy arises primarily when dealing with problem, or "rogue," states. Although the United States often imposes economic sanctions against problem states, U.S. policy toward Iraq from 1988 to 1990 was an exception to that general practice. From August 1988 to August 1990—the period between the end of the Iran-Iraq War and Iraq's invasion of Kuwait—the United States sought to engage Iraq in an effort to moderate its behavior and construct a positive bilateral relationship. During this period, the U.S. government, though under no illusions about Iraqi President Saddam Hussein's past actions, permitted trade of nonmilitary items with Iraq and provided credit guarantees for the Iraqi purchase of U.S. agricultural products.

The U.S. policy of limited engagement with Iraq did not succeed. The Iraqis invaded Kuwait in August 1990, ignored the economic sanctions imposed on them, and ultimately fought and lost a war against an international coalition of more than thirty countries acting with the consent of the United Nations Security Council. Indeed, to this day, Iraq defies the UN Security Council resolutions adopted in the aftermath of the Gulf War and remains committed to developing weapons of mass destruction and the capability to deliver them. These circumstances raise the issues of whether engagement with Iraq was a reasonable policy to pursue from 1988 to 1990 and whether lessons might be gleaned from the implementation of that policy.

U.S. Vital Interests in the Persian Gulf

For nearly three decades, since the United States became the principal foreign power in the Persian Gulf, there has been broad consensus on U.S. vital interests in that region.[2] A primary U.S. interest is to maintain the secure and unfettered flow of oil and gas from the Gulf at reasonable prices. Access to these energy supplies is critical to the economic well-being of the industrialized world. A second, related interest is to preserve regional stability by creating security arrangements to protect against the emergence of a dominant power hostile to the United States and by seeking to stem the proliferation of weapons of mass destruction. A third U.S. interest, which relates more broadly to the Middle East, is to ensure the security of Israel.[3]

Since the early 1970s, the United States has sought to advance these national interests through a variety of policies. Initially, from 1972 to 1979, the United States relied on strong relations with Iran and Saudi Arabia—the "two pillar" policy—to stabilize the region and provide secure supplies of oil and gas. During this period, U.S. relations with Iraq were virtually nonexistent. Iraq had severed relations with the United States at the outset of the Six-Day War in 1967 between Israeli and Arab forces; shortly thereafter, Iraq became one of the Soviet Union's principal client states in the Middle East.

U.S. policy in the Gulf collapsed in 1979 with the Iranian revolution, as Iran shifted from being an ally under the Shah to becoming an adversary under Ayatollah Khomeini. By the time Iraq invaded Iran in 1980, commencing a devastating eight-year war, the United States had adopted a de facto balance-of-power approach to these two regional powers. Although the United States was officially neutral regarding the war itself, as Iraq's military position deteriorated in late 1981 and 1982, the Reagan administration became concerned about Iran's expansionist aspirations—a concern shared at the time by many U.S. allies as well as the other Gulf states.

By 1982, President Ronald Reagan concluded that it was in the U.S. national interest to begin to cultivate relations with Iraq. The Reagan administration was motivated primarily by the strategic calculation that the United States needed to buttress Iraq as a regional counterweight to Iran.[4] Secondary motivations included the hope that Saddam Hussein would play a constructive role in the Middle East peace process; the recognition that Iraq, as a large country with major oil reserves, represented an untapped market for U.S. industry and agriculture; and the desire to cut into Moscow's exclusive relationship with Baghdad.[5]

After Saddam Hussein severed Iraq's ties with the terrorist Abu Nidal in 1982, the U.S. government removed Iraq from its list of nations engaged in state-sponsored terrorism. This move made Iraq eligible for assistance from the U.S. Department of Agriculture's Commodity Credit Corporation (CCC), which administers an export promotion and market development program to assist U.S. agricultural exporters and producers by developing foreign markets for U.S. commodities. In December 1982 (U.S. fiscal year 1983), the CCC agreed to extend credit guarantees of approximately $400 million to U.S. agricultural exporters for the sale of commodities to Iraq.

Two years later, in November 1984, the United States and Iraq resumed diplomatic relations and the U.S. government increased cooperation with Iraq by sharing military intelligence with the Iraqis and continuing economic assistance. This cooperation, however, did not extend to selling weapons or weapons systems to Iraq.[6] Indeed, U.S. support for Iraq was not unqualified; it varied depending on developments in the conflict with Iran. When Iraq was suffering losses, the Reagan administration tilted more in favor of Saddam Hussein. For example, in 1987, when Iran began attacking oil tankers in the hope of denying Iraq revenue from its oil exports, the United States "reflagged" Kuwaiti tankers and registered them in the United States, thereby making those tankers eligible for protection by the U.S. Navy against possible assaults from Iran.[7] The Iran-Iraq War concluded with a cease-fire in August 1988.

Iraq emerged from the conflict as one of the most powerful states militarily in the region. Directly preceding and during its war with Iran, Iraq acquired more than $50 billion worth of conventional arms, primarily from the Soviet Union, China, and France.[8] Saddam Hussein also made a concerted effort during that period to develop nuclear, chemical, and biological weapons. Iraq began a nuclear program in the 1970s, which included a nuclear cooperation pact with France pursuant to which the French agreed to build the Osirak nuclear reactor outside of Baghdad and train Iraqi scientists and technicians to run it. In 1981, as that nuclear plant was about to become operational, Israeli jets bombed and destroyed it. Yet as was subsequently discovered, Saddam continued a major clandestine effort to purchase components for his nuclear program, buying equipment and material primarily from France, the United Kingdom, Germany, Brazil, and Pakistan.[9]

The United States had an embargo on selling arms to either Iraq or Iran during their eight-year war. Although the U.S. Department of Commerce approved export licenses for approximately $1.5 billion in dual-use equipment to Iraq between 1985 and 1990, actual shipments under those licenses were quite limited. In fact, contrary to the assertions by some,[10] only about $500 million worth of the $1.5 billion of dual-use exports licensed between 1985 and 1990 were ever shipped to Iraq.[11] Moreover, of the $500 million in dual-use exports, the overwhelming majority occurred during the Iran-Iraq War. The Department of Commerce granted licenses for only $75 million of dual-use exports during 1989 and 1990, a decrease from previous years.[12] Despite the relatively small quantities of exports delivered, some of these items probably ended up being of assistance to Iraq in its efforts to develop weapons of mass destruction.[13]

Iraq used chemical weapons against Iran on several occasions during the war and, in 1988, also used poison gas against Kurdish villages in northern Iraq.[14] The Reagan administration condemned Iraq's actions, demanding and securing a pledge from Baghdad to refrain from any further use of chemical weapons.[15] However, the administration opposed legislation that would impose economic sanctions against Iraq, believing that such sanctions would be "counterproductive in terms of [U.S.] ability to influence the Iraqis."[16]

During the Iran-Iraq War, there had been broad support for U.S. policy toward Iraq, as most analysts agreed on the need to balance Baghdad against Tehran. With the end of the Iran-Iraq War, that consensus began to break down. Some in the Reagan administration argued that Iraq now presented the major military threat in the region and needed to be countered.[17] Others in Congress pointed to Iraq's use of chemical weapons against the Kurds, along with additional Iraqi human rights abuses, and wanted to impose a trade embargo. However, with the Reagan administration in its final months in office, the cooperative efforts toward Iraq that were implemented during the Iran-Iraq War continued. Any reappraisal of Gulf policy was deferred to the next administration. President George Bush ordered such a review shortly after entering office.

Limited Engagement, 1989–90

The conventional wisdom—within the Bush administration as well as within Western Europe and among Arab countries—was that Iraq had emerged from the war more moderate, more pro-Western, and, at least on the surface, more politically open than it previously had been.[18] Exhausted from its conflict with Iran, Iraq clearly needed to rebuild its ravaged country. To obtain the required economic assistance and investment capital, Iraq thus had to cultivate friendly relations with the wealthy Arab states of the Gulf as well as with the West. During its war with Iran, Iraq's neighbors, including Egypt, Jordan, Saudi Arabia, and other Gulf states, had become closer to Iraq and believed that Saddam Hussein would focus on domestic reconstruction (estimated to cost up to $200 billion). Indeed, Saddam formed the Arab Cooperation Council in February 1989, consisting of Egypt, North Yemen, Jordan, and Iraq, to expand his collaboration with moderate Arabs and as a bloc to resist Iranian hegemony. Saddam also reestablished diplomatic relations with Egypt and, in March 1989, signed a bilateral nonaggression pact with Saudi Arabia.[19]

The moderate Arab countries encouraged the United States to reach out to Iraq. Baghdad had weakened its ties with Moscow in the aftermath of the Iran-Iraq War. Iraq also apparently had curbed its support for radical Palestinian factions, played an important role in supporting the Palestine Liberation Organization's historic recognition of Israel's right to exist in November 1988, and endorsed a peaceful resolution of the Arab-Israeli conflict. In addition, Iraq offered a growing market for U.S. and Western exports, already exemplified by Iraqi purchases of European arms and technology (especially from France and Germany) and American grain. And Iraq had become a major source of oil for the United States and its Western partners. Although in retrospect it was wishful thinking, at the time the widely shared view in the international community was that Saddam Hussein was following a more moderate path. Consequently, there was virtually no international support for ostracizing the Iraqi regime.

It was in this context—and having inherited the Reagan administration's efforts to cultivate ties with Iraq—that the Bush administration undertook its review of U.S. policy in the Persian Gulf region.[20] The product of this lengthy review process was National Security Directive (NSD) 26, entitled "U.S. Policy toward the Persian Gulf," which was completed in June 1989 and signed by the president on October 2, 1989. NSD 26 reaffirmed the framework already in place for a policy of limited engagement with Iraq. The directive noted that "access to Persian Gulf oil and the security of key friendly states in the area" remained vital to U.S. national security and that the United States was "committed" to defending those interests, "if necessary and appropriate through the use of U.S. military force." NSD 26 went on to conclude that the evolution of "normal relations between the United States and Iraq would serve our longer-term interests and promote stability in both the Gulf and the Middle East."

The directive recognized the need to probe and test the Iraqis as part of the effort to moderate their behavior. On the one hand, NSD 26 proposed expanded "economic and political incentives for Iraq" and directed the facilitation of "opportunities for U.S. firms to participate in the reconstruction of the Iraqi economy, particularly in the energy area." On the other hand, the directive provided that, if the positive incentives offered to Saddam Hussein failed to produce the desired behavior, the United States would undertake a series of negative sanctions to encourage constructive Iraqi policies: the "Iraqi leadership must understand that any illegal use of chemical and/or biological weapons will lead to economic and political sanctions, for which we would seek the broadest possible support from our allies and friends." Similarly, any breach by Iraq of international safeguards in its nuclear program also would lead to sanctions. Finally, the directive noted that "human rights considerations" would continue to be an important element in U.S. policy toward Iraq and that Iraq should be called on to "play a constructive role in negotiating a settlement with Iran and cooperating in the Middle East peace process."

A Justice Department probe soon complicated efforts to implement the engagement policy enunciated in NSD 26. The U.S. attorney in Atlanta began to investigate the Atlanta branch of the Italian bank, Banca Nazionale del Lavoro (BNL), which participated in the CCC credit guarantee program for U.S. exporters of agricultural products to Iraq. In the course of the investigation, allegations arose that the CCC program had been perverted to assist Iraq in illegally obtaining arms and other weapons-related materials. These allegations—which were never substantiated—surfaced just as the Bush administration was considering Iraq's request for $1.03 billion in CCC credit guarantees for fiscal year 1990.[21]

The U.S. government, which had provided Iraq with $1.1 billion of credit guarantees in each of the previous two years, chose to modify its approach for fiscal year 1990. The decision to modify the program, which resulted from several interagency meetings in October and November 1989, was due primarily to the BNL allegations. There also was a fair amount of internal debate—and disagreement—about Iraq's creditworthiness. Representatives from the Treasury Department and the Federal Reserve Board expressed concern about the size of Iraq's debt to foreign lenders and about Iraq's default on loans from some other countries. However, they and other senior Bush administration officials also recognized that Iraq had always treated U.S. lenders on a preferred basis, had made full and timely payments under the CCC program, and had substantial oil reserves as a source of future revenue to service its debt.[22] Ultimately, the administration, rather than granting Iraq's CCC request outright, in November 1989 adopted a tiered approach to the credit guarantees.

Under this plan, the Agriculture Department extended a first tranche of $500 million in credit guarantees, with additional guarantees for the fiscal year to depend on the results of the U.S. attorney's investigation into those aspects of the BNL case that related to the CCC program and on the results of the Agriculture Department's own administrative review of the CCC program with Iraq.[23] The Bush administration also warned the Iraqi government that the CCC program could continue only if it were found to be "free from any taint of illegality."[24]

While the BNL allegations were still pending in January 1990, President Bush overrode congressional opposition and signed a directive authorizing the Export-Import Bank to advance $200 million in development loan credits for Iraq. That decision, according to Secretary of State James A. Baker III, "turned out to be the high-water mark of [U.S.] efforts to moderate Iraqi behavior."[25] As the Agriculture Department continued to monitor the BNL investigation, preliminary results of the department's own administrative review of Iraq's CCC program identified some apparent irregularities.[26] Accordingly, in February 1990, the Bush administration deferred a decision to release any portion of the second tranche of $500 million of credit guarantees for export sales to Iraq, a move that triggered complaints from Iraq.[27]

At the same time, a series of Iraqi actions began to raise new questions about Iraq's intentions and whether the U.S. engagement policy was having its intended effect. At the February 1990 summit of the Arab Cooperation Council, Saddam Hussein asserted that Iraq, which had accumulated a foreign debt of approximately $80 billion during its war with Iran, should no longer have to repay "loans" received from other Arab countries (including an estimated $10–30 billion from Kuwait) because Iraq supposedly had fought the war on behalf of the entire Arab world.[28] Indeed, Saddam actually demanded that the Gulf states provide Iraq with additional funds. During the same meeting, Saddam publicly criticized the long-standing U.S. naval presence in the Persian Gulf and called for the U.S. fleet to go home. Iraq also complained to the United States in February about a Voice of America broadcast that was critical of the secret police in Iraq and other countries.

In March 1990, Saddam Hussein's troubling behavior escalated. Iraq brought to trial an Iranian-born British journalist who had been in prison and, despite international pleas for clemency, executed him on charges of espionage for Israel. That same month, British customs officials, working with the United States, interdicted an Iraqi attempt to smuggle into Iraq capacitors with potential missile and nuclear applications. In addition, the U.S. government consulted with the British about the confiscation of materials for Iraq's development of the so-called supergun, at a time that coincided with the mysterious assassination of Dr. Gerald Bull, the Canadian ballistics expert who was largely responsible for developing that weapon. During this period, the U.S. intelligence community also detected Iraqi construction of missile launchers with sufficient range to reach Israel. Shortly after that discovery, on April 2, 1990, Saddam issued the provocative threat that, if Israel attacked Iraq, the Iraqis would use chemical weapons to "eat up half of Israel."[29]

All of these events marked a period during which Saddam Hussein reportedly suspected an American-British-Israeli conspiracy directed against Iraq. There was, in fact, no such conspiracy, and the Bush administration sought to reassure Saddam that it harbored no ill intentions toward Iraq.[30] In April and May 1990, however, the administration took steps—insufficient in the view of critics—to respond to Saddam's alarming conduct. President Bush condemned Saddam Hussein's threat against Israel, and the State Department denounced the threat as irresponsible. In addition, the deputy national security adviser requested the State Department to coordinate with other agencies to develop and implement a multilateral initiative to address Iraq's nonconventional weapons proliferation.[31] The administration also decided, once again, to defer the release of the second tranche of $500 million in CCC credit guarantees for Iraq and suspended the agricultural assistance program, a decision condemned in Iraq as more evidence of a U.S.-led conspiracy against it.[32]

By late June 1990, U.S.-Iraq relations had deteriorated further. Yet whether Saddam Hussein's actions reflected a strategic shift or merely a tactical change in conduct was difficult to discern because the United States lacked good intelligence capabilities within Iraq, especially human intelligence within the Iraqi leadership circle. Under the circumstances, the Bush administration relied heavily on what it heard from Iraq's Arab neighbors, who seemed to be more knowledgeable about Saddam's true intentions. Leaders from both Saudi Arabia and Egypt continued to advise the administration to avoid inflammatory words and precipitate actions.[33] The Bush administration in fact resisted congressional proposals to impose new sanctions against Iraq. In the view of the administration, such legislation would deny the president flexibility in dealing with Iraq and would infringe upon his right to conduct foreign policy. Moreover, there remained the view within the White House— encouraged by Egypt and other moderate Arab countries—that the United

States was more likely to maintain influence over Iraq by continuing limited contacts than by imposing additional sanctions.[34]

In July 1990, as the falling price of oil exacerbated Iraq's economic plight, tensions escalated between Iraq and Kuwait. Iraq accused Kuwait and the United Arab Emirates (UAE) of deliberately exceeding their OPEC production quotas, thereby creating a glut in the oil market. Iraq also charged the Kuwaitis with having established military and police posts and oil installations on Iraqi territory, thus violating the Iraq-Kuwait border, and with siphoning oil from the Rumailah oil field that lay beneath that border. By mid-July, U.S. satellites detected movement of Iraqi troops and equipment toward the Kuwaiti border.[35] However, the countries in the region—including Egypt, Jordan, Saudi Arabia, and even Kuwait—continued to believe that Iraq was seeking only to intimidate Kuwait and urged the United States not to take any provocative actions. Indeed, all of the Arab countries, with the exception of the UAE, rejected as counterproductive an overt American presence in the region. The UAE alone asked the United States to participate in a joint military exercise as a show of solidarity against Saddam Hussein's new threats. President Bush approved the exercise on July 23, and the next day six U.S. ships, including aerial-refueling tankers, engaged in joint maneuvers with the UAE. The State Department also reiterated the U.S. government's commitment to the free flow of oil through the Strait of Hormuz and to the individual and collective self-defense of the countries in the region, a message that U.S. Ambassador April Glaspie gave directly to Iraq's deputy foreign minister on July 24.

The U.S. intelligence community issued a formal "warning of war" on July 25, but Arab leaders continued to believe (optimistically) that matters between Iraq and Kuwait would be resolved peacefully. Egyptian President Hosni Mubarak indicated that he had personal assurances from Saddam Hussein that Iraq would not move against Kuwait.[36] Further, Ambassador Glaspie, following an unprecedented meeting with Saddam on July 25, reported that Saddam had given her assurances that he would seek a diplomatic solution to the crisis at an upcoming OPEC meeting in Saudi Arabia.[37] In light of these mixed signals and in a further effort to defuse the crisis, President Bush sent an upbeat, though balanced, message to Saddam Hussein on July 28. The message indicated "in a spirit of friendship and candor" that the United States would oppose any Iraqi military action but also expressed a desire for "better relations with Iraq." This message reflected the final vestige of the Bush administration's attempt to coax constructive conduct out of Iraq, in line with Arab diplomatic efforts.

The meeting in Saudi Arabia between the Iraqis and Kuwaitis ended without resolution. On August 1 the U.S. intelligence community upgraded its formal "warning of war" to a "warning of attack," though experts actually only expected Iraq to make a limited incursion into Kuwait to take the Rumailah oil field and possibly the islands of Bubiyan and Warba, which controlled access to the Iraqi port of Umm Qasr. On the morning of August 2, before the White House could send a second, more strongly worded message to Saddam Hussein, Iraqi forces rapidly invaded and occupied all of Kuwait.[38]

Lessons of Engagement

U.S. policy toward Iraq was not a prominent issue during the first eighteen months of the Bush administration. Attention was focused instead on the revolutionary changes in Central and Eastern Europe, the situation in China following the Tiananmen Square crackdown, unrest in Central America (Nicaragua and Panama), the process of German unification, and turmoil in the Soviet Union. Even in the Middle East, the primary U.S. focus was on the peace process between the Israelis and the Palestinians and the role that neighboring countries could play to advance that process.[39]

The attention that was given to U.S. relations with Iraq, in congressional hearings and elsewhere, did not spark much debate or controversy. One member of Congress, Representative Tom Lantos (Democrat of California), who later became a sharp critic of the Bush administration's engagement policy, had generous words for that policy at a hearing in June 1990 with the assistant secretary of state for Near Eastern and South Asian affairs, shortly before Iraq invaded Kuwait. At that hearing, Representative Lantos stated: "About a month ago, you testified before us, and I am quoting you, 'If Iraq should seek to play a spoiler's role in the Middle East, we would take appropriate action on behalf of American interests. If Iraq plays an increasingly responsible role, the U.S.-Iraq relationship will improve.' Now, that's a statement that I think we all can subscribe to."[40]

This view reflected concerns held by many (including several Arab leaders) that U.S. actions toward Iraq, if too harsh, might actually provoke a conflict with Saddam Hussein. Yet after the conclusion of the Gulf War, the Bush administration's overall effort to engage Iraq came under attack within the United States for being too tolerant of Iraqi conduct. The post–Gulf War critics ranged from members of Congress seeking to tarnish the administration's success in the Gulf War, to journalists who labeled U.S. policy toward Iraq as one of "appeasement," to academics who branded the engagement policy as "flawed in both its concepts and its execution" and as ill conceived and amoral. Some of these criticisms were politically motivated; virtually all were made only with the benefit of hindsight.[41] But whatever the merits of the engagement policy—a subject about which reasonable people certainly can disagree—several important lessons emerge from the debate about that policy.

First, there are inherent political risks in adopting a policy of engagement, even limited engagement, with a problem state. An engagement policy is necessarily predicated on the expectation that the problem state is willing to take steps to improve its conduct. In the case of Iraq, NSD 26 appeared to lay out a balanced and measured policy of constructive engagement, and if Saddam Hussein had moderated his conduct—as neighboring Arab countries predicted he would—engagement would have been a "success." However, when Saddam invaded Kuwait, engagement drew just the opposite response, and it was attacked as a "failure" and as "appeasement." Indeed, the use of such labels ignores the fact that a problem state, by its very nature, may be beyond the influence of any country's foreign policy. The simplistic use of these labels illustrates another political risk associated with an engagement policy: such a policy, especially in hindsight, is often misunderstood or mischaracterized. The Bush administration was under no illusions about the nature of Saddam Hussein's regime. Nevertheless, based on indications in the aftermath of the Iran-Iraq War that Saddam was prepared to improve his conduct, the administration believed it was worth taking the calculated risk of engaging Iraq to encourage such improvement.

Ultimately, the engagement policy with Iraq must be judged in comparison with alternative policy options under consideration at the time, to determine which course of action, among a series of unattractive choices, might have best advanced U.S. interests in the Persian Gulf. Critics of the Bush administration's policy contend that U.S. sanctions against Iraq would have best served U.S. interests. A sanctions policy certainly would have been a less risky political approach than engagement. Sanctions would have openly signaled that Iraq's conduct was objectionable, thereby making it difficult to criticize the policy if Iraqi conduct remained objectionable and making it easy to praise the policy as successful if Iraqi conduct had improved over time. Yet it is by no means clear that *unilateral* sanctions by the United States—in conflict with the position of Iraq's neighbors in the region and of virtually every Western country—would have succeeded in deterring Saddam Hussein from his aggressive conduct. Indeed, six months of *multilateral* sanctions against Iraq by the world community (August 1990–January 1991), followed by five weeks of massive bombing (January–February 1991), did not convince Saddam to change his position toward

Kuwait. And almost a decade of severe multilateral sanctions against Iraq after the Gulf War have not yet persuaded Saddam to cooperate with UN weapons inspections teams.

Even in hindsight, it is not evident that any policy option could have prevented Iraq from invading Kuwait or could have had a sustained, salutary effect on Saddam Hussein's conduct. The fact that the Bush administration's engagement policy did not succeed does not necessarily mean that the policy was misguided. It actually took Saddam's invasion of Kuwait to galvanize the domestic and international consensus needed to resist his aggression. Because the United States had not previously followed a unilateral policy on sanctions, it had enhanced credibility in dealing with countries in the region and elsewhere as it forged the United Nations coalition that subsequently drove Iraq out of Kuwait. A policy of unilateral sanctions probably would not have had a positive influence on Saddam nor would it have provided the basis to organize later international action against him. It is even conceivable that a sanctions policy could have pushed Iraq to invade Kuwait sooner.

A second lesson concerns the type of influence that groups with economic interests and other actors outside the U.S. government exert on U.S. foreign policy. Over time, a range of domestic and international forces may inexorably press policymakers to move in the direction of an engagement policy with a problem state, even if sanctions are already in place and despite the political risks involved in moving toward engagement. While moral indignation may underlie a policy of sanctions, other factors within the sanctioning country and among its friends and allies, such as commercial interests, people-to-people relationships, humanitarian concerns, and even historical ties, may eventually push policy in the direction of some form of engagement, especially economic engagement—which often is less visible publicly, and thus less contentious, than full-blown political engagement. Elements of this phenomenon certainly occurred with respect to U.S. policy toward Iraq.

Within the United States, agricultural groups interested in exporting their products to Iraq quietly but effectively lobbied the Reagan and Bush administrations to extend increased levels of credit guarantees to Iraq. By 1989, Iraq had become the ninth largest purchaser of U.S. agricultural products. Indeed, the CCC program for Iraq was extremely popular both on Capitol Hill and with farm state politicians, and these groups made their policy preferences known to the executive branch. Thus the trade program had a dual effect: it provided the United States with economic leverage over Iraq, but also pushed those domestic groups that had developed a stake in the program to exert political pressure against using that leverage.[42]

Internationally, both Arab countries and allies in Europe urged the United States to reach out to Iraq, insisting that conditions were favorable for integrating Iraq into the moderate grouping of Arab states in the Gulf region. It would have been quite difficult for the U.S. government to ignore such views because, at the time, the countries involved had more extensive familiarity with, and knowledge about, the internal situation in Iraq than did the United States. In addition, the U.S. government understandably was more attracted to a policy position that enjoyed broad multilateral support than one opposed by virtually all of its friends and allies. Moreover, any effort by the United States to act against Iraq without regional support would have jeopardized improved U.S.-Arab relations and overall U.S. credibility in the Middle East.[43]

This leads to a third lesson: the need for reliable intelligence assets and capabilities when implementing a policy of engagement.[44] Evaluating any country's behavior in the context of an engagement policy is never an easy task. Given the limited relationship between the United States and Iraq, it is not surprising that U.S. intelligence capabilities with regard to Iraq were scant, especially in terms of human assets. This deficiency made it difficult to interpret ambiguous information about Saddam Hussein's actions and intentions.

Although NSD 26 laid out a policy of conditional engagement, it provided neither explicit milestones for determining whether Iraq was responding favorably to positive incentives, nor a precise list of Iraqi actions that might necessitate some form of sanction. The United States thus had adopted a soft, or implicit, form of conditional engagement. The policy sought to promote improved behavior by Iraq without clear guidelines for the specific actions that Iraq was expected to take (or avoid). Nor did the policy provide for specific responses by the United States to particular Iraqi actions. Under these circumstances, proponents of engagement, especially those who were committed to (and thus had a stake in) the policy, may have been more inclined than a neutral observer to interpret mixed conduct favorably, discount negative conduct, and temper U.S. responses to provocative actions by Iraq.[45] Indeed, it was less apparent at the time than in hindsight that Iraqi conduct showed an emerging pattern of irresponsible behavior.

A fourth lesson concerns the process for making judgments when formulating a policy to respond to the conduct of a problem state. Ideally, there should be relatively clear guidelines for desired conduct, especially in the initial, confidence-building stages of what has been a hostile relationship. Setting forth those guidelines as part of a hard, or explicit, form of conditional engagement might have provided a road map for actions that the United States and Iraq could have taken in seeking to normalize relations.

Such a road map, with discrete, reciprocal steps, would have clarified for domestic interest groups the specific conduct expected of Iraq. It also might have facilitated greater scrutiny and more careful assessment of Iraqi actions. And it would have made clear how the U.S. government would respond to a failure by Iraq to meet expectations, thereby reducing the likelihood of criticism of particular elements of U.S. policy.

A fifth lesson relates to engagement with an authoritarian regime. Any policy of engagement, by definition, provides the initiative to the target state to decide whether to acquiesce in the engagement effort or to resist it. An authoritarian ruler such as Saddam Hussein, in whom virtually all state power resides, can readily commit to engagement if he is so inclined. Yet if such a ruler declines to engage, he can just as easily refuse to moderate policy, or decide to reverse course away from recent positive initiatives, without much concern about public opinion. Indeed, because of the authoritarian nature of the Iraqi regime, it was extremely difficult for the United States directly to engage the Iraqi people in a manner designed to put pressure on Saddam to moderate his conduct.

U.S. policy toward Iraq in the 1988–90 period was both helped and hindered by the dilemma posed in dealing with an authoritarian ruler: the regime can easily embrace or scuttle an engagement effort. Initially, in the aftermath of the Iran-Iraq War, Saddam Hussein gave indications that he was willing to moderate his conduct and work cooperatively with Arab neighbors and Western countries. By early 1990, however, he decided for his own reasons to reverse course. Once Saddam made that decision, he headed down a path of collision with the Kuwaitis, regardless of U.S. policy.

A related set of problems engendered by dealing with an authoritarian regime has plagued post–Gulf War policy toward Iraq.[46] At the end of the Gulf War, the United Nations Security Council (UNSC) enacted several resolutions setting forth the terms for ending hostilities with Iraq, including the requirement of weapons inspections and the (temporary) imposition of economic sanctions. The centerpiece of the sanctions regime was UNSC Resolution 687, which established a road map for Iraq to follow to end sanctions. In particular, paragraph 22 of Resolution 687 provided that sanctions against the importation from Iraq of commodities, such as oil, would remain in place until the Security Council agreed that Iraq had complied with all directives in that resolution involving the inspection and destruction of Iraq's weapons of mass destruction and missile delivery systems. Resolution 687 contemplated—and the United States and other members of the Security Council expected—that Iraq would comply promptly with the provisions of Resolution 687, so that sanctions could be lifted. Yet that has not occurred, as Iraq has lied repeatedly to weapons inspectors, sought to conceal its weapons program, and obstructed the inspections process.

Frustrated by these circumstances, the Clinton administration publicly began tying the lifting of oil sanctions against Iraq to compliance by the Iraqis with all UNSC resolutions, rather than just Resolution 687's provisions related to weapons of mass destruction. Indeed, the administration has even suggested on occasion that sanctions would continue in place as long as Saddam Hussein remained in power. This expanded conditionality that the Clinton administration imposed, though intended to increase the likelihood of a military coup against Saddam, has been criticized by some as "moving the goalposts" and, in any event, has not succeeded in changing the situation within Iraq.

Now, after almost ten years of sanctions and with Iraq's expulsion of UN inspections teams from its territory, members of the Security Council have moved in the opposite direction, adopting a new (and apparently less intrusive) inspections program for Iraq, with the prospect that sanctions against Iraq could be suspended within a year merely if the Iraqis cooperate with the inspectors. Yet this approach also is problematic. It rewards Iraq for its prolonged noncompliance with the conditions set forth in Resolution 687, clearly a bad signal to other "rogue" states contemplating activities contrary to international norms.

Conclusion

The legacy of the U.S. engagement policy toward Iraq is a renewed sense of disillusionment and outrage by Americans with Saddam Hussein. On the one hand, having sought to engage Iraq and having forgone the unilateral imposition of sanctions, the United States was well positioned to lead the international coalition against Saddam. On the other hand, the United States emerged from the Gulf War more determined than ever not to allow Iraq to develop weapons of mass destruction or threaten its neighbors in the Persian Gulf. Until it is clear that all of Iraq's weapons of mass destruction have been destroyed, opinion in the United States remains firmly behind a policy of economic sanctions toward Iraq, backed at times, in response to provocative Iraqi actions, with the use of military force. With Saddam Hussein having rejected the conditions for ending the sanctions set forth in UNSC Resolution 687, the road toward again engaging Iraq, at least temporarily, has reached a dead end. Once more, therefore, policymakers are faced with a series of unattractive options for dealing with Iraq.

Notes

1. Kenneth I. Juster was a senior official at the State Department during the Bush administration, though he did not participate in the formulation or implementation of U.S. policy toward Iraq before Iraq's invasion of Kuwait in August 1990.

2. For an excellent summary of U.S. interests in the Middle East, see Robert Satloff, "America, Europe, and the Middle East in the 1990s: Interests and Policies," in Robert D. Blackwill and Michael Stürmer, eds., *Allies Divided: Transatlantic Policies for the Greater Middle East* (MIT Press, 1997), pp. 7–39. For a critique of the standard view of U.S. interests in the Persian Gulf, see Graham E. Fuller and Ian O. Lesser, "Persian Gulf Myths," *Foreign Affairs*, vol. 76 (May-June 1997), pp. 42–52.

3. A fourth interest sometimes expressed in U.S. policy is encouraging political and economic reforms and promoting human rights in the region. This objective, however, has often assumed a lower priority than the other three, particularly when its implementation complicates the pursuit of other goals, such as maintaining regional stability.

4. See Amatzia Baram, "U.S. Input into Iraqi Decisionmaking, 1988–1990," in David W. Lesch, ed., *The Middle East and the United States: A Historical and Political Reassessment* (Boulder, Colo: Westview Press, 1996), pp. 325–27.

5. In the early 1980s, Saddam Hussein appeared to accept in principle Israel's right to exist and expressed his support, privately and publicly, for peace negotiations between Israel and the Arabs. Lawrence Freedman and Efraim Karsh, *The Gulf Conflict, 1990–1991: Diplomacy and War in the New World Order* (Princeton University Press, 1993), p. 21; Judith Miller and Laurie Mylroie, *Saddam Hussein and the Crisis in the Gulf* (Times Books, 1990), pp. 143–45.

6. By the end of the Reagan administration (into fiscal year 1989), the CCC had extended approximately $4.5 billion in credit guarantees to U.S. agricultural exporters for sales to Iraq.

7. In May 1987, however, the "accidental" attack by an Iraqi jet on the USS *Stark*, which killed thirty-seven American sailors, threatened U.S. relations with Iraq. Saddam Hussein apologized for the incident, and Iraq made compensatory payments of $27 million to the families of the victims.

8. Elaine Sciolino, *The Outlaw State: Saddam Hussein's Quest for Power and the Gulf Crisis* (John Wiley and Sons, 1991), pp. 140–42, 144; Miller and Mylroie, *Saddam Hussein and the Crisis in the Gulf*, p. 157; Kenneth R. Timmerman, *The Death Lobby: How the West Armed Iraq* (Houghton Mifflin, 1991), pp. 420–23.

9. Sciolino, *The Outlaw State*, p. 152.

10. See, for example, Douglas Frantz and Murray Waas, "Secret Effort by Bush Helped Hussein Build Military Might," *Los Angeles Times*, February 23, 1992, p. A1; Douglas Frantz, "Bush Exercised Hands-On Role in Iraq Aid Effort," *Los Angeles Times*, April 27, 1992, p. A1.

11. More than $1 billion worth of cargo trucks licensed for export were never sent to Iraq. U.S. Department of Commerce, "BXA Facts: Fact Sheet on Export Licensing for Iraq," December 16, 1991.

12. Eileen M. Albanese, Acting Director, Office of Export Licensing, U.S. Depart-

ment of Commerce, letter to author, June 10, 1993 (responding to Freedom of Information Act request for "a year-by-year breakdown of export licenses granted and goods shipped to Iraq for each of years 1985 through 1990").

13. France, Germany, Italy, and the United Kingdom each provided two to four times as many high-technology exports to Iraq as did the United States. Timmerman, *The Death Lobby,* p. 417. Many of these sales of high-technology items to Iraq came at a time when COCOM—the group established by the United States and its allies after World War II to control technology—had been removing restrictions on high-technology exports to the Warsaw Pact and other communist countries.

14. Sciolino, *The Outlaw State,* pp. 149–51.

15. Miller and Mylroie, *Saddam Hussein and the Crisis in the Gulf,* p. 147.

16. Richard W. Murphy, assistant secretary of state for Near Eastern and South Asian affairs, memorandum to Michael H. Armacost, under secretary of state for political affairs, "U.S. Policy Toward Iraq and CW Use," September 19, 1988 (declassified). In addition, domestic agricultural interest groups objected to a suspension of the CCC program for Iraq, and the oil industry protested against any possible oil boycott. Sciolino, *The Outlaw State,* p. 171.

17. This position was exemplified in a memorandum from Zalmay Khalilzad of the U.S. Department of State's policy planning staff to Secretary of State George P. Shultz. Sciolino, *The Outlaw State,* p. 170.

18. See Freedman and Karsh, *The Gulf Conflict, 1990-1991,* pp. 21–22.

19. Ibid, p. 22.

20. See James A. Baker III, *The Politics of Diplomacy: Revolution, War and Peace, 1989–1992* (G. P. Putnam's Sons, 1995), pp. 270–74.

21. Allegations regarding Iraqi abuse of the CCC program mushroomed over time into more pernicious charges—labeled the Iraqgate scandal—that the Bush administration had illegally aided Iraq in the years before the Gulf War by, among other things, helping divert money to Iraqi arms agents, improperly shipping arms to Iraq, and covering up such alleged malfeasance. Several years of extensive investigations by various executive branch, congressional, and judicial bodies, during both the Bush and Clinton administrations (including a two-year investigation by President Clinton's Justice Department), failed to substantiate any of the Iraqgate charges. See John M. Hogan, acting United States attorney, Northern District of Georgia, and counselor to the attorney general, "BNL Task Force—Final Report," October 21, 1994 (1/16/95), and "Addendum to the BNL Task Force—Final Report," October 21, 1994 (1/17/95). See also Kenneth I. Juster, "The Myth of Iraqgate," *Foreign Policy,* no. 94 (Spring 1994), pp. 105–19.

22. Statement by John E. Robson, deputy secretary, U.S. Department of the Treasury, in *The Banca Nazionale del Lavoro (BNL) Scandal and the Department of Agriculture's Commodity Credit Corporation (CCC) Program for Iraq, Part 1,* Hearing before the House Committee on Banking, Finance and Urban Affairs, 102 Cong. 2 sess., May 21, 1992, pp. 26–28.

23. See U.S. General Accounting Office, "International Trade: Iraq's Participation in U.S. Agricultural Export Programs," GAO/NSIAD-91-76, November 1990, pp. 2–3, 12.

24. U.S. Department of State cable, "Message from Secretary to Iraqi FonMin [*sic*] on CCC," November 9, 1989 (declassified).

25. Baker, *The Politics of Diplomacy*, p. 267.

26. These irregularities included what appeared to be abnormally high prices being charged by U.S. exporters to Iraq and reports that the Iraqi government was requiring exporters to pay a stamp tax, which is prohibited under the CCC program. See statement by Richard T. Crowder, under secretary for international affairs and commodity programs, U.S. Department of Agriculture, in *The Banca Nazionale del Lavoro (BNL) Scandal, Part 1*, pp. 216–18.

27. Ibid., p. 217.

28. Amatzia Baram, "The Iraqi Invasion of Kuwait: Decision-making in Baghdad," in Amatzia Baram and Barry Rubin, eds., *Iraq's Road to War* (St. Martin's Press, 1993), pp. 9–10.

29. "President [Hussein] Warns Israel, Criticizes US," Baghdad Radio, April 2, 1990, *Foreign Broadcast Information Service, Daily Report: Iraq*, April 3, 1990, pp. 32–36.

30. As part of this effort, ten days after Saddam Hussein's threat to Israel, a group of five U.S. senators visited Iraq. The senators delivered a letter to Saddam denouncing Iraq's efforts to obtain chemical and nuclear weapons, while also reassuring Saddam that President Bush did not support a campaign against Iraq.

31. Edward W. Gnehm, acting assistant secretary of state for Near Eastern and South Asian affairs, memorandum to James A. Baker III, secretary of state, "DC Meeting on Iraq," April 16, 1989 (declassified). In July 1990, the Bush administration formally initiated the process of implementing a revised set of export controls with particular focus on Iraq. See Secretary of State James A. Baker III, letter to Secretary of Commerce Robert A. Mosbacher, July 25, 1990. This process came to be known as the enhanced proliferation control initiative.

32. Baram, "U.S. Input into Iraqi Decisionmaking, 1988–1990," p. 334.

33. Ibid, pp. 344, 347.

34. See John F. Kennedy School of Government, Case Program, "Prelude to War: US Policy toward Iraq 1988–1990" (Harvard University, 1994), pp. 18–20.

35. In July 1990, the Bush administration also intercepted the export to Iraq of an induction-melting furnace that potentially could have been used for nuclear explosive purposes.

36. Baram, "The Iraqi Invasion of Kuwait," p. 18.

37. U.S. Department of State cable, "Iraq/Kuwait: Ambassador's Meeting with Saddam Husayn," July 25, 1990 (declassified); U.S. Department of State cable, "Saddam's Message of Friendship to President Bush," July 25, 1990 (declassified).

38. See John F. Kennedy School of Government, Case Program, "Prelude to War," pp. 26–29.

39. See, for example, George Bush and Brent Scowcroft, *A World Transformed* (Alfred A. Knopf, 1998); Baker, *The Politics of Diplomacy*.

40. *Developments in the Middle East*, Hearing and Markup before the Subcommittee on Europe and the Middle East of the House Committee on Foreign Affairs, 101 Cong. 2 sess., June 20, 1990, p. 17.

41. Chief among the congressional critics was Henry Gonzalez (Democrat of

Texas), then-chairman of the House Committee on Banking, Finance and Urban Affairs. Also see William Safire, "Crimes of Iraqgate," *New York Times*, May 18, 1992, p. A17; Bruce W. Jentleson, *With Friends Like These: Reagan, Bush, and Saddam, 1982–1990* (W. W. Norton, 1994), p. 250; Zachary Karabell, "Backfire: U.S. Policy Toward Iraq, 1988–2 August 1990," *Middle East Journal*, vol. 49 (Winter 1995), pp. 28–47; Senator Al Gore, Address before the Center for National Policy, Washington, D.C., September 29, 1992.

42. See Jentleson, *With Friends Like These*, p. 244.

43. See Bush and Scowcroft, *A World Transformed*, p. 313.

44. Of course, the implementation of economic sanctions also requires reliable intelligence to monitor trade with the target state and to prevent any leakages in the sanctions program.

45. Similarly, opponents of engagement may have been more likely to view mixed conduct by Iraq in a negative light and propose harsh U.S. responses.

46. See Kenneth I. Juster, "Iraq: An American Perspective," in Richard N. Haass, ed., *Transatlantic Tensions: The United States, Europe, and Problem Countries* (Brookings, 1999), pp. 102–23.

5

The United States and North Korea: Cooperative Security on the Agreed Framework and Beyond

LEON V. SIGAL

Since the 1990s, the United States has had four main interests at stake with North Korea. It has wanted to ensure that, whatever happened internally in North Korea, the artillery that Pyongyang placed within range of Seoul was never fired in anger. Second, it has desired to keep Pyongyang from acquiring nuclear arms. Third, it has endeavored to prevent North Korea from developing, testing, deploying, and selling any more medium- or longer-range ballistic missiles. Finally, it has sought reconciliation between the two Koreas and the peaceful reunification of the peninsula. Although all these objectives have framed U.S. policy toward North Korea, the second interest had top priority in both the Bush and Clinton administrations.

The question of how best to satisfy these interests has been the subject of much debate. Coercion was unlikely to work; it would only ensure that North Korea deployed more artillery near the demilitarized zone, sought more aggressively to acquire nuclear arms, and tested, deployed, and sold more missiles. Encouraging the collapse of North Korea, which some thought was in America's interest, was far too risky a course, especially if the United States had not achieved its first three aims. Even benign neglect of North Korea would only lead to more mischief-making by Pyongyang. Others wanted to condition U.S. aid on change or reform in North

Korea. Yet it was doctrinaire to put free market ideology ahead of security. Change would only come to North Korea when it let in more outsiders from the international community, both governmental and nongovernmental. That, too, could not happen without Pyongyang's cooperation.

The most appropriate way to satisfy U.S. interests was to use diplomacy to test North Korea's willingness to cooperate with the United States.[1] Nevertheless, it was regarded as politically risky to conduct a diplomatic probe of North Korean intentions because of the mistaken belief, widely shared in the American foreign policy establishment and reflected in the press, that cooperation was likely to fail. This shared image was especially prevalent among experts on Korea and on nuclear proliferation, who assumed that North Korea was hell-bent on acquiring nuclear arms and missiles and unwilling to live up to any commitments it might make. At the same time, the communist regime was believed to be on the verge of collapse. Operating under these assumptions, government agencies were reluctant to commit resources to a package of inducements, and Congress was wary of appropriating funds for such a purpose. Top policymakers were unwilling to expend scarce time and political capital mustering support for any policy as unpromising as deal making with North Korea. Threats seemed cheaper and more expedient than promises, at least in the political currency of Washington.

As a consequence, from 1989 until the spring of 1994, the United States was unwilling to engage in sustained diplomatic give-and-take with North Korea. Instead it adopted a crime-and-punishment approach in the belief that the way to get states to abandon nuclear arming was to demonize them as outlaws and force them to disarm. The United States at first insisted that North Korea comply with inspectors from the International Atomic Energy Agency (IAEA) as a precondition for talks. Then America entered into high-level talks with extreme reluctance. Even when it did so, it was unwilling to specify what it would give North Korea in return for abandoning nuclear arming. Moreover, when it did make promises, they were not always kept, often because South Korea and the IAEA were unwilling to carry them out. As a result, the talks went nowhere.

Perhaps the most egregious example of this interplay came after the Democratic People's Republic of Korea (DPRK) and the United States agreed, on December 29, 1993, on four steps to be taken simultaneously.[2] The United States and South Korea would suspend their joint Team Spirit military exercises for 1994. North Korea would allow the IAEA to begin "inspections necessary to ensure the continuity of safeguards," assuring itself that the North was not diverting spent nuclear fuel to bomb making.[3] North Korea would resume working-level talks with South Korea; and the United States, in turn, would hold a third round of high-level talks with the DPRK. However, Seoul refused to call off joint Team Spirit military exercises until an exchange of special envoys took place with Pyongyang and until IAEA inspections were completed. Washington backed Seoul, thereby reneging on its agreement with Pyongyang. This action led to the collapse of talks and very nearly to war in June 1994.

In this instance, as in others, North Korea was unwilling to comply with U.S. demands first and hope for rewards for its actions later. It was loathe to give up its nuclear program unless it got something in return. It was widely assumed in Washington that North Korea was engaged in blackmail. However, evidence suggests that North Korea's most inflammatory actions were not blackmail attempts, but instead responses to American acts of noncooperation. North Korea was playing tit-for-tat—cooperating when the United States cooperated, retaliating when the United States reneged—in an effort to get the United States to negotiate in earnest.[4] When Washington unilaterally withdrew its nuclear arms from Korea and suspended Team Spirit military exercises, Pyongyang reciprocated in December 1991 by signing a denuclearization accord with Seoul and a safeguards agreement with the IAEA. To demonstrate its interest in cooperating, North Korea halted reprocessing in 1991 and delayed removing spent nuclear fuel from its reactor until 1994. Similarly, when Washington resumed high-level talks in June 1993 and pledged in a joint statement to refrain from nuclear threats and respect North Korean sovereignty, Pyongyang agreed to suspend its withdrawal from the Nuclear Nonproliferation Treaty (NPT) and to resume nuclear inspections for the purpose of ensuring that no diversion of spent nuclear fuel or further reprocessing was taking place. By contrast, when Washington refused to engage in high-level talks after January 1992, Pyongyang was slow to let the safeguards agreement come into force. Moreover, Washington ignored Pyongyang's proposal for replacement reactors in June 1992 and instead resumed Team Spirit military exercises after the IAEA demanded special inspections. In response, on March 12, 1993, Pyongyang announced its intent to renounce the NPT; however, it left in place the seals and cameras installed by the IAEA as a safeguard against diversion of reactor fuel to bomb making.

Resisting Engagement: Assessing Options for Coercive Diplomacy

Ideally, the DPRK would have lived up to its obligations under the Nuclear Nonproliferation Treaty voluntarily. But what if it did not? What if it wanted something in return for complying? Both the Bush and Clinton administrations were reluctant to spell out the inducements and instead tried to attain North Korean compliance by threatening economic sanctions.[5] The viability of most options was hampered by the attitude of U.S. allies and the difficulty of using military force. As a result, the United States was forced to turn to negotiations with North Korea.

In the early 1990s, the U.S. domestic political climate was inhospitable to cooperative threat reduction, that is, using positive inducements, reassurances, and reciprocity rather than threats to enhance U.S. security. Although the American public consistently preferred talks to war, the U.S. foreign policy establishment was skeptical of negotiations, even hostile to them. Proliferation experts, following the IAEA's lead, preferred to have North Korea renounce the NPT than to bribe it to comply.[6] Korea experts, following Seoul's lead, were opposed to having Washington engage Pyongyang. The very thought of accommodation with a hateful communist regime in Pyongyang also antagonized unilateralists on the right wing of the Republican Party, who tended to distrust international cooperation and to prefer that the United States go it alone in the world. They pushed strenuously to derail diplomacy and confront North Korea. Collapse, not cooperation, was their idea of how to deal with the North's nuclear program.

With implacable opposition outside and skepticism inside, the Clinton administration moved to resume talks with North Korea. Secretary of State Warren Christopher, Secretary of Defense Les Aspin, and National Security Adviser Anthony Lake met with South Korea's foreign minister, Han Sung Joo, in Washington on March 29, 1993. Afterward, Han said that they had reached a general understanding on a stick-and-carrot approach to the North Koreans: "The threat of sanctions plus certain face-saving inducements will help them comply." Han emphasized the need for carrots, arguing that "pressure alone will not work." A senior State Department official, when told of Han's comments, said Pyongyang "always had the kind of assurances" he was talking about and that Washington had no plans to offer a more explicit quid pro quo.[7] His comment strongly implied a policy of all stick, no carrot.

The carrot-and-stick policy was aptly characterized by one proponent: "To get a mule to move, you have to show it the carrot and hit it with a stick at the same time."[8] The mule may be struck repeatedly, but is fed the carrot only when it reaches the mule driver's destination, if at all. The metaphor was not lost on the DPRK. In May 1993, just before high-level talks resumed in New York, North Korean negotiators asked an American visitor in Pyongyang, "What is the meaning of 'sticks and carrots'?" One of them showed the visitor the entry "carrot-and-stick" in an old Merriam-Webster dictionary, which had a drawing of a donkey with a bunch of carrots hanging before it; next to the donkey stood its master, stick in hand.[9]

An appreciation of North Korea's insecurity might have led America to abandon coercive diplomacy altogether. Instead, the United States pursued what it called "the step-by-step approach," setting preconditions for high-level talks and insisting that North Korea take the first step. Only after the North complied fully with IAEA safeguards and resumed North-South talks would the United States engage in diplomatic negotiations. Washington did not get very far going step-by-step.

North Korea wanted specific promises and intended to hold the United States to them. "We watched how you dealt with the Russians," said a senior North Korean at that time, referring to Washington's fitful cooperation with Moscow. "We will not let that happen to us."[10] The day after South Korea's foreign minister met with senior U.S. officials, North Korea's minister of atomic energy "categorically" rejected the IAEA's demand for a special inspection, but invited consultations on "implementation of the Safeguards Agreement"—inspections of areas apart from the nuclear waste sites.[11] On April 1, the IAEA declared the DPRK in violation of the Nuclear Nonproliferation Treaty. There were twenty-eight ayes; China and Libya voted no; India, Pakistan, Syria, and Vietnam abstained. The IAEA referred the matter to the UN Security Council to enforce compliance. On April 8, in a move designed to avoid a veto by China, the Security Council president issued a statement urging further consultations between the IAEA and the DPRK.

In what was to become a leitmotif of U.S. nuclear diplomacy, the IAEA vote and Security Council action stirred yearnings to romance China. It was a case of looking for love in all the wrong places. Certainly, Beijing had its own interests in a nonnuclear North Korea. It wanted to discourage Japan from nuclear arming and to prevent South Korea from eventually inheriting North Korea's nuclear program. As Foreign Minister Qian Qichen put it in November 1991, "We do not want to see the existence of nuclear weapons on the Korean Peninsula."[12] China disagreed with the United States over how best to achieve that aim, however. Having suffered from a U.S.-led embargo in the past, Beijing was opposed in principle to economic sanctions.[13] Whether it vetoed a Security Council resolution or just abstained, China was unwilling to enforce stringent sanctions, such as an oil embargo against North Korea, for fear of destabilizing its next-door neighbor. China was also sensitive about control of its border with North Korea, which resembles that between the United States and Mexico. Smuggling runs rampant, often with the connivance of local authorities, who benefit both politically and financially from the profitable cross-border traffic in goods and currency. With ethnic Koreans in substantial numbers on the Chinese side of the border, it could serve as a convenient escape route for those fleeing deprivation in North Korea in the event of an economic embargo. For the central government in Beijing, already struggling with assertive regional authorities throughout China, trying to enforce sanctions could prove embarrassing or, even worse, could set off local unrest.[14]

The Clinton administration tried to exploit China's reluctance to support sanctions by getting Beijing to exert pressure on Pyongyang. "The threat of sanctions," said a top official in the administration, "moved the Chinese to help lean on the North Koreans because the Chinese didn't want to go through that."[15] Just how hard Beijing leaned on Pyongyang is open to question. For its part, Beijing emphasized the limits of its influence in Pyongyang and never linked its stance toward the North with its continued most-favored-nation trading status.[16] Yet China did lend tacit political support to American efforts by abstaining on UN Security Council resolutions and by helping draft statements for the council president urging North Korean compliance. It reportedly showed its displeasure in March by turning down a request by Kim Jong Il to see Deng Xiaoping during a visit to Beijing. Subsequently, Kim canceled the visit. In turn, a high-level Chinese visit to Pyongyang on April 15, on the occasion of Kim Il Sung's birthday, was canceled, and the DPRK briefly sealed its border with China after North Korean guards had fired on the Chinese.[17] China was reluctant to assist North Korea by supplying oil at concessionary "friendship prices," but it did send food and other aid to sustain the North's economy against collapse. China also offered the country a strategic alternative to nuclear arming by reaffirming Chinese-North Korean solidarity and reassuring the DPRK about the strength of the Sino-Korean alliance. Yet rather than embracing the role of middle-man between the West and North Korea, China in effect kept telling Washington, "Forget about us. Talk to Pyongyang."

This Chinese position prompted the American diplomatic effort that was to follow. As one U.S. official admitted, "The only way we could build a consensus at the UN Security Council to impose sanctions was to demonstrate that the North Koreans were unwilling to make a deal."[18] Yet Chinese officials would not be easy to convince. They remained in close contact with North Korea, putting them in a good position to judge which side was impeding a deal and leaving the North Koreans unconvinced of China's willingness to impose sanctions. Without Chinese cooperation, sanctions would be an empty threat.

Further difficulties with relying on sanctions to curb North Korean behavior became obvious in November 1993, when Defense Secretary Les

Aspin, en route to the annual Security Consultative Meeting in Seoul, stopped off in Tokyo. His Japanese interlocutors showed some willingness to curb high-technology exports to North Korea but refused to stanch the flow of remittances from Koreans in Japan to their kin in North Korea. Both Japan and South Korea were concerned about allowing this [behavior] to go on in a "chronic, gnawing way," Aspin acknowledged in a background briefing, "but no one really wants to move to sanctions yet."[19]

The likelihood that sanctions would prove politically provocative and economically ineffective was one major premise of trying for a diplomatic deal; the risk of war was another. It was a risk that the armed services were reluctant to run. North Korea regarded sanctions as a breach of the Korean War armistice with the United Nations and sanctions under Chapter 7 of the UN Charter were, as the North Koreans repeatedly said, tantamount to an act of war. Although North Korea had never quite threatened to start a war if sanctions were imposed, the Pentagon needed to be prepared for that possibility. Before sanctions were imposed, it was prudent for the United States to send reinforcements to Korea.

The trouble was, however, that these precautions in themselves could provoke war. North Korea was weaker than South Korea, even without U.S. help. Every time the allies ran military exercises in Korea, the North mobilized its forces. "Anything that we do, however defensive it looks, is offensive to them," explained General James Clapper, Defense Intelligence Agency (DIA) director at the time. "That's why they don't even like to see logistical exercises."[20] Large-scale reinforcements could easily be mistaken by North Korea as a prelude to war, triggering preemptive moves. Even lesser reinforcements would lead the country to mobilize, prompting the United States and South Korea to countermobilize. As both sides readied their forces and stepped up reconnaissance on land and sea, a helicopter straying across the demilitarized zone or a submarine running aground offshore could inadvertently set off a war.

Applying military pressure also posed problems. In the summer of 1993, the administration began planning a graduated campaign of coercive diplomacy, using sanctions and military deployments to pressure Pyongyang. This strategy put the U.S. commander in Korea, General Gary Luck, in a quandary. A high-ranking officer with the U.S. forces in Korea said, "You've got to make your military moves so they don't drive your diplomatic actions." This reality required "playing our cards just right so that in the process of getting proliferation under control we didn't cause a ground war to be fought on the peninsula, a ground war which we thought we could win, but winning would come at great cost."[21]

The possibility of air strikes and covert operations against North Korea's nuclear facilities also encountered resistance in the Pentagon. Air strikes had support among intrepid enthusiasts of air power, but those skeptical of this strategy included members of the Joint Staff and senior civilians in the Defense Department. Some air force officers contended that they had a high probability of destroying all the known nuclear sites without causing massive collateral damage or starting fires, spewing radioactivity across Japan. Others in the Pentagon, aware of air power's poor performance against Iraq's weapons of mass destruction, had their doubts. These hesitations were fueled by the speculation of intelligence analysts about clandestine sites in North Korean tunnels. Bombers could not target what they could not locate. "We can't find nuclear weapons now, except by going on a house-to-house search," Air Force Chief of Staff Merrill McPeak told reporters at a breakfast backgrounder. Even if the nuclear sites could be found, McPeak added, "If you put them deep enough underground, we can't get down to [them]."[22]

Air options ranged in scope from a surgical strike on known nuclear sites to other suspect sites, to chemical and biological weapons facilities, to air defenses that guarded those sites, to other military targets. The attitude was "while we're at it, why not get them all," said a Pentagon official.[23] This outlook was understandable because of the widespread belief in the Pentagon that air strikes were likely to trigger all-out war. One civilian privy to the planning revealed that Pentagon officials "felt there would be a war, but they were very optimistic the mission would be a success."[24] For these reasons, air strikes—while not ruled out if North Korea were to unload spent fuel from its reactor and resume reprocessing—were not an attractive option.

Facing Crisis: Going to the Brink of War

While the drawbacks of each of these policy options were apparent in the abstract, the risk of war became all too palpable in the spring of 1994. In December 1993 Washington had agreed to a package deal with North Korea in principle, but not in practice. When Seoul did not suspend Team Spirit and put preconditions on North-South talks in March 1994, reneging on promises the United States had made to Pyongyang, the North again impeded the IAEA's access. The Pentagon began taking precautions in the event that sanctions were to be imposed. Depending on the severity of the sanctions, General Luck recommended dispatching Patriot antimissile batteries, expediting delivery of Apache helicopters and Bradley armored vehicles, stationing an aircraft carrier off Korea, and reinforcing air and ground units.

"General Luck feels that sanctions are a dangerous option," said an administration official. "As the commander of 37,000 men there he will want to try to increase deterrence if we go that route."[25]

President Clinton scheduled a well-publicized briefing on Pentagon plans in February 1994 by Joint Chiefs of Staff Chairman John Shalikashvili and General Luck. According to a top official, such preparations indicated the serious nature of the plans. He found the discussion of reinforcement options sobering: "The intelligence people were saying this could be very provocative."[26] General Luck's assessment, recalls a participant, was just as sobering: "You could win and you could punish the North, but in the process you would punish everyone else who's a participant. The North has and will continue to have a tremendous capacity to do great damage to the South even in its weakened state."[27]

On March 19, 1994, North-South talks broke off. The Principals' Committee met and opted for coercive diplomacy. It decided to resume Team Spirit exercises, to consult with Seoul on dispatching Patriot antimissile batteries to Korea, and to mobilize support for sanctions in the UN Security Council.[28] Yet in trying to ratchet up the crisis by mustering support for sanctions, Secretary of State Christopher found little enthusiasm in Seoul or Tokyo. He sought to put the best face on his talks in Beijing: "I would say that if we work at it carefully and patiently in the United Nations and bring the Chinese along, that they will not block the imposition of sanctions." Enforcing them was another matter. Appearing on *Face the Nation* on March 20, Christopher acknowledged that he had no assurances of a Chinese abstention in the Security Council: "What we do have is their encouragement to pursue patient diplomacy."[29] Two days later Prime Minister Li Peng left no doubt about China's opposition to coercing North Korea, "If pressure is applied on this issue, that can only complicate the situation on the Korean peninsula, and it will add to the tension there."[30]

North Korea had told the IAEA it was ready to let the agency resume the March inspection, and it invited inspectors to witness the long-delayed refueling of the Yongbyon reactor to verify that spent fuel was placed in nearby cooling ponds and not diverted to bomb making. However, it balked when the IAEA insisted on setting aside a cross section of the 7,500 rods in the reactor for analysis to determine the reactor's operating history: how many bombs' worth, if any, of spent fuel might have been removed in the past. On May 12, Pyongyang shut down the reactor and began removing the plutonium-laden spent fuel. On May 31, President Clinton met again with the Principals' Committee to determine the U.S. sanctions strategy. Tokyo and Beijing were still cool to sanctions, and the Pentagon, concerned about appearing too provocative, preferred to "go low and slow."[31] The administration adopted a phased approach: first a warning by the Security Council, then a thirty-day grace period, to be followed by a gradual tightening of sanctions. The initial steps were modest: a halt to all cooperation that could contribute to North Korea's nuclear know-how, an end to UN economic aid, a cutback in diplomatic activities with the North, a curtailment of cultural, technical, scientific, commercial, and educational exchanges, and a UN ban on arms trade with the North.[32] The administration discreetly sounded out South Korea, Japan, and China on the possibility of attacking Yongbyon, should North Korea begin removing spent fuel from the cooling ponds and reprocessing it. The reaction was negative. "Japan does not regard North Korea as its adversary," Tokyo responded; "Every action has an equal and opposite reaction," replied the Chinese official who was contacted. Asked how he thought North Korea would react, he replied, "Not North Korea, China."[33]

In consultations with Japan and South Korea, the United States broached the idea of imposing economic sanctions without a Security Council endorsement to get around a possible Chinese veto. Both were prepared to proceed with the first phase of sanctions but were unenthusiastic about going ahead without Security Council approval.[34] Japan had already taken steps to impede remittances to North Korea, despite opposition to sanctions by the Social Democratic Party, a partner in the ruling coalition.[35] Japan's representative, Shunji Yanai, told a reporter, "The US wants to apply sanctions faster than we do."[36] Nevertheless, the three countries issued a joint statement that the United Nations should "urgently consider an appropriate response, including sanctions."[37] President Clinton did not sound too eager to impose them, either. "There's still time," he declared, "for North Korea to avoid sanctions actually taking effect if we can work out something on the nuclear inspectors."[38] The sanctions strategy did gain some ground in Moscow, but only after Washington dropped its opposition to Russia's proposal for an international conference on North Korea before the imposition of sanctions.[39] Officials used the talk of economic sanctions to put pressure on Pyongyang, but with insufficient backing, the administration decided to opt for political pressure, while postponing the imposition of economic sanctions.[40]

On June 10, the IAEA suspended technical assistance to North Korea, the only sanction it had at its disposal. China's Foreign Minister Qian Qichen expressed regret, saying sanctions would be "ineffective," and appealed for the resumption of dialogue.[41] Pyongyang reacted by notifying Washington of its intent to withdraw from the IAEA. Such a move was not the same as abandoning the Nuclear Nonproliferation Treaty, which would have crossed one of the red lines drawn by the United States. On June 13, a Foreign Ministry spokesman declared that "the inspections for the continuity of safeguards, which we have allowed in our unique status, will no longer be allowed. Any unreasonable inspections can never be allowed until it has been decided whether we should return to the Nuclear Nonproliferation Treaty or completely withdraw from it." The spokesman "strongly [reaffirmed] our position that the UN 'sanctions' will be regarded immediately as a declaration of war." A declaration of war was not the same as the start of hostilities, but it did portend an end to talks: "Sanctions and dialogue are incompatible. It is our inevitable option to counter expanded sanctions by hostile forces with expanded self-defense measures."[42] With Washington on the verge of dispatching reinforcements, there were signs of panic in Seoul. The South Korean stock market plummeted, and shoppers emptied store shelves of provisions. As one State Department official remarked shortly thereafter, "This is what it looks like when two countries blunder into war."[43]

Former president Jimmy Carter arrived in Pyongyang on June 15, the very day the United States began circulating a draft resolution in the UN Security Council on the plan for graduated sanctions. Sanctions were to be imposed only if North Korea expelled the remaining IAEA inspectors, withdrew from the Nuclear Nonproliferation Treaty, or resumed reprocessing.[44] During the first phase, the U.S. draft included a mandatory ban on the sale of arms and their components; suspension of all development aid; a ban on air traffic other than passenger flights; a ban on technical and scientific cooperation; a ban on cultural, commercial, and educational exchanges; a ban on participation in athletic events; and a request, though not a requirement, to curtail the size and scope of diplomatic activities. A second phase would freeze most remittances. The third phase was not spelled out but could include a total trade embargo, including oil.[45] Because of fear of a violent reaction in North Korea, the gradual imposition of sanctions was the most that South Korea and Japan—or the Pentagon—would accept. Even so, Chinese acquiescence was still unlikely. If the Security Council was unable to act, the United States was prepared to form a coalition to impose sanctions without UN authorization.[46]

On June 16, Washington time, the day of Carter's first meeting with Kim Il Sung, President Clinton convened a Principals' Committee meeting to authorize reinforcements for Korea in anticipation of sanctions. The Pentagon proposed three options, depending on the severity of the sanctions. Its low option was to deploy 10,000 troops, mostly to handle logistics, in preparation for the 400,000 additional troops General Luck had said he would need in the event of war. A second option would be to dispatch another thirty to forty aircraft, including fighter planes, to South Korea and F-117 stealth fighter-bombers and other bombers to Guam. An even more robust option would also station a second aircraft carrier in the region and send more army and marine combat troops there. National Intelligence Officer for Warning Charles Allen briefed President Clinton on the sobering possibility that reinforcements could trigger North Korean mobilization, raising the risk of preemptive war. Such war warnings are customarily given to the president only when war seems imminent. "I don't recall a big alarm bell going off," said a top official who was there. One reason was that the CIA and the DIA disagreed: "CIA was more worried about the danger of war."[47] The risks of not sending reinforcements were also noted by Defense Secretary Perry and Joint Chiefs of Staff Chairman Shalikashvili. The president approved the Pentagon plans.

A phone call from Carter in Pyongyang interrupted the meeting. In a triumph of Track II diplomacy, Carter said he had the makings of the deal and was about to go on CNN to tell the world. He did that, and more. After talking up the chances of a deal, Carter publicly repudiated the administration's sanctions strategy. "Nothing should be done to exacerbate the situation now," he declared. "The reason I came over here was to try to prevent an irreconcilable mistake."[48] The White House immediately disavowed the statement, to no avail. Carter had gone public deliberately. "It was obvious," Carter himself wrote at the time, "that the threat of sanctions had no effect on them whatsoever, except as a pending insult, branding North Korea as an outlaw nation and their revered leader as a liar and criminal."[49] "His intent was to kill the sanctions movement," said a diplomat who was directly involved. "The North Koreans had reiterated that a sanctions resolution in the UN would be the breaking point. . . . Carter didn't know where it stood, but he wanted to make sure he killed it. He knew some countries were wavering and I think he figured that if he went on CNN and said we have the makings of a deal . . . it would cause any nation that was wavering to stand back and say, wait a minute, let's not rush to sanctions."[50]

The stratagem succeeded. The next day, June 16, Foreign Ministry spokesman Shen Guofang hardened China's stance against sanctions: "China in principle does not subscribe to the involvement of the Security Council in the nuclear issue on the Korean peninsula or the resort to sanctions to solve it."[51] Russian Foreign Minister Andrei Kozyrev also bridled at the U.S. draft on grounds that Russia had not been consulted in advance.[52] By overturning administration policy and publicly disavowing sanctions, Carter ensured that China and other fence-sitters in the UN Security Council would be in no hurry to vote. Putting off sanctions delayed the dispatch of reinforcements to Korea, defused the immediate crisis, and once again, opened the door for diplomatic give-and-take.

Embracing Engagement: The Agreed Framework and Beyond

Jimmy Carter managed to move the United States and North Korea away from the brink and back to the negotiating table. Once he did, it would take negotiators just four months to conclude an Agreed Framework on October 21, 1994. In a diplomatic victory, this accord mapped out reciprocal steps to resolve the nuclear issue.

The Agreed Framework was just that: an agreed framework, not a treaty, sidestepping the need for Senate action and avoiding diplomatic recognition of the DPRK that a treaty would imply. The accord carefully avoided obligating the United States to supply two replacement reactors and set just one fixed date, pledging U.S. best efforts to complete the first reactor by the end of 2003. Instead, it laid out a detailed road map of reciprocal steps, leaving both sides some leverage against reneging. The DPRK pledged to remain a party to the Nuclear Nonproliferation Treaty and to freeze its nuclear program by not refueling its reactor, to cooperate in arranging temporary safe storage of the spent fuel rods pending their eventual removal, and to seal its reprocessing plant to prevent it from extracting plutonium from those fuel rods. A confidential minute barred nuclear reactors or related facilities at other sites. Implementation of the freeze under IAEA monitoring was an immediate test of the North's good faith. In return, the United States promised to move toward political and economic normalization, exchange liaison offices, and "reduce barriers to trade and investment." The North pledged to "engage in North-South dialogue, as the Agreed Framework will help create an atmosphere that promotes such dialogue." Linking normalization with the United States to progress in North-South reconciliation cut both ways. Diplomatic relations between the sides would be upgraded "as progress is made on issues of concern to each side," a reference to missiles and North-South relations. A U.S.-organized consortium would construct two new nuclear reactors and provide the North a supply of heavy fuel oil in the interim.

In elaborately choreographed steps, nuclear dismantling would proceed along with construction of the replacement reactors. With construction of the plant and turbines for the first reactor complete, but before any nuclear components were supplied, the North would have to come into full compli-

ance with its safeguards agreement by "taking all steps that may be deemed
necessary by the IAEA, following consultations with the agency, with regard
to verifying the accuracy and completeness of the DPRK's initial report on
all nuclear material in the DPRK." Unspecified but clearly implied were two
steps that the agency could well deem necessary: special inspections and the
safeguarding of any previously undeclared nuclear material. In the next phase,
as the reactor's nuclear components were installed, the North would ship
out its fuel rods. As the second replacement reactor neared completion, the
North would complete the dismantlement of its gas-graphite reactors and
reprocessing plant.[53]

The United States committed itself to very little: it would supply a por-
tion of the heavy fuel oil needed to generate electricity while nuclear construction was underway and help arrange and pay for the storage of the
spent nuclear fuel. The bulk of the estimated $4.7 billion cost of construct-
ing the reactors and supplying the spent fuel would be borne by others, especially South Korea and Japan, although it would take several years to work
out exact cost-sharing arrangements. If these steps failed to meet the North's
energy needs, President Clinton in a letter to Kim Jong Il promised to "use
the full powers of my office to provide, to the extent necessary, such interim
energy alternatives from the United States, subject to the approval of the
U.S. Congress." The letter contained a similar obligation for the replacement
reactors.

Cooperative threat reduction under the Agreed Framework gave Washington the negotiating leverage it lacked. At the same time, the Agreed Framework was structured so that the United States would not have to give anything
away without getting something in return. It could also retract its inducements if North Korea did not comply. The agreement meant that the world
would still have to live with some ambiguity about North Korea's nuclear
past for at least five years, perhaps forever. What it does not have to live with
is the near certainty that by now the North could have nuclear weapons.

The Clinton administration tried hard to convince observers that North
Korea had backed down under the threat of sanctions and military actions.
"The Agreed Framework is the product of months of determined diplomacy and firm negotiation," Secretary of State Christopher later testified to
the Senate Foreign Relations Committee. "We negotiated from a position of
strength."[54] Most observers have uncritically accepted the claim that North
Korea changed course under threat of sanctions, but there is little evidence
to support the notion that Pyongyang relented under duress. Rather it appears that coercive diplomacy failed to secure full inspections or an end to
North Korea's nuclear program and showed little sign of succeeding any

time soon. North Korea's neighbors were unwilling to go along with more than symbolic sanctions. Worst of all, the dispatch of reinforcements, as a precaution in the event of a vote on sanctions, placed the United States on the brink of war. Given these drawbacks, the sanctions strategy was moribund long before Jimmy Carter prompted Washington to abandon it. Air strikes had also been set aside, to be considered only as a last resort if the North Koreans began removing spent fuel from the cooling ponds.

Nor did North Korea accede to the Agreed Framework because it had undergone a sudden change of heart. Rather, it had been trying for more than three years to strike a nuclear deal with the United States. One indication of this desire was the possibly self-imposed limits that North Korea had placed on its nuclear program in 1991 and its willingness to allow international inspectors to verify them. Consistent with a tit-for-tat strategy, North Korea became more accommodating as the threats evaporated. Only after Carter's repudiation of sanctions did Kim Il Sung agree to freeze the North Korean nuclear program. Moreover, an exchange of letters between Washington and Pyongyang followed in which North Korea clarified that no refueling would take place. Again, this step occurred after sanctions were no longer politically viable. In just four months of talks, the United States and the DPRK concluded the Agreed Framework, which, if fully implemented by both sides, could put an end to North Korean nuclear arming. This deal, too, was done without any credible threat of sanctions or use of force.

This much-maligned and misunderstood history is relevant today. Contrary to the conventional wisdom in Washington that Pyongyang is engaged in blackmail, there is significant evidence that North Korea has been trying to cooperate with the United States. North Korea had begun its nuclear program with the intent of making weapons, but by 1991 it had changed its aim. If North Korea had been determined to acquire nuclear arms in the early 1990s, as most people in Washington believed at the time, it could have shut down its nuclear reactor any time between 1991 and 1994, removed the fuel rods, and quickly reprocessed the spent fuel to extract plutonium, the explosive ingredient in bombs. Yet the North did not reprocess any spent fuel from 1991 on, nor did it shut down its reactor until May 1994, long after it was anticipated that it would. Moreover, North Korea allowed inspectors from the IAEA to verify these moves. These actions seem inconsistent with the assumption that North Korea was intent on acquiring nuclear arms. North Korea's actions suggest that, starting in 1991, it was restraining itself somewhat in hopes of concluding a nuclear deal with the United States. On November 11, 1993, it said as much in public.[55]

Similarly, if, as most experts now believe, North Korea is determined to develop, deploy, and export longer-range ballistic missiles, it should have been testing and perfecting its No Dong, Taepo Dong-I, and Taepo Dong-II missiles for the past few years. Yet the North conducted just two such tests in the past decade, one on May 29, 1993, and another on August 31, 1998, both of them failures. Again, this inactivity suggests that North Korea is restraining itself somewhat in hopes of concluding a missile deal with the United States. Pyongyang has been expressing interest in such a deal since 1992. On June 16, 1998, it said as much in public.

Why would North Korea show self-restraint? There is no way to know for sure, but Pyongyang seems to want the United States to help ensure its security against a South Korea it fears, a Japan it hates, and a China it distrusts. What better way to restrain South Korea and Japan and have a counterweight to China than to engage with the United States? Security is paramount for North Korea, but economically, the collapse of communism in the Soviet Union and Eastern Europe and the economic transformation of China led the North to seek aid, investment, and trade from South Korea, Japan, and the West. When the United States tried to impede closer North Korean ties to South Korea and Japan in the 1988–92 period, Pyongyang learned that Washington held the key to opening doors to the World Bank, the Asian Development Bank, and economic engagement with the West.

If North Korea wants engagement with the United States, why does it dig holes and test missiles? Quite possibly, Pyongyang has learned that threats are the only way to get Washington to negotiate in earnest—a lesson Washington keeps reinforcing by its own inaction absent such threats. Yet threats to break the 1994 Agreed Framework are not the same as breaking it. By resuming excavation at a long-suspect and well-watched site at Kumchangni and causing the United States to worry that the site was nuclear related, North Korea may have been deliberately manipulating what the intelligence community was seeing and hearing to get the United States to negotiate in earnest. Why? In Pyongyang's view, until recently Washington has been unwilling to extend cooperation beyond the Agreed Framework or even to keep its end of the nuclear bargain. In hopes of coaxing its allies to ante up more, the Clinton administration initially understated its appropriations request to Congress to pay for the heavy fuel oil that it had pledged to provide North Korea under the accord. Fearful of congressional reaction, the administration was slow to seek additional funding; Congress was slower to authorize it. As a result, fuel deliveries fell behind schedule, and by the end of 1997 the United States had not fulfilled its obligations under the Agreed Framework. That happened again in 1998. Only in the final days of debate on the fiscal year 1999 budget did Congress agree to the administration's full request of

$35 million to fund U.S. obligations under the accord, allowing the Korean Peninsula Energy Development Organization (KEDO), the multinational consortium set up to implement the agreement, to continue its work.

Moreover, construction of the first of two light-water reactors to replace the reactors to be dismantled under the terms of the Agreed Framework got off to a slow start because previous governments in South Korea and Japan refused to provide the necessary funding. Consistent with the Agreed Framework, the delay in construction has further postponed the removal of up to six bombs' worth of plutonium in the spent nuclear fuel now in North Korea, as well as Pyongyang's obligation to clear up the anomalies in its initial material declaration to the IAEA. Both of these steps, once regarded as urgent, especially by critics of the Agreed Framework, have been delayed by allied inaction. Even worse, from Pyongyang's point of view, Washington was reluctant to move beyond the 1994 accord to greater political and economic engagement. After all, Pyongyang reasoned, if Washington was willing to supply nuclear reactors, improved diplomatic, trade, and other ties would surely follow. Yet Washington did not even take the modest steps to ease U.S. unilateral sanctions that North Korea was promised in February 1995: unfreezing assets seized during the Korean War, allowing commercial loans from U.S. banks, and licensing private investment projects in mining and agriculture.

When these steps were not taken, North Korea, believing it was adhering to the letter of the Agreed Framework and not getting much in return, began warning in January 1998 that it would abandon the accord unless Washington proceeded with implementation. In particular, North Korea pressed for the timely shipments of heavy fuel oil, a speedup of construction of the replacement reactor, and easing of economic sanctions. In late April 1998, the North stopped the canning of the plutonium-laden spent fuel at Yongbyon but only after all the 8,000 or so intact fuel rods were put in casks and nothing but nuclear sludge from a few disintegrating rods remained. On May 7, Pyongyang said it would need to "open and readjust" its other nuclear facilities, including the reactor, for maintenance, but in the presence of IAEA inspectors. The North also hinted it might end its freeze on reprocessing. The spurt of activity at the suspect underground site at Kumchangni in autumn 1997 should be understood in this context. Had North Korea wanted to break the nuclear accord, it could have thrown out the international inspectors, opened the casks, and removed the spent fuel for reprocessing. Instead, the North resumed excavation at the long-suspect underground site, which U.S. intelligence has been observing for over a decade and had reassessed in spring 1999 to be nuclear related. Even if that assessment had been correct, it would have taken Pyongyang years to complete such an installation, hardly a sign of its eagerness to break the Agreed Framework.

After talks in New York in early September 1998, Pyongyang allowed the canning of the spent fuel to resume. In May 1999, it allowed the United States access to the tunnels at Kumchangni, where U.S. inspectors found nothing nuclear related. In return, the North received the additional food it had expected more than two years earlier. In short, North Korea has been threatening to break the October 1994 accord without actually violating it. It appears to be another instance of tit-for-tat behavior by Pyongyang— cooperate when the United States cooperates and retaliate when it reneges— intended to get Washington to deal in earnest.

North Korea may be playing tit-for-tat on missiles as well. North Korea's willingness to terminate its missile exports for a price first became evident in negotiations with Israel starting in October 1992. In March 1993, two months after Israel had offered to establish diplomatic relations and provide investment and technical assistance worth hundreds of millions of dollars to induce North Korea to end its missile sales to the Middle East and Iran, the United States intervened and got Israel to break off the talks. North Korea responded by conducting the only test of its Rodong missile, in the presence of Iranian officials. Israel later resumed its negotiations with North Korea, although the United States was again instrumental in seeing that the deal was never consummated. Yet despite this activity and the avowed desire of America to strike a deal concerning missiles, the United States did not hold a first round of missile talks with the DPRK until April 1996. The second round was called off by Washington in September 1996, at Seoul's insistence after a North Korean submarine incursion into South Korean waters. Pyongyang began preparations for another missile test, but halted them after talks with U.S. officials in New York on October 18. The second round of missile talks was held in June 1997. However, these talks did not catalyze further cooperation, as the United States was unwilling to present Pyongyang with adequate inducements for dealing with the missile issue. At the same time, North Korea was disappointed by the lack of urgency Japan was demonstrating in moving toward normalization with it. Rather than engaging in normalization talks with the North, the Japanese remained preoccupied with the cases of at least ten Japanese whom officials in Tokyo suspect were kidnapped by North Korean agents and taken to North Korea over the years.

In this context, Pyongyang publicly proclaimed its willingness to end exports in a June 16, 1998, statement that also threatened to resume missile testing: "If the United States really wants to prevent our missile export, it should lift the economic embargo as early as possible and make a compensation for the losses to be caused by discontinued missile export." The June 16 statement went much further, suggesting readiness to negotiate an end to development as well: "The discontinuation of our missile development is a matter which can be discussed after a peace agreement is signed between the DPRK and the United States and the U.S. military threat [is] completely removed."[56] The price for an end to missile development, which is not necessarily the same thing as testing, is a peace agreement with the United States, which is not necessarily the same as a peace treaty. Such an accord, which could be considered tantamount to ending the "U.S. military threat," would establish a "peace mechanism" to replace the Military Armistice Commission set up at the time of the Korean War cease-fire.

There was little American or Japanese reaction to this public statement. In the face of what North Korea probably perceived as American and Japanese reluctance or disinterest in addressing the question of North Korean missiles, North Korea conducted its Taepodong test on August 31, 1998—a test that violated Japanese airspace—and eventually resumed test preparations for further tests in the summer of 1999. Only when the Clinton administration pledged in September 1999 to end sanctions under the Trading with the Enemy Act did North Korea agree to a moratorium on missile tests while negotiations proceed. Again, when the United States behaved cooperatively, the DPRK reciprocated.

Compensation may not be the key to a missile deal. Pyongyang's interest in a deal could be indicative of its larger objectives: to reinvigorate the U.S.-DPRK dialogue and to end its long-standing enmity with the United States. American economic sanctions, dating back to the Korean War, are a monument to that enmity. Putting an end to sanctions would also improve the political conditions for an even more far-reaching deal in four-party talks to defuse the conventional military confrontation in Korea that nearly sparked war in June 1994. Without meaningful political and economic engagement, North Korea is unlikely to agree to meaningful military disengagement.[57]

The Lessons of Nuclear Diplomacy with North Korea

Economic sanctions have been the tools of choice for American counterproliferation policy. Targeted sanctions have been used to deny would-be proliferators the means to make nuclear arms and other weapons of mass destruction. Economic embargoes have been employed to coerce states into giving up their nuclear ambitions. Symbolic sanctions have been deployed as a shield against resorting to military force when the U.S. government faces domestic political pressure to "do something" to counter proliferation. Experience with North Korea shows the limitations of all three forms of sanctions and the need for alternative counterproliferation strategies.

Targeted sanctions might have slowed bomb making by North Korea, but they could not prevent it. It is likely that North Korea already had whatever it needed to make nuclear arms. Even in the best of circumstances, targeted sanctions to deny states the means of bomb making are inadequate. Denial can buy time and provide early warning, but it cannot succeed forever. The interdiction of supply has to be supplemented by efforts to reduce demand. States that seek nuclear arms are insecure. Trying to isolate them or force them to forgo nuclear arming could well backfire. They need reassurance to ease their insecurity, a lesson most proliferation experts have been loathe to learn. Unlike a strategy of pure denial, which threatens proliferators with economic and political isolation, convincing countries not to build nuclear bombs requires cooperating with them, however unsavory they may be.

The use of economic embargoes to pressure states into giving up their nuclear weapons programs has had questionable success. In the case of North Korea, that strategy was a dangerous bluff. The United States already had a near-total embargo of its own on trade and contact with the North. For an embargo to work, all of North Korea's neighbors would have to enforce it. A cutoff of oil might have caused the North's economy to collapse, but the prospect worried South Korea, Japan, China, and Russia, which would have to suffer the consequences of its collapse: mass migration, instability, and possibly war. They were unwilling to enforce sanctions stringent enough to strangle North Korea. Without their full backing, the Clinton administration would have to settle for symbolic sanctions.

The threat of military force was no more credible than an embargo. Force is a proven failure in preventing proliferation. Short of attacking, defeating, and occupying a nuclear-arming state, the use of armed force—like sanctions—can at best set back a nuclear weapons program or drive it underground; it cannot stop it. If North Korea had nuclear arms or enough plutonium to make bombs, U.S. intelligence had no idea where they were; air strikes could not target what could not be found. Even striking the reactor at Yongbyon risked spewing radiation over Japan. The option of conquering North Korea seemed the only feasible military strategy to stop nuclear proliferation, but for good reason, neither the United States nor South Korea wanted to take the risk of all-out war, especially with a possibly nuclear-armed North. In short, economic sanctions and military force were empty threats. Only political and economic engagement would give the United States the leverage it needed with North Korea.

For a government that feels politically compelled to try coercion and faces a choice between doing nothing and doing something excessive, symbolic sanctions have some utility. The Clinton administration was attracted to them as a stopgap measure to forestall pressure to use military force. In time, however, symbolic sanctions were likely to fail, leaving it vulnerable to being outhawked by critics. Worse yet, they would greatly increase the risk of war, a problem for a president who had been assailed for dodging the draft during the Vietnam War.

The alternative to coercion is cooperation or engagement, or cooperative threat reduction in the well-chosen words of Senators Sam Nunn (Democratic of Georgia) and Richard Lugar (Republican of Indiana). An engagement strategy of nuclear nonproliferation that combines reassurance with conditional reciprocity, promising and providing inducements to potential proliferators on the condition that they accept verifiable restraints on their nuclear activities, might just persuade them to give up their quest. The strategy requires identifying allies inside the target state who have no interest in nuclear arming, probing their willingness and ability to attain common ends, and then working with them. This type of engagement, or cooperative threat reduction, has a long record of accomplishment in this field. American reassurances and inducements have helped convince South Korea, Taiwan, Sweden, Brazil, Argentina, South Africa, Ukraine, Belarus, and Kazakhstan to abandon nuclear arming.[58] Only in Iraq, Israel, and Pakistan have inducements failed, although the United States chose not to dwell on evidence that Israel and Pakistan were nuclear arming.

Cooperative threat reduction may be especially difficult, yet all the more imperative, when the state in question has a history of egregious or seemingly irrational international behavior, when evidence of internal change is difficult to discern or deliberately obscured, and when contact with the country is so limited that potential allies within its political system are not easy to find. North Korea is a case in point. Critics of engagement could always play on fear of the unknown, making policymakers reluctant to risk diplomatic give-and-take or to defend the deals they did make. While those implementing a policy of engagement could argue that North Korea was being induced to do what the United States wanted, the possibility always existed that North Korea could at any moment renege on the deals made. Even threats by Pyongyang to break the accord—whether inspired by U.S. foot-dragging or otherwise—fueled U.S. domestic criticism of the engagement policy. Certainly, a policy of political and economic isolation would have been easier for the administration to defend to the American public. Talking tough and brandishing sticks may be politically advantageous in the short run, but they are no substitute for making promises and keeping them or for being direct about defending deal making to Congress and the American people.

The North Korean case demonstrates that cooperative threat reduction is difficult without congressional support. It used to be axiomatic around Washington that politics stop at the water's edge. Like most Washington axioms, the notion that foreign policy was insulated from domestic politics does not withstand close scrutiny. In nuclear diplomacy with North Korea, it was demonstrably false. Time and again, politics inside the Beltway prompted the Bush and the Clinton administrations to adopt postures of toughness and inhibited them from making anything like acceptable offers to North Korea. The result was diplomatic deadlock, and worse, a crisis that nearly got out of hand.

The United States will undoubtedly face that predicament again, in Iran and elsewhere. So long as the United States persists in criminalizing proliferation and demonizing so-called rogue states in order to confront them, it will leave itself with politically unpalatable options: to live with more nuclear-armed states or to go to war to disarm them, temporarily, as it did in Iraq. The alternative—intense coordination between the executive and congressional branches, which serves as the basis for carefully crafted and implemented engagement strategies—is unquestionably much more difficult and demands leadership on both sides of Pennsylvania Avenue. However, it is the only choice that holds out the possibility of solving the problems of proliferation, rather than simply prolonging or even exacerbating them.

Notes

1. As a result of the policy review conducted by former secretary of defense William Perry in 1998–99, the Clinton administration has come to this conclusion.

2. Leon V. Sigal, *Disarming Strangers: Nuclear Diplomacy with North Korea* (Princeton University Press, 1998), pp. 95–108.

3. Statement by State Department spokesman Michael McCurry on Resumption of U.S.-DPRK Negotiations on Nuclear and Other Issues, March 3, 1994.

4. Robert Axelrod, *The Evolution of Cooperation* (Basic Books, 1984), demonstrates experimentally how cooperation can emerge from conflict between distrustful adversaries by following a tit-for-tat strategy.

5. At the time, America already had the full gamut of unilateral sanctions in place against North Korea; therefore, U.S. threats of further sanctions implied multilateral efforts.

6. Sigal, *Disarming Strangers*, pp. 70, 114.

7. Douglas Jehl, "Seoul Eases Stand on Nuclear Inspections of North," *New York Times*, March 30, 1993, p. A13. Compare Don Oberdorfer, "South Korean: U.S. Agrees to Plan to Pressure North," *Washington Post*, March 30, 1993, p. A14.

8. Senator John McCain, remarks at conference, "The US–North Korea Nuclear Agreement: Current Status and Prospects for the Future," Heritage Foundation, Washington, D. C., June 15, 1995.

9. Memorandum by K. A. Namkung, June 7, 1994. Namkung was a key intermediary with North Korea.

10. Senior DPRK diplomat, interview by author, March 9, 1993.

11. IAEA, "Safeguards in the DPRK: Chronological Background," February 15, 1994, p. 12.

12. Thomas L. Friedman, "China Undercuts U.S. Anti-Atom Effort on Korea," *New York Times*, November 15, 1991, p. A12.

13. The sole exception had occurred in the case of Iraq, when China did not exercise its veto after vigorous diplomacy by UN Ambassador Thomas Pickering.

14. Chinese officials, interviews by author, March 10, 1993, and March 2, 1994.

15. Senior administration official, interview by author, May 1, 1997.

16. Chinese officials, interviews by author, February 10, June 23, and August 11, 1993.

17. Lena H. Sun and Jackson Diehl, "N. Korea Reportedly Snubs China," *Washington Post*, April 28, 1993, p. A13.

18. U.S. official, interview by author, February 15, 1996.

19. David E. Sanger, "U.S. Presses Japan on Missile Project," *New York Times*, November 3, 1993, p. A12. On the high-tech exports, see David E. Sanger, "Tokyo Raids Seek to Halt Aid For North Korea on Missiles," *New York Times*, January 15, 1994, p. A6; Jathon Sapsford and David P. Hamilton, "Japan Probes Illegal Exports to North Korea," *Wall Street Journal*, January 17, 1994, p. A6.

20. General James Clapper, interview by author, October 31, 1996.

21. Senior military officer, interview by author, May 2, 1997.

22. Barton Gellman, "Trepidation at Root of U.S. Korea Policy," *Washington Post*, December 12, 1993, p. A1; Peter Grier, "On US Wish List: Ability to Detect Nuclear Arms Diplomacy, Sanctions Are Seen as Inadequate," *Christian Science Monitor*, December 28, 1993, p. 1. Compare Robert D. Novak, "Aborted Ultimatum," *Washington Post*, December 16, 1993, p. A25.

23. Member of the Joint Staff, interview by author, December 14, 1995.

24. Defense Department official, interview by author, May 20, 1996.

25. Michael R. Gordon, "Pentagon Studies Plans to Bolster U.S.-Korea Forces," *New York Times*, December 2, 1993, p. A1.

26. Senior administration official, interview by author, May 1, 1997.

27. Senior military officer, interview by author, May 2, 1997.

28. Michael R. Gordon, "U.S. Will Urge UN to Plan Sanctions for North Korea," *New York Times*, March 20, 1994, p. A1. R. Jeffrey Smith and Ann Devroy, "U.S. Backs Maneuvers in S. Korea," *Washington Post*, March 20, 1994, p. A1. Team Spirit exercises could not be held at that late date; an alternative was to rename the scheduled exercise.

29. Stephen Barr and Lena H. Sun, "China's Cooperation on N. Korea Seen," *Washington Post*, March 21, 1994, p. A12.

30. Steven Greenhouse, "Christopher Says U.S. Stays Firm on Korea, but Pledges Diplomacy," *New York Times*, March 23, 1994, p. A12.

31. Michael R. Gordon, "U.S. Finds It Hard to Win Consensus over North Korea," *New York Times*, June 10, 1994, p. A1.

32. Daniel Williams, "U.S. Considers Gradual Path for North Korea Sanctions," *Washington Post*, June 2, 1994, p. A1. Briefing by Madeleine Albright, U.S. ambassador to the United Nations, Associated Press, June 15, 1994.

33. Chinese and Japanese sources, interviews by author.

34. Senior South Korean official, interview by author, June 7, 1994.

35. Christopher W. Hughes, "The North Korean Nuclear Crisis and Japanese Security," *Survival*, vol. 38 (Summer 1996), p. 90; William Dawkins, "Japan's SDP Opposes Korean Sanctions," *Financial Times*, June 6, 1994, p. 16.

36. T. R. Reid, "Accord Near on N. Korea Sanctions," *Washington Post*, June 12, 1994, p. A1.

37. John Darnton, "Clinton Says That North Korea Can Still Avoid UN Sanctions," *New York Times*, June 5, 1994, p. 6.

38. Ibid.

39. R. Jeffrey Smith and William Drozdiak, "U.S. Officials Claim Progress on Tougher N. Korea Sanctions," *Washington Post*, June 11, 1994, p. A17.

40. Michael R. Gordon, "U.S. Is Considering Milder Sanctions for North Korea," *New York Times*, June 12, 1994, p. 1.

41. Patrick E. Tyler, "China Tells Why It Opposes Korea Sanctions," *New York Times*, June 13, 1994, p. A5.

42. "Statement by the Spokesman of the Ministry of Foreign Affairs of the Democratic People's Republic of Korea, Pyongyang, June 13, 1994," no. 41, June 14, 1994.

43. Mitchell Reiss, *Bridled Ambition: Why Countries Constrain Their Nuclear Capabilities* (Washington, D.C.: Woodrow Wilson Center Press, 1995), p. 271.

44. R. Jeffrey Smith, "U.S. to Propose Delay in N. Korea Sanctions," *Washington Post*, June 15, 1994, p. A32.

45. Reuters, "Highlights of U.S. Draft Resolution on North Korea," June 15, 1994.

46. Reuters, "Clinton Hews to Carrot, Stick North Korea Policy," June 15, 1994.

47. Senior administration official, interview by author, May 1, 1997.

48. Former president Jimmy Carter, telephone interview with CNN, June 15, 1994.

49. Former president Jimmy Carter, "Report of Our Trip to Korea, June 1994," p. 2.

50. State Department official, interview by author, June 28, 1996.

51. Lena H. Sun, "North Korea Presents China with Dilemma," *Washington Post*, June 17, 1994, p. A20.

52. Alessandra Stanley, "Moscow Is Miffed by U.S. Draft on Sanctions," *New York Times*, June 17, 1994, p. A10.

53. Walter B. Slocombe, "Resolution of the North Korean Nuclear Issue," in Henry Sokolski, ed., *Fighting Proliferation: New Concerns for the Nineties* (Maxwell Air Force Base, Ala.: Air University Press, 1996), pp. 192–93.

54. Secretary of State Warren Christopher, testimony before the Senate Foreign Relations Committee, 104 Cong. 1 sess. (January 24, 1995).

55. Statement by Kang Sok Ju, "The Nuclear Problem of the Korean Peninsula Can Never Be Solved by Pressure, But Be Solved Only by Means of Dialogue and Negotiation," November 11, 1993.

56. "Daily Says DPRK May Have 'At Least 1 Nuclear Weapon,'" *Kyodo,* June 3, 1998, *Foreign Broadcast Information Service, Daily Report: East Asia,* June 16, 1998.

57. Such reasoning has now led former secretary of defense William Perry in his 1998–99 review of U.S. policy toward North Korea to conclude that a missile deal is worth exploring without further delay. William J. Perry, "Review of United States Policy toward North Korea: Findings and Recommendations" (U.S. Department of State, October 12, 1999) (www.state.gov/www/regions/eap/991012_northkorea_rpt.html [January 2000]).

58. Reiss, *Bridled Ambition,* ably details all but the first two cases. Inducements also played a part in earlier efforts to keep Sweden and Australia nonnuclear. In all these cases, domestic political considerations were important influences on decisions to disarm or refrain from nuclear arming.

6

The United States and South Africa: Persuasion and Coercion

PAULINE H. BAKER

The contentious debate over U.S. policy toward South Africa in the 1980s was unusual in its intensity, duration, scope, and consequences. In America, it led to a clash between the executive and legislative branches of government, stoked partisan bitterness, strained domestic race relations, and penetrated many sectors of society, from college campuses to corporate boardrooms, over a two-year period. Nonetheless, the desired changes occurred within South Africa, and U.S. policy objectives were eventually achieved. Apartheid retreated in favor of negotiations for domestic political change within South Africa, and regional settlements were signed by three countries—with the cooperation of the superpowers and other African countries—that led to the removal of Cuban troops from Angola and the independence of Namibia.

These developments occurred, paradoxically, not because one continuous American foreign policy approach prevailed throughout the period, but rather because two opposing approaches became unintentionally entangled and mutually reinforcing. In the end, parallel policy tracks operated simultaneously to exert pressure on Pretoria for internal changes, on the one hand, while leaving the door open for South Africa to turn toward strategic negotiations, on the other. The best way to understand this case is to view it as a dialectical process. Policy progressed from the *thesis,* which exclusively used incentives to pursue strategic objectives, to the *antithesis*, which employed sanctions and some incentives to effect change in internal South African politics, and finally to a *synthesis*, in which both sanctions and incentives helped achieve progress in both strategic and internal realms.

The United States had been quietly engaging the South African government from the 1950s through military, intelligence, and economic cooperation. However, it had not adopted an explicit, structured, official policy of offering concrete incentives to influence Pretoria until the administration of President Ronald Reagan. *Constructive engagement* was the name given to this approach. By offering broad incentives of closer diplomatic ties based on common strategic objectives, publicly expressing sensitivity to the dilemma of the white population, and reshaping South Africa's image to end its pariah status, Washington believed it could positively influence what it described as a modernizing elite in South Africa to take the steps needed to end the region's conflicts. While not indifferent to the domestic situation in South Africa, inducing domestic political reforms was decidedly a second priority of the Reagan administration under this policy.[1] What the United States sought in return for the incentives it offered was South Africa's cooperation in working toward a peace settlement in Namibia, the removal of Cuban troops from southern Africa, and, last, eventual reforms in South Africa itself. As articulated by Assistant Secretary of State for African Affairs Chester Crocker, in a May 1981 memo to Secretary of State Alexander Haig,

> After twenty years of generally increasing official U.S. Government coolness toward South Africa and concomitant South African intransigence, the possibility may exist for a more positive and reciprocal relationship between the two countries based upon shared strategic concerns in southern Africa, our recognition that the government of P. W. Botha represents a unique opportunity for domestic change, and a willingness of the Reagan Administration to deal realistically with South Africa.[2]

Namibia—particularly linking its independence from South Africa to the removal of Cuban troops from Angola—became the key to this approach. Holding out the promise of a reduction of the Soviet-Cuban threat in the region and warmer bilateral ties with the United States, Crocker reasoned that constructive engagement would put relations with Pretoria on a new footing. In this scheme of thinking, there was no place for sanctions or penalties because, as Crocker's memo to Haig indicated, "we ... need Pretoria's cooperation."[3] Indeed, as Jeffrey Herbst observes, the policy derived its distinction from the fact that it forswore sanctions altogether. "A commitment not to sanction was in effect an incentive."[4] Thus at the outset, the United States adopted a position of unconditional engagement with the South African government. However, it became apparent after a couple of years that the approach was not yielding the promised results. As some analysts concluded, "Crocker's strategy contained two basic problems. First, it failed to take into account the changing military situation inside Angola; and second, it assumed that South Africa was interested in a settlement."[5]

When violent unrest erupted in South Africa in 1983, a backlash ensued against constructive engagement as well as against the white regime. The thesis triggered the antithesis, a policy of conditional engagement that held internal change in South Africa as its primary objective. This antithesis involved a mix of incentives and penalties enacted by Congress over the veto of a popular president after two years of grassroots anti-apartheid activism in the United States. The new approach was not merely an adjustment to existing policy, but a totally different form of engagement, aimed at different targets and using different policy instruments. Engagement was no longer directed at the government, but at supporting the anti-apartheid opposition in South Africa. At the same time, the South African government was also targeted with limited trade and financial sanctions, which would be lifted if Pretoria adopted specific measures that would lead to negotiations with the black opposition. A commitment to lift sanctions when those steps were taken was the new incentive for Pretoria. The measures were spelled out in a clear road map defined in the legislation, the Comprehensive Anti-Apartheid Act of 1986 (CAAA). The measures did not call for total isolation or abdication of the white government, but rather defined a set of five "do-able" actions that would level the playing field for negotiations.

The struggle over U.S. policy—the tensions and contradictions represented by the thesis and the antithesis—had a high political cost in America and may well have prolonged conflicts in the region. However, in the end, the combination of incentives and sanctions resulting from these tensions contributed to real change in the region. Not only were strategic goals (the object of the thesis) met, but internal political changes (the object of the antithesis) also occurred, resulting in a synthesis.

The Thesis

For three decades, U.S. policy toward South Africa had traveled a fairly well-defined path, with little public opposition outside a small constituency of

Africanists, liberal activists, and concerned African Americans. South Africa first emerged as a foreign policy issue for the United States in the 1950s, when other nations criticized Washington for its own racial practices and for its failure to condemn apartheid. Civil rights activism and the emergence of independent black states in Africa generated a somewhat stronger U.S. posture against apartheid, but military, nuclear, intelligence, trade, and investment links between the United States and South Africa continued uninterrupted. Under President John F. Kennedy, the United States expressed even greater anti-apartheid criticism and imposed a unilateral arms embargo against South Africa in 1964, but other relationships remained intact. During the Nixon administration, geopolitical and strategic concerns took precedence over human rights concerns. The arms embargo was relaxed, bilateral relations were improved, and anti-apartheid rhetoric was subdued. After the 1974 military coup in Portugal, which led to the independence of Angola and Mozambique under Marxist governments, U.S. policy continued heavily to favor geopolitical concerns. In particular, Secretary of State Henry Kissinger focused on bringing about majority rule in Rhodesia in an effort to stem the spread of Marxism in southern Africa.

However, with the Carter administration, the pendulum swung back to emphasize human rights, a keystone of Carter's foreign policy. President Carter felt that African nationalism, not communist aggression, was the biggest threat to stability on the continent. Relations between the United States and South Africa were strained in the 1970s and deteriorated rapidly when a nuclear weapons site was detected by the Soviet Union in the Kalahari Desert. Moreover, Pretoria launched a brutal crackdown on black opposition groups following the 1977 death in detention of Steve Biko, a popular black leader, further straining U.S.–South African relations. Against this backdrop, the United States joined other nations in supporting a mandatory UN arms embargo against South Africa in 1977. Diplomatic contacts continued, nonetheless, as the United States continued to work toward the independence of Rhodesia and Namibia. Carter became more wary of Soviet and Cuban intentions in southern Africa during the second half of his term, and this sensitivity contributed to a division within the administration on how best to approach South Africa. As a result, mixed signals were sent by the United States concerning what it expected of South Africa and the extent to which it would back up its anti-apartheid rhetoric.

Despite these shifts in foreign policy strategies from the 1950s to the late 1970s, U.S. policy objectives in southern Africa remained constant over this period. All administrations engaged the white-ruled states in the regime, supported majority rule through peaceful change in those states (Rhodesia,

Namibia, and South Africa), and sought to limit Soviet influence in the region. The differences among the various administrations' policies were more of style than substance, with the key distinction being whether Washington should be more confrontational or cooperative with Pretoria in public. However, no administration supported the broad use of economic sanctions to achieve U.S. objectives and, while the United States tried to get South Africa to sign the Nuclear Nonproliferation Treaty, concern over the nuclear question never caused an open breach in the relationship.

The Reagan administration came to office in 1981, effusing a strong sense of setting a new course. Reagan's principal emphasis focused on limiting Soviet influence in the region, particularly in Angola. There, the United States, along with South Africa, backed a rebel group, the National Union for the Total Liberation of Angola (UNITA), in opposition to Soviet and Cuban support for the Popular Movement for the Liberation of Angola (MPLA), a self-styled Marxist party that took over after the collapse of Portuguese rule. This proxy war in Angola became the focal point of superpower rivalry in the region, superseding concerns over the domestic situation in South Africa. Reagan had a natural empathy with South Africa, based on his perception of the country being a close historic U.S. ally. Steered by Assistant Secretary of State Chester A. Crocker, Reagan also viewed South Africa as a key player in achieving regional settlements and checking communist influence. To repair relations with Pretoria that had been strained during the Carter administration, Crocker felt he had to offer concrete incentives to the regime.

First, he underscored a common interest in opposing the Soviet bloc, citing Reagan's conservative credentials and strong anticommunist rhetoric as the basis for "constructive engagement" with South Africa. Reagan frequently spoke in warm tones about South Africa as "a country that has stood beside us in every war we've ever fought."[6] This played well in Pretoria, for it validated its theory of "total onslaught," a view of the world that portrayed black nationalist groups as communist-inspired or controlled organizations fronting for Moscow. Pretoria's perception was that these groups, including Nelson Mandela's African National Congress (ANC), wanted to deny the West access to South African strategic minerals.

Second, in regional diplomacy, the United States discarded the Carter administration's multilateral initiative, which had relied on a five-nation "contact group" (Canada, France, Great Britain, the United States, and West Germany) to negotiate a settlement in Namibia. Instead, Crocker adopted a unilateral approach, based on a strategy of formally linking two previously disparate issues: South African withdrawal from Namibia and Cuban withdrawal from Angola. Carter had also recognized that South Africa was reluctant to withdraw from Namibia as long as Cuban troops were in Angola, but Reagan went further by making progress on one issue contingent upon progress on the other. This linkage likewise played well in Pretoria, for it shifted the responsibility for achieving Namibian independence from South Africa to Angola and the United States. There were also military advantages to this changed posture. Linkage gave South Africa reason to continue its military forays into Angola, for, in doing so, it would ensure that the Cubans would remain there. As long as the Cubans stayed, South Africa could justify retaining its grip on Namibia, a territory it considered strategically important for security operations against rebel forces in the region, including guerrilla bases of the African National Congress.

Third, the Reagan administration promoted better relations with South Africa by downplaying the issue of racial injustice. President Reagan spoke sympathetically of a white government under siege that the United States could not abandon due to historic friendship. He misleadingly attributed turmoil in the country to tribalism, not racism, and in depicting South Africa as a World War II ally missed the fact that many members of the National Party had sided with Nazi Germany.

Through quiet diplomacy, Crocker promoted closer bilateral ties with South Africa on regional issues and tried to reshape American perceptions of the apartheid regime. He argued that meaningful political reforms were being adopted under the leadership of President Pieter W. Botha and that they would eventually lead to wider black political participation. Botha did institute some reforms, but they were aimed at modernizing apartheid, not abolishing it. Nonetheless, in Crocker's view, the government represented a modernizing autocracy whose behavior could be moderated if the United States took account of white fears. Public presentation of this more moderate image of South Africa constituted an incentive for Pretoria to cooperate more with the Reagan administration, given the pariah status it had in the international community at the time. Even the South African military, which had gained political influence under Botha, was depicted in benevolent terms, despite its repeated interventions in the region. "It would be unwise to view the South African Defense Force as an instrument of domestic brutality or as the rogue elephant of southern Africa, crashing across borders and wrecking Western interests," Crocker wrote.[7] The fundamental assumption of constructive engagement was that the South African regime represented a reformist, pro-Western government that, with U.S. encouragement, would work toward regional settlements, check communism in Africa, and eventually give blacks political rights. Crocker used this image of a changing South

Africa both to justify his policy at home and to induce the South African regime, then highly distrustful of the United States, to work with Washington, setting aside for the time being the domestic situation in South Africa itself. By eschewing sanctions, Crocker was also presenting the Reagan administration as Pretoria's best friend. The international community had utilized arms and oil boycotts in the past, and there was growing talk of economic as well as sports and cultural sanctions.

Beyond a small circle of anti-apartheid activists, concerned spokespersons in the African American community, and African experts, there was little sustained public criticism of the policy at first. By the end of 1982, two years into constructive engagement, dissent began to grow as the perception took hold in America that the policy was failing to achieve any meaningful progress on black political rights, regional diplomacy, or containment of communism. The attacks came from both liberal and conservative circles. Liberal opponents argued that constructive engagement was tacitly encouraging aggressive regional destabilization by Pretoria and was not leading to any significant internal political progress within South Africa on opening a dialogue with credible black leaders. The policy was also creating concern in Africa and in the U.S. Congress, where a number of resolutions and bills were submitted that began to urge the use of sanctions. In response to these developments, Vice President George Bush was dispatched to Africa to quell anxieties on the continent, and, to subdue criticism at home, Undersecretary of State Lawrence Eagleburger gave a strong speech criticizing the white minority government more harshly.

The right wing was also critical of the policy but from a very different perspective. It was critical of Crocker's pragmatic approach to Marxist regimes. For instance, Crocker responded to Mozambique when it sought economic and other assistance from the West in order to stem South African support for antigovernment rebels. In response, Maputo began to soften its socialist dogma and to negotiate with South Africa on security issues. Also to the chagrin of many U.S. conservatives, Crocker believed that Washington should provide economic assistance and extend closer political relations to the newly independent government of Zimbabwe (formerly Rhodesia), Africa's second most developed country.[8] Despite the government's socialism and harsh anti-apartheid rhetoric, Crocker saw an opportunity to draw Harare closer to the West. Zimbabwe's leader, Robert Mugabe, had been backed by China, had poor relations with Moscow, pursued a policy of racial reconciliation with whites, fostered a mixed economy, and supported a foreign policy that denied ANC guerrillas bases to launch attacks against South Africa—all of which made him an appealing ally in Africa. While the incentives Crocker offered to the black-ruled states opened doors for the United States in checking Soviet influence, it created tensions with Pretoria, which was wary of Washington tilting too far, possibly selling out white interests. As a result, many U.S. conservatives opposed Crocker's action in southern Africa at large.

Initially, Crocker kept criticism from both political camps in check, citing some diplomatic progress. In early 1984, the high-water mark of constructive engagement, Crocker succeeded in negotiating agreements between South Africa and Angola (the Lusaka Agreement) and between South Africa and Mozambique (the Nkomati Accord), both of which required Pretoria to cease its support of rebel groups in those countries. These agreements bred optimism that constructive engagement was working, but this hope was dashed when it was revealed a few months later that South Africa had not lived up to its commitments. Instead, South Africa continued to aid the Mozambique rebels and increased its assistance to UNITA, exposing the fact that American and South African strategic objectives in the region actually diverged. Meanwhile, the Cuban troop buildup in Angola continued, regional violence escalated, Namibia remained in Pretoria's grip, and the internal situation in South Africa grew more tense.

The flashpoint that unleashed the forces that undermined constructive engagement was the attempt by South Africa in 1983 to promulgate a new constitution. It created junior-status, racially segregated parliaments for Indians and Coloureds, but excluded Africans, who represented three-quarters of the population. Crocker endorsed the constitution as evidence of domestic reform. However, in reality, the new constitution was meant to co-opt minorities in order to continue to keep black Africans without political representation, an updated version of apartheid meant to quell opposition. Protests broke out the day the constitution went into effect, with Coloureds and Indians—the groups targeted to be beneficiaries of the change—in the forefront of the opposition. In short order, this protest spiraled into an anti-apartheid insurrection across the country, engulfing South Africa in spasms of violence that the government could not contain. The uprising triggered the greatest repression ever seen in South Africa, with security forces firing on unarmed black demonstrators, mostly teenagers, often using methods that lured demonstrators out of hiding and attacked them with maximum force. Rising black fury was evidenced in "necklace killings," a gruesome form of lynching in which flaming gasoline-soaked tires were thrown by enraged mobs around the necks of blacks suspected of collaborating with police. Victims of police violence were given emotional funerals, which often doubled as political rallies because they were the only circumstances under which large numbers of people could legally assemble. In this charged atmosphere, South Africa appeared to be heading toward a full-scale race war. With little progress on strategic or regional issues, constructive engagement was seen by many Americans as a policy that placed the United States in the position of being an apologist for an oppressive racist government.

These developments precipitated the end of constructive engagement by making it impossible for the Reagan administration to continue to prioritize strategic objectives over domestic concerns in South Africa. However, the policy—as one that sought to use incentives to impel South Africa to cooperate in resolving regional conflicts—was riddled with dilemmas long before the events of 1984. First, the separation of strategic issues from domestic concerns, even if possible in theory, was not plausible in practice; South Africa's regional policies were an extension of its domestic situation. Both were designed to keep the region safe for white rule. Despite the reality of having multiple objectives, there were few unrelated incentives available to the United States to spur action on these different agendas.[9] The offer or promise of international legitimacy—a vague, intangible incentive to begin with—might have been sufficient to goad the South Africans into making concessions at the regional level. However, once this incentive was granted, it would be difficult for U.S. policymakers to extend it again in efforts to secure changes in the domestic South African arena. Finally, because the policy employed only incentives, it was essentially reliant upon Pretoria's willingness to comply with American demands and desires. As demonstrated vividly by Pretoria's disregard for the Nkomati Accord, the absence of coercive tools left U.S. negotiators with few mechanisms for exacting cooperation when Pretoria resisted compliance.

The Antithesis

The South African experience points to the vulnerabilities of engagement strategies that do not sufficiently take internal politics into account, both in the country of origin, where in this case the administration failed to anticipate the strength of domestic opposition, and in the targeted country, where the administration failed to anticipate the strength and duration of the black uprising. In tying events in South Africa to the wider global struggle to combat Soviet influence, constructive engagement was a politically astute way of getting a conservative administration that otherwise would not have been very interested in the region to focus on South Africa.[10] However, the policy neglected to take into account several other important factors: it had few allies (most of the Western countries, except for Margaret Thatcher's Britain, opposed it); it had no credible penalties for South Africa for failing to reciprocate; and it ignored the human rights component of the issue by giving exclusive attention to the strategic dimension of the policy. Ultimately, these weaknesses proved to be the undoing of the policy as public opposition mounted.

Organized opposition in the United States was launched by African American grassroots activists during a protest over the Thanksgiving weekend of 1984. A group of prominent African American leaders led a peaceful demonstration in front of the South African embassy in Washington, D.C., announcing the birth of the Free South Africa Movement, a loose coalition of organizations and activists protesting both apartheid and the U.S. policy of constructive engagement. The campaign attracted major media attention and spread rapidly across the country, drawing an array of church, student, labor, and civil rights backers. Thousands of these supporters volunteered to be arrested while picketing the South African embassy and consulates, invoking the days of civil disobedience in the American civil rights movement. These protests were fed by a serious deterioration in the South African domestic scene, an iron-fisted response by the apartheid government, and extensive media coverage of the upheavals. Charismatic individuals such as South African Archbishop Desmond Tutu, a Nobel Peace Prize winner who called for comprehensive economic sanctions against Pretoria, also helped fuel opposition to the regime. Also of crucial importance was the campaign for divestment—the sale of stock in U.S. firms operating in South Africa—which had been under way for a decade. The seasoned network of activists who had been exerting pressure at the state and local government levels for divestment joined forces with the Free South Africa Movement and other domestic groups, including labor unions, churches, and student organizations, to mobilize popular sentiment into a call for comprehensive economic sanctions at the federal level.[11]

Constructive engagement was under frontal attack by its critics for misreading the nature of the South African regime and for offering incentives without reciprocity based on the promise of achieving strategic objectives. The charge was given credence when President Botha gave a much advertised speech in 1985 in which he stated that he had "crossed the Rubicon" in embracing reform, but would act at his own pace, on his own terms, and that he would not be pressured.[12] Billed in advance as a speech that would announce major new steps, it was instead the articulation of a defiant stand in which Botha blamed the violence in his country on "barbaric communist agitators." He ruled out any compromise on power-sharing with blacks.

This event pulled the rug out from the U.S. policy of constructive engagement. Along with the speech, South Africa in 1985 declared a state of emergency, gave security forces virtually unlimited powers to crush the two-year-old uprising, and banned media coverage of the disturbances. However, even though the issue was pulled off the television screens, it was too late to stop the campaign in the United States. Botha's censorship merely reinforced the commitment by American campaigners to place South Africa on the agendas of legislative, academic, religious, corporate, and civic organizations across the nation. Bank loans to South Africa started drying up, multinational firms began to pull out, and Republicans as well as Democrats called for action. South Africa had shown itself to be a recalcitrant ally that had behaved, as Crocker put it years earlier, as a rogue elephant crashing across borders and opposing Western interests. For the United States, regional and strategic concerns were swept aside by fears of a race war in southern Africa and by popular opposition to the United States seeming to take the side of the white government. Moral considerations, in sum, superseded strategic goals. The issue split the Republican Party down the middle. The right wing, represented by Patrick Buchanan, a strong supporter of South Africa and Reagan's communications director, called for closer ties with South Africa to defend an anticommunist ally under siege. The moderate wing, represented by Senators Nancy Kassebaum (Republican of Kansas) and Richard Lugar (Republican of Indiana), held that U.S. strategic considerations would not be advanced unless the United States also addressed moral and political concerns within South Africa itself.

Gradually a consensus emerged that a policy shift was needed to correct the perceived tilt of America in favor of the white government. Washington needed to engage broader elements of South African society, press for negotiations between the government and legitimate black leaders to end apartheid, and exact a price on Pretoria for its intransigence. New policy instruments were also advocated, including more aid to black civil society, targeted economic sanctions, and high-level diplomatic contacts with opposition political groups, especially the ANC. In these respects, liberal and conservative views were beginning to converge. The Conservative Opportunity Society (COS), a group of young House members led by Newt Gingrich (Republican of Georgia) and Vin Weber (Republican of Minnesota) distanced themselves from the administration's policy. This group warned the South African ambassador that it would support sanctions if Pretoria construed constructive engagement as "an excuse for maintaining the unacceptable status quo" and if there was no "demonstrated sense of urgency about ending apartheid."[13]

However, while consensus was building around a new approach toward internal politics in South Africa, contradictory strands were still evident in U.S. policy toward Angola. The COS, while moving toward punitive sanctions against South Africa, pushed for assistance to UNITA, based on its opposition to communism. On the other hand, Crocker opposed aid to UNITA, calculating that it would set back delicate negotiations with the Angolan government and force Luanda to depend even more on Cuban troops. The White House overruled Crocker and authorized covert aid to UNITA. In retaliation, Angola broke off negotiations with the United States, as Crocker predicted, and talks did not resume until two years later.

While these disagreements were occurring within the executive branch, congressional opinion was coalescing into a common position that culminated in the Comprehensive Anti-Apartheid Act (CAAA) in October 1986, roughly two years after the Free South Africa Movement was launched and a year after Reagan tried unsuccessfully to ward off tougher measures by imposing mild sanctions of his own. The CAAA was passed, it was vetoed by President Reagan, and the veto was overturned by Congress in an overwhelming bipartisan vote that constituted one of Reagan's biggest foreign policy defeats. This was only the second foreign policy law since World War II to be voted into existence by Congress over a presidential veto, the first being the War Powers Act enacted over the veto of President Richard Nixon. The strength of the anti-apartheid vote reflected the intensity of American feelings on the issue from both sides of the aisle.

Interestingly, however, the legislation did not incorporate all the demands of those campaigning for sanctions. It imposed sanctions that were designed to persuade the government of South Africa to move toward negotiations with the black opposition, not to get the government to abdicate.[14] The law included a clear road map for the future, laying down doable conditions for Pretoria to meet before the status quo could be changed. The terms of engagement with the government were clearly spelled out. For sanctions to be lifted, the government had to release Nelson Mandela and other political prisoners, repeal the state of emergency, legalize proscribed political parties, repeal two fundamental apartheid laws, and agree to enter into good faith negotiations without preconditions with truly representative members of the black majority population.[15] The message to white South Africans was that the United States would no longer do business as usual with their country unless blacks were given equal political rights; the message to South African blacks was that the United States was moving away from a policy unsympathetic to their aspirations.

The law included a ban on new investments and bank loans and an end to direct air links. Importation of a range of South African goods was prohibited, the bilateral tax treaty was terminated, U.S. agencies were proscribed from promoting trade and investment in South Africa, and additional sanctions were threatened if sufficient progress toward negotiations was not made. Tougher measures, such as those taken against North Korea, Cuba, and Iraq, were rejected. For example, the law did *not* require compulsory disinvestment, restrict travel, end cultural, sports, and educational exchanges, impose a full-scale embargo, or break off diplomatic relations.

Most important, Congress not only laid down punitive measures but also provided resources to reach out to nonstate actors in society. The CAAA provided for up to $40 million in economic assistance to expand contacts with and support of black civil organizations. This allocation transformed and enlarged a small existing program to further the education of South African blacks. Whereas the earlier program had been accused of being a palliative to the American conscience, post-CAAA aid to South African civil society took on greater significance.[16] By the close of the Reagan administration, largely due to pressure from Congress, a total of $91 million had been channeled to nonracial, grassroots organizations with no connection with the apartheid government. These initiatives composed the first U.S. development assistance program that specifically aimed at aiding civil society, did not go through the host government, and had an avowedly political objective—to strengthen anti-apartheid forces.

Similarly, rather than sharply curtailing the involvement of the private sector in South Africa, the CAAA encouraged American private enterprises to remain engaged under certain circumstances. While praising U.S. firms that stayed in the country, the legislation required them to adopt fair labor practices based on the principles developed by the Reverend Leon Sullivan.[17] By not forcing U.S. firms to withdraw, the law succeeded in walking a fine line that, in the long term, proved to be an example of the careful targeting that make sanctions most effective. The law restricted corporate expansion through new investment, thus denying the South African government access to capital that it needed badly. At the same time, the law did not require U.S. firms to disengage, but rather allowed them to retain a foothold in the South African economy. By 1999, five years after the first election on a universal, nonracial franchise, the United States stood as South Africa's largest trading partner, with approximately $10 billion invested in a range of industries, from telecommunications to soft drinks. The flow of foreign investment has fallen short of government expectations in the postapartheid period, with unemployment at nearly 40 percent, a high crime rate, and other legacies from the apartheid era crippling the economy.[18] However, even existing levels of U.S. investment would not have been likely had U.S. companies been forced in the 1980s to withdraw completely, as many anti-apartheid activists advocated at the time.

Still, the Sullivan principles also came under attack from activists, many of whom felt that they were being used as a substitute for sanctions. These principles were initially confined to breaking down racial barriers in the workplace and did not advocate openly confronting apartheid laws, as activists had hoped. The principles nonetheless set a standard of corporate social responsibility that encouraged all corporations, including South African firms, to adopt more progressive policies toward their work force and contribute more generously to black educational and business endeavors. This reinforced the U.S. policy shift toward empowering civil society, including the black private sector. Today the ANC is courting U.S. investors, reassuring them that it will continue its conservative fiscal policies implemented since the 1994 election, which have been widely praised in Western circles.[19]

The Synthesis

The thesis pursued primarily strategic objectives in South Africa at the expense of pushing for domestic reforms by Pretoria; the antithesis was willing to put these goals aside in its quest to effect progress in the domestic sphere. The first approach relied exclusively on incentives, while the latter employed both inducements and penalties. In the end the two approaches came together in a synthesis under which both incentives and sanctions played a critical role in securing strategic and domestic goals. Like the policy instruments employed by the United States, the departure of Cuban troops from Angola, South Africa's withdrawal from Namibia, and the dismantling of apartheid all reinforced one another. In the late 1980s and early 1990s, this synthesis helped to end the cold war, colonialism, and apartheid in southern Africa.

Of course, many factors account for the final political turnaround in South Africa, the most important being events in South Africa itself. Nonetheless, in addition to the cooperation between the United States and the USSR in southern Africa, U.S. economic sanctions were among the most important international variables that had a meaningful, and perhaps decisive, impact.[20] As Marina Ottaway notes,

> to what extent South Africa's economic problems were the result of sanctions, rather than the consequence of [internal] policy choices and struc-

tural deficiencies, is a matter on which there is no agreement. But by the government's own admission, sanctions did contribute to change.[21]

Some, including former President Frederik de Klerk, argue that sanctions had only a negligible, if any, impact.[22] Others argue that there was also serious economic mismanagement causing economic decline. However, the data suggest that sanctions had both material and political impact, especially on white attitudes and the political calculations of the white regime.

South Africa's economic decline began in the mid-1970s, as it began to take steps to prepare for the threat of sanctions. From a history of roughly 5 percent per annum growth rate, "between 1975 and 1991 the annual rate of growth fell to only 1.6 percent, well below the 3 percent annual population increase."[23] By the 1980s, economic decline was eroding the National Party's political base. Robert Schrire reports that by the time Frederik de Klerk came to power in 1989, three years after U.S. sanctions were imposed, inflation was running at over 15 percent. Moreover,

> real white incomes were static or declining. . . . Economic adversity was a major factor in the alienation of the white working class, small-scale farmers, and petty officials in the government [most of whom were Afrikaners] . . . [who] took it as their due to receive special treatment and economic privileges.[24]

In protest, they began to shift toward the political right. The National Party expected to balance these losses by picking up support from the English-speaking middle- and upper-class whites. But they, too, after first supporting the National Party in 1987, shifted to the more liberal Democratic Party in 1989, protesting "higher taxation . . . the erosion in the value of currency, high inflation, and declining real standards of living."[25] Recognizing that a continuation of current policies would result in a further splintering of National Party support, de Klerk identified the "reform constituency" as representing 70 percent of the electorate, combining National Party support and votes for the Democratic Party.[26] There were many reasons, including rising black protest, that pushed the National Party toward taking the steps necessary to make a fundamental break with the past, but shifting white political support, fueled by economic decline, was a vital element in that equation.

On February 2, 1990, less than six months after being elected president, de Klerk announced that he had decided to lift the emergency, release Nelson Mandela, legalize the ANC and other banned political parties, repeal the

Population Registration Act and the Group Areas Act, the two legislative pillars of apartheid, and enter into negotiations that eventually led to elections in 1994 on the basis of a universal franchise. In short, South Africa complied with all the conditions set forth in the CAAA.

Although bilateral relations had cooled when sanctions were first imposed and diplomatic progress seemed to have reached an impasse, momentum suddenly picked up during Reagan's last year in office. Diplomatic efforts concerning Namibia and Angola were revived due to a fortuitous set of factors.[27] Sanctions had resulted in a pause in regional diplomacy, but did not kill the diplomacy as some had feared. In fact, sanctions may have even enhanced the chances for diplomacy by convincing Pretoria that the costs of intransigence were increasing and that the terms of a deal made with the Reagan administration would be far better than those it could negotiate with a subsequent Democratic administration.

With barely a year left to the Reagan administration term in office, U.S. policy came back to where it had begun, with a focus on regional and strategic issues. Crocker fulfilled his eight-year diplomatic quest for a breakthrough when he orchestrated marathon negotiations in several capitals, negotiations that ended with Angola, Cuba, and South Africa signing agreements in 1988 that resulted in the withdrawal of Cuban troops from Angola and the independence of Namibia. It was a triumphant conclusion to a long and difficult ordeal that had included a massive political defeat on Capitol Hill and a series of on-again, off-again negotiations that raced to the finish line at the final conclusion.

The success of these negotiations also had an impact on the domestic situation in South Africa, although the Reagan administration was out of office by the time the political breakthrough came in 1990. For South Africa, regional negotiations on Namibia "underscored the point that the Red Scare was no more."[28] De Klerk's watershed speech in 1990, announcing the political breakthrough in South Africa, came two years after Pretoria had agreed to withdraw from Namibia, a former German territory that it had administered under the terms of an old League of Nations mandate for nearly three-quarters of a century. Pretoria allowed a free election, which it knew would end inevitably in handing over power to the South West African People's Organization, the largest Namibian liberation organization, which Pretoria had been fighting for thirty years. As Robin Renwick, the British ambassador to South Africa at the time, noted: "Namibia showed the South Africans this kind of change would not necessarily have catastrophic results."[29]

The possibility of a viable political outcome combined with the mounting costs and uncertainties of a declining economy played a role in Pretoria's calculations on internal change. Pretoria was concerned that sanctions would erode its support base by undermining white morale, especially in the English-speaking community, which largely ran the commercial sector. As the internal crisis mounted, this segment of the population began emigrating, dodging the draft, and shipping assets abroad. The South African business community regarded sanctions as a disaster, a further tightening of the noose that was first slipped around its neck in 1985 when Chase Manhattan Bank and other creditors unexpectedly called in South African loans. Relations between the government and business, which ranged from collaboration to outright hostility, became tense in the 1980s. Schrire reports that

> the worsening crisis in the country and Botha's inability to "normalize" business conditions placed acute stress on government-business relations. . . . In sharp contrast to the cooperative spirit of Botha's early years, the second half of the 1980s witnessed often acrimonious exchanges between him and leading businesspeople.[30]

Botha's belligerent "Rubicon" speech in 1985, which rejected meaningful political change, had plunged the country into economic crisis, triggering a chain reaction of disasters. A large number of Western banks refused to roll over short-term loans, the rand plunged in value, the stock and currency markets were forced to close temporarily, and South Africa had to stop payment of its foreign debt. Leading publications called for Botha's resignation, and ads were taken out in the local newspapers by prominent industrialists calling upon the government to lift the state of emergency, end statutory racism, and begin negotiations with black leaders. Opposition whites and the business community criticized the government for failing to comprehend the economic consequences of its political mistakes. A meeting was held in Lusaka, Zambia, between the ANC and leading members of the Anglo-American Corporation, South Africa's largest conglomerate, in defiance of attempts by the government to clamp down. Emigration of whites began to go up sharply. Schrire wrote that "the loss to the South African economy of accountants, doctors, lawyers, and qualified management personnel during this period was incalculable."[31] The South African business community vigorously opposed international sanctions, but many blamed the government for failing to adopt political reforms that could have thwarted them.

In the most comprehensive study ever done on the impact of sanctions on South Africa, the Investor Responsibility Research Center (IRRC) concluded in 1990 that sanctions had an important effect on both the economy and white attitudes.[32] Financial sanctions were more effective than trade ones, but overall attempts to evade restrictions had cost South Africa between $15 billion and $27 billion. The IRRC reported that the economy had shrunk by 20–35 percent as a result of limits on capital flows and the expensive import substitution strategies that Pretoria adopted as far back as 1967, when the threat of economic sanctions first surfaced after the Soweto student uprising. Most important, the IRRC found that by the time the first "talks about talks" between Nelson Mandela and the newly installed President F. W. de Klerk were due to begin, nearly half of all white South Africans, representing the "reform constituency," were prepared to make political compromises to get sanctions lifted. This attitude signaled a significant shift in the support base, representing the political center of white opinion, which allowed de Klerk to move forward by 1990. He did so both at home and in the region, setting the stage, along with his U.S. interlocutors, for de-escalation of tensions throughout southern Africa.

Engagement Guidelines

In the end, a mix of U.S. policy instruments contributed to the dramatic changes that occurred in southern Africa. However, the outcome was not carefully planned, the methods employed were hammered out in a prolonged debate, and the price paid in U.S. domestic political terms was high. Such a rancorous political debate over foreign policy had not occurred in America since the Vietnam War.

Nevertheless, the dichotomy between incentives and sanctions, when they came into balance, is what actually made U.S. policy effective. Proponents of each strategy have claimed credit for the success. In part, each can legitimately declare to have played a positive role in achieving some part of the outcome—the tenacity of Crocker's engagement led to success in regional diplomacy when the timing was ripe, and the tenacity of activists for pressing for internal political change and sanctions helped bring an end to apartheid in South Africa. Both approaches were needed to accomplish the full range of U.S. policy objectives in the region. Neither policy alternative, engagement or disengagement, was applied fully. The "good cop, bad cop" synthesis applied coercion and incentives, leaving the Pretoria government a way out.

It is important to understand that, contrary to statements by the Reagan administration at the time that nothing had really changed, the targets and tactics of engagement had fundamentally shifted from Reagan's first term to his second. Moving from a policy that aimed at engaging the South African government, the U.S. Congress insisted on engaging civil society and the political opposition at the risk of alienating Pretoria and freezing regional negotiations. Moving from the use of unconditional incentives to influence Pretoria, the United States applied conditional negative incentives in the form of sanctions, with a clear road map on what steps had to be taken to get them lifted. And the United States switched from little engagement with civil society and the political opposition to unconditional engagement with nongovernmental groups and organizations.

The policy instruments also changed. An economic aid program unique for its time was applied to assist a broad group of civic organizations. It bypassed the South Africa government, becoming the first U.S. economic aid program with avowedly political, not developmental, objectives that did not go through the government. The United States also withdrew the ambassador associated with constructive engagement, appointed a new one, and met with high-level officials in the ANC—the first time in the seventy-five-year history of the ANC. Moreover, Washington changed its public characterization of the organization. Rather than describing the ANC as using calculated terror, the United States portrayed the organization as having a legitimate voice in South Africa. Finally, the United States dropped the term *constructive engagement*, sparking humor that this was a policy that dares not speak its name.

While the policy of constructive engagement was seen to have failed with the enactment of sanctions, the administration continued to play a positive role in persistently pursuing regional diplomacy. This paid off when circumstances changed in the last year of the Reagan administration, when the South African government was prepared to act, because of internal and international pressures. The United States helped bring about change in southern Africa, partially through luck, partially through persistence, and partially through the complex interplay of two approaches that mixed incentives and engagement strategies into a complicated web of relationships.

Nevertheless, the tensions between these two approaches resulted in a costly exercise that undermined the conduct of foreign policy, set back regional diplomacy for at least two years, heightened partisanship, and bruised race relations in America. Looking back, one can only speculate how much more effective it might have been to have employed incentives and sanctions simultaneously from the start. How many lives might have been saved in South Africa if targeted sanctions had been applied sooner? How many casualties in southern Africa could have been avoided had Pretoria's destabilization policy against its neighbors been curtailed earlier? How many years might Cuban troop presence in Angola been cut short had the United States not backed UNITA "freedom fighters," who were later blamed for continuing the war in Angola and placed under UN sanctions? How much more effective would U.S. policy have been had it engaged the entire spectrum of political groupings in South Africa, rather than just the government, from the outset? And how much political heat would the American political system been spared had incentives and penalties been used judiciously from the beginning?

Whatever the answers to these questions, the South African case provides insights useful to current crafters of similar engagement strategies. First, since such approaches aim to influence both targeted elites and influential constituencies, a keen understanding of what motivates elites and constituencies is essential for engagement to work. In South Africa, the Reagan administration started out by addressing white fears of externally inspired communism, on the assumption that a strategic alliance with the United States was the way to influence the behavior of South African elites. It turned out that whites were far more interested in protecting the economy and averting a race war that would overwhelm them. By the same token, sanctions and aid became vehicles for engaging the country's most important disenfranchised constituencies, showing concretely that the United States identified with their aspirations for political equality.

Second, an engagement strategy with an oppressive government is a risky endeavor if it disregards international human rights standards. Any administration that fails to take human rights into account risks loss of credibility and a political backlash against that policy at home. In today's world, engagement must incorporate human rights or the United States will likely be seen, rightly or wrongly, as an apologist for that regime. Engagement strategies that focus narrowly on strategic objectives can also encourage a form of clientism, in which decisionmakers feel compelled for tactical reasons to downplay negative aspects of the regime. For example, in South Africa, constructive engagement would not even have been possible if it had been publicly known then just how far the country had gone in manufacturing nuclear weapons, conducting research on biological and chemical weapons, sponsoring guerrilla groups that committed atrocities, maintaining death squads that hunted down and killed opponents of white minority rule in other countries, covering up crimes by police units, and supporting terrorist activities by the secret police.[33] While there were allegations and rumors of all these activities, no systematic official investigation or inquiry by the United States to determine the veracity of such charges was ever made, possibly because policymakers did not want to unearth evidence that would jeopardize their strategy.[34] Downplaying these suspicions in the interest of a U.S. policy that was to portray South Africa in a positive light was not simply morally questionable, it also increased the probability that America would be confronted with far larger problems in South Africa further down the road. We now know that South Africa had become not only a pariah state but a "rogue" nuclear state as well; it is a stroke of good luck that the United States and the international community did not have to face a rude awakening with an openly hostile, racist nuclear state in the 1990s.

A final guideline to current policymakers concerns incorporating congressional participation and consultation into foreign policy. Hybrid policies, which use both incentives and sanctions, can be highly divisive for the American political system if not managed carefully. In almost all instances, unless there is congressional support, controversial policies can drive the congressional branch to take the lead with sufficient public outcry. If Congress is the driving force behind a new foreign policy initiative that the executive branch strongly opposes, deep congressional-executive divisions ensue that can leave a residue of resentment that undermines the effectiveness of U.S. policy. In the case of South Africa, Congress overrode the veto of a popular Republican president, who was reluctant to act against South Africa even in the face of overwhelming opposition to his policy. A hybrid approach from the outset would likely have been far more effective.

The road to achieving a hybrid policy toward countries with recalcitrant regimes is not an easy one, and there is no template that can be easily transferred. But goals should be framed modestly, articulated clearly, be doable (such as the five conditions in the CAAA), and reflect both the values and the interests of the United States. Moreover, to have an impact, proper timing, nuanced application, and careful cultivation of domestic political support for the policy are essential. Targeted sanctions against China, for example, geared to relevant issues such as human rights or intellectual property, may be coupled with multilateral diplomacy to obtain allied support and unconditional engagement with civil society and the burgeoning private sector. At the same time, the United States could encourage discourse with China on regional security issues, from Taiwan to North Korea. Such a policy would not only have to be carefully crafted, however, but also continually explained at home so that collaboration on security or economic issues is not mistaken for acquiescence on human rights issues.

Failure to resolve foreign policy tensions between Congress and the executive branch can leave a legacy of lingering domestic political battles. For example, skirmishes occurred over who should replace the American ambassador to South Africa, who had been closely associated with constructive engagement. In a hasty search to select an African American, three candidates were announced before one was confirmed. The first was a businessman, who was eliminated when it was discovered that he had ties with a Nigerian who had been accused of corruption. The second was a career foreign service officer, who publicly disqualified himself when he stated from his diplomatic post that he could not consider the job because he felt that U.S. policy toward South Africa lacked credibility. The third was a career foreign service officer, who was confirmed quickly after the passage of the CAAA.[35] While a capable candidate was eventually found, the messy process caused the United States considerable embarrassment overseas. Such debacles could have been avoided.

Paradoxically, the bitter U.S. debate over South Africa did have some positive benefits. It exposed the complexities of the South African issue, allowed the public to consider the strengths and weaknesses of two alternative policy approaches, and engaged Americans in a debate on how to respond to human rights violations abroad. Americans had to weigh strategic and economic interests against moral considerations, foreshadowing debates, at least partially, on a range of subsequent issues a decade later, from China to Kosovo. Never before had an African foreign policy issue assumed such salience in the United States. However, these positive elements may have been achieved with diminished political polarization had a more balanced approach been achieved from the outset. Policy success need not extract as high a political price as was paid in the South African debate.

Notes

1. Assistant Secretary of State Chester Crocker spelled out the policy before his appointment in a widely quoted article in which he wrote, "when our officials speak only the language of ticking clocks and time bombs—it is not likely that we will be taken seriously by the leadership [in South Africa]. A tone of empathy is required not only for the suffering and injustice caused to blacks in a racist system, but also for the awesome political dilemma in which Afrikaners and other whites find themselves." Chester A. Crocker, "South Africa: Strategy for Change," *Foreign Affairs,* vol. 59 (Winter 1980–81), pp. 350–51.

2. Chester A. Crocker, memo published in *Counterspy* (August-October 1981), p. 54, reproduced in Michael Clough, "The Superpowers in Southern Africa: From Confrontation to Cooperation," in Robert S. Jaster and others, *Changing Fortunes: War, Diplomacy, and Economics in Southern Africa,* South Africa Update Series (Ford Foundation and Foreign Policy Association, 1992), pp. 116–17.

3. Clough, "The Superpowers," p. 117.

4. Jeffrey Herbst, "Incentives and Domestic Reform in South Africa," in David Cortright, ed., *The Price of Peace: Incentives and International Conflict Prevention* (Rowman and Littlefield, 1997), p. 208.

5. Clough, "The Superpowers," p. 117, argues that the military situation inside Angola at the time was unfavorable to a political settlement because UNITA's growing strength, helped by repeated incursions by the South African Defense Force on UNITA's behalf, made it more difficult for the Angolan government to reduce Cuban military support. South Africa's increasing attacks in southern Africa, deepening the dependence of African states on Soviet and Cuban assistance, eventually made the Reagan administration rethink its assumption of common strategic objectives between Pretoria and Washington, but it never abandoned the central tenets of the policy.

6. Office of the Historian, Bureau of Public Affairs, *The United States and South Africa: U.S. Public Statements and Related Documents, 1977–1985* (U.S. Department of State, 1985), p. 58.

7. Crocker, "South Africa: Strategy for Change," p. 338.

8. Zimbabwe had become independent just nine months before Reagan took office.

9. This point was also made by Herbst, "Incentives and Domestic Reform in South Africa."

10. Clough, "The Superpowers," p. 117, writes correctly that "linkage offered Crocker a means of winning support from senior administration officials for continued U.S. diplomatic engagement in southern Africa. Without the promise of removing the Cuban-Soviet presence from Angola, President Reagan and Secretary of State Haig would have had little interest in promoting Namibian independence."

11. For a more detailed description of the events leading up to sanctions, see Pauline H. Baker, *The United States and South Africa: The Reagan Years* (Ford Foundation and Foreign Policy Association, 1989), pp. 29–47.

12. Address by State President P. W. Botha at the opening of the National Party Natal Congress, Durban, August 15, 1985. (Botha stated: "I believe that we are today crossing the Rubicon. *There can be no turning back*.") While this statement implied that he was committed to reform, Botha also warned the international community, "Don't push us too far," and affirmed that he was "not prepared to lead white South Africans and other minority groups on a road to abdication and suicide." This speech was seen by the international community as one of the most hard-line statements resisting reform that Botha had ever given. Full text can be found in Robert Schrire, *Adapt or Die: The End of White Politics in South Africa*, South Africa Update Series (Ford Foundation and Foreign Policy Association, 1991), app. A.

13. Baker, *The United States and South Africa*, p. 36.

14. The intention of the Comprehensive Anti-Apartheid Act of 1986, as the legislation stated, was to "set forth a comprehensive and complete framework to guide the efforts of the United States in helping to bring an end to apartheid in South Africa and lead to the establishment of a nonracial, democratic form of government." In short, the law was intended to create a new U.S. policy to replace constructive engagement, with a wide range of directions on how the United States was to accomplish its new policy goals.

15. The two apartheid laws were the Population Registration Act, the cornerstone of apartheid that required racial classification of every South African, and the Group Areas Act, requiring segregated residential areas.

16. The earlier, small aid program had come under attack from U.S. conservatives, who wanted the money disbursed through established institutions, even if they were controlled by the South African government. However, congressional liberals, who ultimately prevailed, wanted the program to bypass state schools and remain independent of government control.

17. Specifically, the Sullivan principles required desegregating employment facilities; providing equal employment opportunity for all employees; ensuring that the pay system be applied to all employees; establishing a minimum wage and salary structure; increasing the number of persons in managerial, administrative, clerical, and technical jobs who are disadvantaged by apartheid; taking responsible steps to improve the quality of employees' lives outside the work environment; and implementing fair labor practices by recognizing the right of all employees to unionize.

18. When Congress approved the sanctions in 1986, there were 360 U.S. companies doing business in South Africa. By 1991, only 125 remained, even though the sanctions did not require any U.S. firms to disinvest. Those that did withdraw did so based on their own political risk assessments. However, by 1999 there were 386 U.S. firms in South Africa, slightly more than the number before sanctions were applied. Many in South Africa had hoped that the number would be far higher after the end of apartheid, but "South Africa's entrance into the pool of emerging market countries came just as competitors in Asia and Latin America—almost all with larger populations than South Africa's 42 million—were becoming darlings of investors and receiving most available money." Crime, unemployment, AIDS, powerful labor unions, and a poorly educated work force are other legacies of apartheid that will take time to overcome and have provided disincentives for investors. See Jon Jeter, "South Africa's Image Problem Deters Investors," *Washington Post*, October 17, 1999, p. A21.

19. Rachel Swarns, "South African to Court U.S. Investors," *New York Times*, September 20, 1999, p. A14.

20. The other major international influence affecting events in South Africa was the changes in the Soviet Union under Gorbachev. Allister Sparks wrote that the reforms that began to unravel the communist empire "eased Pretoria's phobia that the black struggle against apartheid was a conspiracy directed from Moscow. It took the monkey off de Klerk's back and enabled him to justify to his people what would otherwise have appeared a suicidal course of action." Allister Sparks, "Letter from South Africa: The Secret Revolution," *New Yorker*, April 11, 1994, p. 71.

21. Marina Ottaway, *South Africa: The Struggle for a New Order* (Brookings, 1993), p. 210. This conclusion is also supported by confidential interviews conducted with government officials by the author in South Africa during the late 1980s and early 1990s.

22. Frederik W. de Klerk, *The Last Trek—A New Beginning: The Autobiography* (St. Martin's Press, 1999).

23. See Hermann Giliomee, "Surrender without Defeat: Afrikaners and the South African 'Miracle,'" *Daedalus* (Spring 1997), p. 127.

24. Schrire, *Adapt or Die*, pp. 127, 130.

25. Ibid., p. 130.

26. De Klerk's political calculations were discerned from interviews conducted at the time by the author with government representatives and many close political observers of the National Party in South Africa.

27. These factors included a change in the U.S.-Soviet relationship in the waning days of the cold war when Moscow was seeking cooperative ways to reduce its international commitments from Afghanistan to southern Africa; a visit by Bavarian leader Franz Josef Strauss, a friend of South Africa, to Pretoria to inform the government that Moscow had concluded that no military solution was possible in Angola and that the Soviets would be prepared to support a negotiated solution; a shift in the military balance of power in the region largely as the result of Cuba's decision to increase its military commitment to Angola to 45,000–50,000 troops that would take a more frontline role, causing more South African combat deaths and a loss of air supremacy over southwestern Angola; a willingness by the United States to admit Cuba to the negotiations on Angola over the objections of the anti-Cuban faction in the State Department, which wanted to shut out Castro; rising economic costs for all the warring parties in the region; a realization by South Africans that with U.S. presidential elections approaching they could get a better deal with the Reagan administration than with a possible Democratic one; and a change in the leadership of South Africa's ruling National Party, which replaced P. W. Botha, following his stroke and a power struggle within the party, with the more pragmatic F. W. de Klerk.

28. Sparks, "Letter from South Africa," p. 71.

29. Ibid.

30. Schrire, *Adapt or Die*, p. 82.

31. Ibid., p. 84.

32. Charles M. Becker and others, *The Impact of Sanctions on South Africa, Part 1: The Economy,* and Jan Hofmeyr, *The Impact of Sanctions on South Africa, Part 2: Whites' Political Attitudes* (Washington, D.C.: Investor Responsibility Research Center, 1990).

33. See, for example, "Senior Officer Admits Role in Killing Foes of Apartheid," *New York Times,* May 25, 1999, p. A8.

34. Even a confirmed nuclear test site in 1977, discovered by the Soviet Union, and a subsequent intelligence report of a signal that suggested a nuclear device had exploded in the South Atlantic in 1979 did not provoke a thorough or sustained investigation of Pretoria's nuclear capabilities.

35. The three candidates were Robert J. Brown, a businessman from North Carolina, Terence A. Todman, then serving as ambassador to Denmark, and Edward J. Perkins, who was ambassador to Liberia at the time.

7

The United States and the Soviet Union: Lessons of Détente

JAMES M. GOLDGEIER

The indispensable nation, the lonely superpower, the reluctant sheriff—policymakers, professors, and pundits have spent a great deal of time discussing what it means for America to stand atop the world's hierarchy of nations. The subtext to much of the conversation about this country's current position is speculation about its ability to manage whatever follows this unipolar moment. How long, many ask, can the United States preserve its hegemony before its likeliest challenger—China—emerges as a major economic and military power seeking to disrupt U.S. interests in Asia and beyond? Is there anything the United States can do about what history suggests will be an inevitable trend away from hegemony toward greater pluralism in international affairs? In addition to the "China problem," can the United States ensure Germany's commitment to Europe's multilateral institutions, engage Russia during its continued transition, manage India's emergence as a nuclear power, and keep Japan as its major ally in Asia?

The last time an American administration consciously developed a strategy to preserve this country's political and military position in the face of a rising challenger was in the late 1960s and early 1970s. When President Richard Nixon and National Security Adviser Henry Kissinger took the reins of American foreign policy in January 1969, the U.S. position in the world had eroded dramatically since the beginning of the decade. Forced to back down during the Cuban missile crisis in 1962, the Soviet Union had embarked on a massive military effort and achieved nuclear parity with the United States by the start of the new administration. The war in Vietnam was having devastating consequences at home and abroad. Europe and Japan had recovered fully from World War II and were poised to compete economically. Independence movements throughout the third world challenged American interests in Latin America, Africa, the Middle East, and Asia.

To respond to this set of challenges and preserve a world America had created at the end of World War II, Nixon and Kissinger developed their strategy of détente. A complex strategy that linked progress in different areas of competition to one another, détente was designed to lessen the risk of nuclear war and to channel rising Soviet power constructively into a less dangerous competition. Hoping that combining carrots and sticks effectively would induce the Soviet Union to accept the U.S. vision of international order, Nixon and Kissinger thereby sought to end the war in Vietnam, to ensure that Europe and Japan stayed firmly allied to the United States, and to contain revolutionary movements in the third world.

Those hoping to combine carrots and sticks to co-opt a rising China into America's vision of the post–cold war order would be wise to examine closely the successes and failures of the Nixon-Kissinger approach. The heyday of détente was a brief period, 1972–73, after which the policy lost momentum rather quickly. By the end of the decade, events in the Middle East, Angola, and Afghanistan had resulted in the resumption of the cold war. While Nixon and Kissinger were quite successful in using Soviet and Chinese interest in special relationships with the United States to play the two communist giants against one another, their strategy faced an overwhelming obstacle: it required tremendous control over the different levers of policy, and the American Congress, the bureaucracy, and allies were not always subject to control. Although détente was an impressive strategy conceptually, it produced meager results in limiting strategic nuclear weapons, enhancing economic ties, and promoting regional peace efforts.

The Nixon-Kissinger Strategy

In 1947 George F. Kennan publicly articulated the doctrine of containment that guided U.S. policy during the cold war. The Soviet regime, argued Kennan, promulgated the Marxist-Leninist cause abroad because of the need to justify monopoly power at home by the Communist Party. U.S. foreign policy should work to contain Moscow's efforts to expand its power by protecting core American interests "and in this way to promote tendencies which must eventually find their outlet in either the break-up or the gradual mellowing of Soviet power."[1] Once the regime changed its stripes, a different relationship might become possible. Although Kennan later argued that he meant to emphasize diplomatic, political, and economic containment, American policy after 1950 became highly militarized. The Korean War sparked an enormous increase in the American defense budget, and it turned a Eurocentric policy into a global strategy. The United States sought to block communist expansion in Korea and later Vietnam, and superpower crises developed in Berlin, the Middle East, and most notably, Cuba.

The Soviet arms buildup of the 1960s, along with the huge domestic and international cost of the Vietnam War, led the Nixon administration to shift American policy away from a confrontational cold war approach toward an "era of negotiation" in order to moderate Soviet behavior. The economic and military costs of maintaining America's position in the world, under tremendous assault due to the debacle in Vietnam, meant that the United States had to find a lower-cost strategy to accommodate changing global circumstances and an increasingly militant antiwar population at home. As Kissinger wrote later,

> For us to have launched the grandiloquent anti-Soviet crusade which our critics later (though not at the time) chastised us for not undertaking would only have driven our domestic crisis out of control. For, at the time Nixon entered office, the American public was drained by twenty years of cold war exertions and the increasing frustrations with Vietnam. It had lived through two Berlin crises, the Korean War, Soviet invasions of Hungary and Czechoslovakia, and the Cuban Missile Crisis, and had already sustained over 35,000 casualties in Indochina. Americans were growing tired of defending distant frontiers against a seemingly irreconcilable ideological opponent in a protracted conflict with no end in sight.[2]

A remark Kissinger made to the president in March 1973 captures the essence of the overall Nixon-Kissinger strategy. "If we play our cards right," wrote Kissinger, we can "continue to have our mao tai and drink our vodka too."[3] What had the president and his national security adviser sought after January 1969? They needed a way out of Vietnam, and they believed Moscow and Beijing could help them by pressuring North Vietnamese leader Ho Chi Minh to accept a deal. Kissinger in particular feared U.S. isolation resulting from a successful Soviet military attack on China that then would cause Europe to kowtow to Moscow's demands; a closer relationship with

Beijing could deter such behavior. Nixon and Kissinger were concerned lest U.S.-Soviet competition in the third world escalate into all-out nuclear war. Economic carrots for better behavior and accords limiting strategic nuclear arsenals would limit those dangers. What China and the Soviet Union did to their own citizens had no place in this view of the world; as Nixon told Chinese leader Mao Zedong, "What is important is not a nation's internal political philosophy. What is important is its policy toward the rest of the world and toward us."[4]

In pursuing détente with the Soviet Union, Nixon and Kissinger benefited from the strong position Leonid Brezhnev had achieved within the Soviet leadership. There would be critics of the policy from ideological hard-liners in Moscow, but the Twenty-Fourth Communist Party Congress in 1971 publicly declared détente and peaceful coexistence as the general line of Soviet foreign policy. In 1972–73, at the height of his political and physical health, Brezhnev could pursue the foreign policy he desired, although having personally benefited from the plot to overthrow Soviet leader Nikita Khrushchev in 1964, he understood the need to buy off the leading economic, military, and ideological elites.[5] Unfortunately, while Nixon should have been able to deal from a similarly strong position (albeit within the different constraints of a democracy) given his landslide victory in 1972 over George McGovern, Watergate would soon shatter that dream.

Why did the Brezhnev Politburo want détente? Although the Soviet Union had achieved military parity, it lagged behind economically and required Western technological assistance. Border conflicts with China in 1969 reminded the Soviets that Beijing posed a greater threat than Washington, and the USSR hoped for an alliance with the United States against China. Most important, the Soviet Union sought recognition that military equality gave it political equality, that is, the right to be involved in the settling of issues anywhere in the world. Only one country could grant that recognition—the United States. At a time when the Soviet regime was paying greater costs to preserve the empire (having invaded Czechoslovakia in 1968 to subdue the Prague regime and its population) and was facing the rise of a dissident movement internally, détente could provide Moscow with economic, political, and military benefits that could strengthen Brezhnev's hold on power even further.

The Elements of Détente

The most public features of détente were the presidential summits and the arms control agreements, but the policy was much more, including agreements dealing with postwar European borders, trade, cultural exchanges, and rhetorical promises regarding codes of conduct. In 1971, the United States, Britain, France, and the USSR signed the Quadripartite Agreement on Berlin, which resolved issues of Western access and removed this long-standing problem as a potential flash point. In May 1972, the superpowers signed the Anti-Ballistic Missile (ABM) Treaty, limiting development and deployment of defensive systems, and agreed on an interim accord (which became known as SALT I) to limit the number of offensive nuclear launchers. They also signed a document known as the Basic Principles Agreement, which stated that the two countries would "proceed from the common determination that in the nuclear age there is no alternative to conducting their mutual relations on the basis of peaceful coexistence"; they would develop "normal relations based on the principles of sovereignty, equality, non-interference in internal affairs and mutual advantage"; they pledged to avoid confrontations that might lead to nuclear war; and they stated their recognition "that efforts to obtain unilateral advantage at the expense of the other, directly or indirectly, are inconsistent with these objectives."[6]

In January 1973, the United States signed the agreement that essentially ended its involvement in Vietnam, and six months later, the United States and the Soviet Union signed an Agreement on the Prevention of Nuclear War. Then in 1975, all members of NATO and the Warsaw Treaty Organization signed the Helsinki Final Act (giving rise to the Conference on Security and Cooperation in Europe, or CSCE), which recognized Europe's postwar boundaries, promoted confidence-building measures to reduce the dangers of the military face-off in Europe, created trade opportunities, and established human rights provisions.

Linkage

What gave the strategy its unique characteristics was not the pursuit of particular agreements, however, but the explicit decision by Nixon and Kissinger to link the pursuit of arms control agreements, solutions to regional conflicts, and the other elements of détente to one another. Kissinger wrote in his memoirs, "Events in different parts of the world, in our view, were related to each other; even more so, Soviet conduct in different parts of the world. We proceeded from the premise that to separate issues into distinct compartments would encourage the Soviet leaders to believe that they could use cooperation in one area as a safety valve while striving for unilateral advantages elsewhere. This was unacceptable."[7] Harvard professor Stanley Hoffmann put it slightly more colorfully: "The bear would be treated like one of B. F. Skinner's pigeons: there would be incentives for good behavior, rewards if such behavior occurred, and punishments if not. It may have been a bit pedantic, or a bit arrogant; it certainly was rather theoretical."[8]

In theory, the United States could offer the Soviet Union a variety of carrots: agricultural exports, technology transfers, increased credits, most-favored-nation trade status (which dramatically lowers barriers to trade), acceptance of postwar boundaries in Central and Eastern Europe, and recognition of Moscow's global political status. But these carrots would only be released if the Soviets played ball on limiting the buildup of strategic nuclear weapons, helped end the Vietnam War in a way that satisfied the administration's hope for an honorable withdrawal, did not restrict Western access to its part of Berlin, and avoided the pursuit of unilateral advantage in third world conflicts.[9] If the Soviet Union failed to behave as desired in Africa or Southeast Asia, then trade goodies would be pulled back.

The problem was, if the Soviets did engage in arms control or showed restraint in regional conflicts, they were supposed to be rewarded. But Congress, and particularly Senator Henry M. "Scoop" Jackson (Democrat of Washington), had different ideas of the proper linkage strategy. To Jackson, linkage meant providing rewards based on Soviet *internal* behavior. If Brezhnev and company adopted better human rights practices, and in particular loosened restrictions on Jewish emigration, then the Soviet Union could be granted most-favored-nation trade status. But if it did not, then regardless of external behavior, it would be denied. Although no individual frustrated Kissinger's efforts more than Senator Jackson, conceptually the policies were quite similar. In Kissinger's view, "Expanding trade without a political quid pro quo was a gift; there was very little the Soviet Union could do for us economically. It did not seem unreasonable to require Soviet restraint in such trouble spots as the Middle East, Berlin, and Southeast Asia in return."[10] Substitute language on human rights for the last section on trouble spots, and one had the Jackson version of linkage.

The Jackson challenge would illuminate a larger problem for the policy. Its complexity and subtlety left both liberals and conservatives unhappy, and the base of public support eroded rather quickly. Partly that was due to the prism of Vietnam and Watergate. Liberals never trusted the Nixon administration to pursue anything but a cold war strategy and wanted to see withdrawal from Indochina as quickly as possible; they always feared the U.S. role in exacerbating the cold war. Watergate then added to their animus toward Nixon. Conservatives meanwhile were dismayed that the administration did not do what it took to win the war and believed the administration was too soft on Moscow. In their view, the Soviet Union was to blame for conflicts like Vietnam and the cold war and needed to be defeated.

Liberals believed arms control was important as an end in itself, a sign that the relationship was less adversarial, and they feared that linkage would derail the pursuit of the various accords. Their goal was not just the relaxation of tensions implied by the word *détente*, but rather they sought full-blown cooperation. Conservatives meanwhile came to resent the accommodation of Soviet internal practices and the acceptance by Nixon and Kissinger of Soviet domination of Eastern Europe. They wanted a more confrontational policy whose goal was victory. Despite the criticisms, linkage and détente appeared to be working at the 1972 Moscow summit. The two superpowers signed the ABM Treaty, SALT I, and the Basic Principles Agreement. It seemed that they had agreed both to limits in the arms race and to mutual restraint in regional conflicts. As they moved to consideration of economic ties later in the year, Nixon and Kissinger appeared vindicated in their view that the Soviet Union would grant concessions in the political-military sphere in exchange for trade carrots.

Feelings of success regarding the ability to link different parts of the relationship to one another were, however, short-lived. Right under the noses of Nixon and Kissinger, the Soviet Union purchased the 1972 U.S. grain surplus at bargain prices. President Nixon had been pushing the Agriculture Department to increase exports to assist American farmers, and the United States extended significant credits to Moscow for grain purchases. Skillfully dealing with individual trading companies, the Soviet government then succeeded in concealing their purchase of an enormous amount of U.S. wheat at prices subsidized by the American taxpayer. Tagged the "Great Grain Robbery" after the purchases became publicly known, this Soviet coup meant that the United States had not been able to link agricultural exports to other parts of the relationship. Then in October 1972, Senator Jackson introduced an amendment tying most-favored-nation status for the Soviet Union to Soviet policy on Jewish emigration from the Soviet Union; once passed, this initiative would further diminish the U.S. ability to provide economic rewards for the earlier political-military accords. In October 1973, with the outbreak of war in the Middle East, the Soviet Union threatened unilateral intervention to save the Egyptian army, and the United States responded by going on nuclear alert. The notion that a détente strategy predicated on linkage could either be carried out or could limit U.S.-Soviet competition in any meaningful way appeared a farce, and both the American public and the Soviet leadership saw their expectations for the fruits of the policy dashed.

The greatest successes of the policy during the 1970s were the Anti-Ballistic

Missile Treaty, which closed off an entire segment of the superpower arms race, and the opening to China, which fundamentally changed American foreign policy. Accepting the doctrine of mutual assured destruction, which meant that the two countries deterred one another through the capacity to launch an overwhelming nuclear attack even after suffering a first strike, the two countries forswore the deployment of a national missile defense. Even after the arms race continued unabated on the offensive side, even after trade got caught up in American domestic politics, even after the rhetoric about codes of conduct did little to restrain competition in the third world, the ABM Treaty held for nearly thirty years and saved America billions of dollars. As for China, the opening was a diplomatic coup for the Nixon administration. The combination of the alliance the United States had with Western Europe and Japan and its new relationship with China left the Soviets alone diplomatically, facing a situation of encirclement they had always feared and had done so much to bring about.

Major Lessons

There are features of this policy that are worth emulating, particularly the ability at the top to conceptualize a grand strategy. The policy was quite logical if perhaps too clever; it dealt with issues central to international politics; it resulted in modest achievements in arms control, particularly in limiting an arms race in defensive systems; and it did lead both the Soviets and the Chinese to believe they had more to gain from the relationship with the United States than they had to gain from a relationship with one another. But there were numerous problems in carrying out the strategy that resulted from differing expectations, a limit to the array of carrots, the difficulty in maintaining control of engagement strategies in democratic systems, unintended consequences, and Soviet linkage practices. Furthermore, a strategy predicated on a continued rise in Soviet power demonstrates the challenges of forecasting global trends. Each of these issues provides important lessons for present policymaking.

Lesson One: Unrealistic and opposing expectations can be deadly to the process

For Nixon and Kissinger, engaging with the Soviet Union on arms control and offering economic carrots for good behavior was intended to result in Soviet help in ending the war in Vietnam and generally in Soviet restraint throughout the third world. The Soviets would also limit their nuclear weapons program. By moderating Soviet behavior and preventing further advances in Soviet strategic weapons capabilities, the United States would thereby preserve its position at the top of the international system.

Kissinger and Nixon were smart enough to understand that the Soviets would continue to compete in some places, just as Kissinger aggressively sought to reduce Soviet influence in the Middle East. But they sold the American public on the peaceful prospects for a real détente relationship, and the public quickly grew disillusioned with the policy. The Soviets did not settle for parity in land-based strategic nuclear missiles, embarking on a major buildup of launchers equipped with multiple, independently targetable reentry vehicles (MIRVs). They also continued to extend their conventional military reach in Southeast Asia, southern Africa, and the Middle East. As Robert Osgood noted in the early 1980s, "The [Brezhnev] leadership has been bolder than Stalin and more effective than Khrushchev in capitalizing on a growing number of opportunities to project Soviet arms and forces into the Third World."[11] As is often a problem for U.S. democracy, gaining public support meant overselling the policy initially, and thus what should have been unsurprising Soviet behavior in the third world led to a backlash by the American public against détente in the late 1970s.

Meanwhile, the Soviets were disappointed at the American response because they had precisely the opposite expectations. Whereas Nixon and Kissinger viewed détente and the new relationships with both China and the USSR as a means for preserving American influence, the Soviet Union believed détente would make their competitive efforts at weakening U.S. influence in the third world less dangerous. This is how Moscow defined *peaceful coexistence*, a term that they had taken great pains to write into the 1972 Basic Principles Agreement. The Soviets believed that the "correlation of forces" (their term for the balance of power) was shifting in their favor, but they wanted some way to dampen the dangers that nuclear weapons posed to their anticipated rise to global power. The Soviets sought détente precisely so that their efforts on behalf of clients in the third world did not result in another world war, whereas the United States hoped they would abandon many of these efforts.[12]

Thus Moscow never understood, for example, the American reaction to Soviet and Cuban efforts to help their clients in the Angolan civil war in 1975. Furthermore, the Soviet Union was frustrated because its leaders believed that the achievement of military parity should translate into a recognition of political equality. The United States and the Soviet Union would run the world together and thereby reduce the influence of China. When

Kissinger continued to seek to isolate Moscow, as he did by cultivating Beijing or by his efforts in the Middle East after the 1973 war, it was the Soviets' turn to be disappointed in the achievements of détente. The Soviets also hoped that the bilateral achievements of 1972 would result in the realization of most-favored-nation status, and they grew increasingly frustrated with the growing emphasis from Congress on linkage to internal behavior.

Lesson Two: You have to have something to offer

The Kissinger era reminds us that a carrot-and-stick policy requires real carrots (as well as, of course, real sticks). Once Congress imposed limits on what the United States could offer on the economic front, Kissinger was playing the game with one hand tied behind his back. Even if he had not had congressional difficulties, it still is not clear that Kissinger had that much to offer, particularly since he was unwilling to give the Soviets what they wanted most: an alliance against China. One of Kissinger's chief aides, William Hyland, wrote, "at one point [Soviet ambassador Anatoly] Dobrynin bluntly asked what was in it for Moscow if the Vietnam War ended. And Kissinger rather lamely suggested trade and a summit meeting."[13]

We often look at the policy from the U.S. perspective, but look at how little the Soviet Union achieved. Moscow could not obtain most-favored-nation status, nor could the Soviet leadership use the relationship to isolate China. The USSR certainly did not get America's acquiescence to Soviet competitive activity in the third world. A linkage strategy has to be viewed on both sides as win-win, as it was at its peak in 1972 but not after 1973. Having little to offer the Soviets made continued pursuit of a linkage strategy increasingly difficult. If, as was the case with détente, domestic politics preclude the offering of certain incentives, other inducements must be substituted or the process will lose its momentum.

Lesson Three: Control in a democracy is essential but elusive

A sophisticated strategy of linkage requires tight control over the entire process, which requires control of the bureaucracy, the Congress, and at times, allies. Controlling all three to any great extent is impossible, and with Congress and allies, the best one can hope for is to co-opt each group into accepting the general thrust of the policy. Tight control also requires full information as well as in-depth knowledge of all the issue areas, and this too gets more difficult the smaller the number of those in the know. Kissinger was often highly effective at shutting the bureaucracy out, using his private channels to conduct business. However, he did not make enough effort to co-opt Congress, and he overestimated both American and Soviet abilities to control allies.

Only a national security adviser or secretary of state can manage a complex linkage strategy, since no assistant secretary or undersecretary has the portfolio to control all elements of the process.[14] Kissinger's ability to shut out the bureaucracy (including Cabinet colleagues) from what he was doing was impressive. In December 1971, he told Huang Hua, the Chinese ambassador to the United Nations, "Just so everyone knows exactly what we do, we tell you about our conversations with the Soviets; we do not tell the Soviets about our conversations with you. In fact, we don't tell our own colleagues that I see you. [U.S. ambassador to the UN] George Bush is the only person outside the White House who knows I come here."[15] Kissinger negotiated arms control secretly with Dobrynin, completely bypassing his arms control team, which was working on these issues with their Soviet counterparts. He and Dobrynin negotiated the 1971 Berlin agreement in secret with U.S. ambassador to Bonn Kenneth Rush and German national security adviser Egon Bahr. The State Department found out only when a draft of the accord was completed. However, although Kissinger knew the security issues extremely well and maintained tight control, he had much less interest in economics. He was blindsided by the Great Grain Robbery because the White House did not pay close attention to the Agriculture Department's activities in 1972.[16]

Yet even the most successful back channels had their constraints. As Kissinger recalls concerning arms control efforts in the spring of 1972,

> The negotiations on SALT, however facilitated by the backchannel, also revealed its limits. For SALT involved too many vested interests of both the Defense Department and the uniformed military to allow these issues to be settled conclusively in the backchannel. As a result, both the open and backchannel negotiations often took place simultaneously, imposing nerve-racking requirements of coordination on the NSC staff. Once the Soviets caught on, they sometimes tried to play the two channels against each other by putting into the open channel some proposals Nixon had already rejected in the backchannel.

He adds that there was so much at cross-purposes in the different channels that in April 1972, "Nixon . . . lost track of who was saying what to whom."[17]

If Kissinger could for the most part control the executive branch, he could not control Congress or America's allies. Nixon and Kissinger held out the incentive of trade agreements as they worked political-military issues in early 1972, but then could not deliver this primary carrot when Senator Jackson entered the picture. Most-favored-nation status simply means that a country cannot be discriminated against and gets the same tariff levels as the other nations in the global trading regime. The Senate was supposed to agree to grant this status to the Soviet Union in exchange for Moscow's agreement to fulfill its obligations under the World War II lend-lease program. Yet when Nixon submitted the proposal to Congress in April 1973, Jackson stood in his way. The senator's amendment denied most-favored-nation status to any communist country that restricted emigration. Moreover, Jackson wanted to force an annual review process even if the country eventually passed muster.

It is unclear how much most-favored-nation status would have meant in terms of U.S.-Soviet trade. Regardless, it would have given the Soviet Union equal status with all the other countries in the world that were granted this provision through their participation in the General Agreement on Tariffs and Trade (the forerunner of the World Trade Organization). Emigration had been increasing during the previous few years, but Jackson's efforts to get a public, binding Soviet commitment to specific levels backfired. To add to Kissinger's headaches, in June 1974, Jackson tied the usually pro forma renewal of presidential authority to use the Export-Import Bank as an occasion to limit the amount of Ex-Im loans extended to the Soviet Union.[18] The final straw was Senator Jackson's publication of letters between Kissinger and Jackson in October 1974 that disclosed Soviet concessions to gain U.S. approval and led Jackson to declare his victory over the White House. Brezhnev used the letters to embarrass Kissinger in their discussions in Moscow later that month, since Kissinger had referred directly to the Soviet harassment of its citizens in order to placate Jackson. At that meeting, Kissinger responded to Brezhnev's complaint about interference in Soviet internal affairs and about Jackson's apparent victory by acknowledging: "What burns me up is that a lot of what the General Secretary has said is true."[19]

Later in their discussion, Kissinger noted, "On MFN [most favored nation], it was in this room, or a similar room, that we agreed on MFN . . . in 1972. I had never heard of the Jackson Amendment at that time. Nor had I ever mentioned Jewish emigration. . . . [The release of letters] was a trick of Jackson's. . . . The Administration, under extremely difficult circumstances, attempted to fulfill a promise to the Soviet Union, and I regret the behavior of Senator Jackson." He further apologized for his own discussion with Jackson of Soviet internal matters: "The intention of the Administration was to state those things we had been told in order to make MFN possible. There is a mistake that I made, in retrospect. I have believed and have said publicly that it was a mistake for the United States to involve itself in an internal Soviet issue."[20]

Allies are even more difficult to control because they have their own regional needs. The Germans began their own détente policy in the late 1960s—the *Ostpolitik* of Chancellor Willy Brandt—which they did not always coordinate with the United States. In 1973, controlling Israel's behavior during the Middle East war was extremely difficult. Meanwhile, the United States assumed that Moscow could control Cairo, Damascus, and Hanoi, which it could not. Failures to control allies are usually taken by the adversary as a sign of bad faith, further undermining expectations, when in fact it may be beyond even a superpower's reach to rein in the smaller power.

Lesson Four: Engagement has unintended consequences

Because Kissinger was steeped in a diplomatic tradition of great statesmen dealing privately with one another on issues of the highest magnitude, he failed to foresee the unintended consequences of a policy whose greatest effect was on societies: the so-called basket three of the 1975 Helsinki Accords. The Soviets agreed to the human rights provisions of basket three only because of what they would gain from baskets one and two, on security and economic issues, respectively. The Soviet Union achieved its long-standing goal of Western recognition of the inviolability of the postwar boundaries in Central and Eastern Europe and achieved the promise of greater economic assistance. At the time, most analysts believed that the rhetoric of basket three meant nothing in the tightly controlled Soviet society, and President Gerald Ford was criticized by conservatives for consenting to a Soviet sphere of influence in the East. The entire CSCE issue was of little interest to Kissinger, who saw it as a rhetorical bone to throw to the Europeans and domestic human rights lobbies.

As it turns out, however, the human rights provisions had a profound effect in undermining Soviet control in Central and Eastern Europe. With their leaders' signatures on the Helsinki document, dissidents had much more room to operate inside authoritarian regimes. They developed networks throughout Eastern Europe and built ties to the West. Not only did these movements grow in the late 1970s, but when regimes then began to crumble from within a decade later, the dissidents—like Vaclav Havel in Czechoslovakia—were much better prepared to take power.

Lesson Five: Two can play the linkage game

William Hyland argues that at the June 1974 U.S.-Soviet summit, Brezhnev refused to grant concessions on arms control because the United States was not taking him up on an offer to form a superpower alliance against China. Hyland suggests that this alliance was Brezhnev's most cherished goal at that time, and arms control concessions might have helped Nixon as he was attempting to extricate himself from the Watergate crisis.[21] Whether anything could have helped Nixon at that point is not the issue, but Brezhnev was only prepared to offer his carrot on arms control if he got what he wanted on China. There was no benefit, however, to the United States for creating an explicit superpower alliance against Beijing.

This episode serves as a useful reminder that one needs to think through how the target country views the web of relationships, since it may seek to practice its own linkage strategy. In 1973, Leonid Brezhnev was a strong leader of an authoritarian state, but he still had his own domestic constituencies to placate, which is why he pursued his own linkage approach. Brezhnev had consolidated power by promising certain things to key elites. The economic managers would get technological assistance. The military would get a continued nuclear and conventional buildup. Ideologues would get support for Marxist-Leninists in the third world.[22] To give arms control concessions that would displease the military and the ideologues would require something in return, that is, an alliance against China.

Lesson Six: Going beyond the five-day forecast is not easy

Whereas Nixon and Kissinger were concerned that the rise of Soviet power was the greatest challenge to U.S. dominance in the international system, Soviet decline set in by the early 1980s. As the historian John Lewis Gaddis puts it, "Kissinger, it turns out, was wrong about many things, not least of which was the direction in which historical circumstances were proceeding. He saw himself as desperately sticking fingers in dikes when in fact the ocean on the other side was receding."[23] The lesson for today is an obvious one: China may seem the likeliest to emerge as the next great economic and military challenger to U.S. supremacy, but it too could go the other way.[24] Societal pressures such as those that undermined the Soviet system may burst forth, and a breakup of the country is also not out of the question. Given the confident writings regarding Japan's rise to number one in the late 1980s, one should be circumspect about planning a strategy whose main focus is to prevent an emerging China from disrupting the U.S.-led system.

Final Thoughts

The analogy of today's international environment to that of the late 1960s is not completely apt. No power comes close to matching U.S. capabilities as did the Soviet Union then. Still, the expectation should be that unipolarity cannot last forever, and thinking sooner rather than later about how to co-opt or weaken potential challenges to the United States is the best way to preserve American interests. The linkage strategy that underlay détente offers valuable lessons particularly as the United States considers how best to engage or contain rising Chinese power (or, for that matter, any other potential major power). Practicing linkage effectively means recognizing that one is holding hostage to the broader relationship specific items that one may care about. Those who believed the SALT process was important as an end in itself would have preferred that arms control not be tied to behavior in other areas. In their view, achievable elements of SALT were lost to the broader strategy. However, if the adversary's general behavior is the overriding concern, then such costs will be bearable.[25]

Détente showed that the type of control necessary to carry out an effective linkage strategy is hard to achieve. Today, U.S. high-technology companies will seek their own deals and will receive assistance from the Commerce Department, just as American farmers acted with Agriculture Department help in the early 1970s. And members of Congress will practice their own version of linkage, tying carrots to the internal behavior of authoritarian regimes. Any administration will have its hands full on both fronts. A successful linkage policy depends on early and sustained consultation with leading members of Congress. When a president becomes as weak as Nixon did during Watergate (and as Clinton did after the impeachment hearings), even this may not be enough, but to ignore those in Congress who have their own agendas and their own notions of linkage is a recipe for disaster.[26]

In the end, Kissinger's emphasis on traditional realpolitik was both his greatest strength and his greatest weakness. His ability to work the strategic triangle and conceptualize the broader interests of the major powers was at times profoundly perceptive, although he seriously overestimated Soviet intentions to attack China. Most important, no anti-U.S. coalition emerged among major or potentially major powers during that time, and the opening to China was a diplomatic triumph. But Kissinger's emphasis on great power realpolitik led to his failure to appreciate the lack of control that big powers had over little ones and to his failure to recognize how his own society and their representatives in government could disrupt his strategy. Most important, he did not appreciate the role that Soviet society could play in weakening the second superpower. The world is not simply one in which statesmen represent pieces on a chessboard; rather, these diplomats represent societies, and societies can act in ways that confound them.

Notes

1 . X, [George F. Kennan] "The Sources of Soviet Conduct," *Foreign Affairs*, vol. 25 (July 1947), pp. 566–82 (quotation, p. 582).

2. Henry A. Kissinger, *Years of Renewal* (Simon and Schuster, 1999), p. 96.

3. William Burr, ed., *The Kissinger Transcripts: The Top Secret Talks with Beijing and Moscow* (New Press, 1999), p. 115. Good sources on the policy include the memoirs of Richard Nixon and Henry Kissinger as well as Raymond L. Garthoff, *Détente and Confrontation: American-Soviet Relations from Nixon to Reagan*, rev. ed. (Brookings, 1994); William G. Hyland, *Mortal Rivals: Superpower Relations from Nixon to Reagan* (Random House, 1987); John Lewis Gaddis, "Rescuing Choice from Circumstance: The Statecraft of Henry Kissinger," in Gordon A. Craig and Francis L. Loewenheim, eds., *The Diplomats, 1939–1979* (Princeton University Press, 1994), pp. 564–92; Robert S. Litwak, *Détente and the Nixon Doctrine: American Foreign Policy and the Pursuit of Stability, 1969–1976* (Cambridge University Press, 1984).

4. Burr, *Kissinger Transcripts*, p. 64. For Kissinger's assessment of the policy, see Kissinger, *Years of Renewal*, chaps. 3, 4.

5. See, for example, Garthoff, *Détente and Confrontation*, pp. 16–17; George W. Breslauer, *Khrushchev and Brezhnev as Leaders: Building Authority in Soviet Politics* (George Allen and Unwin, 1982).

6. See Garthoff, *Détente and Confrontation*, p. 327.

7. Henry Kissinger, *White House Years* (Little, Brown, 1979), p. 129. See also Helmut Sonnenfeldt, "Linkage: A Strategy for Tempering Soviet Antagonism," *NATO Review*, vol. 27 (February 1979), pp. 3–5, 20–23; Hyland, *Mortal Rivals*.

8. Quoted in Litwak, *Détente and the Nixon Doctrine*, p. 96.

9. See Gaddis, "Rescuing Choice from Circumstance," p. 578.

10. Kissinger, *White House Years*, pp. 152–53.

11. Robert E. Osgood, *Containment, Soviet Behavior, and Grand Strategy* (Berkeley: Institute for International Studies, 1981), pp. 7–8.

12. The best concise discussion of Soviet views remains Coit D. Blacker, "The Kremlin and Détente: Soviet Conceptions, Hopes, and Expectations," in Alexander L. George, ed., *Managing U.S.-Soviet Rivalry* (Boulder, Colo.: Westview Press, 1983), pp. 119–37; see also Garthoff, *Détente and Confrontation*, pp. 40 ff.; Burr, *Kissinger Transcripts*, p. 35.

13. Hyland, *Mortal Rivals*, p. 25.

14. For a good discussion of this point, see Gaddis, "Rescuing Choice from Circumstance," pp. 578–80.

15. Burr, *Kissinger Transcripts*, pp. 48–49.

16. On Germany, see ibid., p. 79, n. 28. On the general issue of control, see Garthoff,

Détente and Confrontation, p. 36. On the grain issue, see William Bundy, *A Tangled Web: The Making of Foreign Policy in the Nixon Presidency* (Hill and Wang, 1998), pp. 339–41; Garthoff, *Détente and Confrontation*, pp. 343–44.

17. Kissinger, *Years of Renewal*, pp. 84–85.

18. For a good discussion, see ibid., pp. 129–34.

19. The letters can be found in ibid., pp. 1088–90. Soviet Foreign Minister Andrei Gromyko's response is on p. 1091. For the meeting quote, see Burr, *Kissinger Transcripts*, pp. 332–34.

20. Burr, *Kissinger Transcripts*, pp. 332–34, 340–41.

21. Hyland, *Mortal Rivals*, pp. 62 ff.

22. See Breslauer, *Khrushchev and Brezhnev as Leaders*; James M. Goldgeier, *Leadership Style and Soviet Foreign Policy: Stalin, Khruschev, Brezhnev, Gorbachev* (Johns Hopkins University Press, 1994), chap. 2.

23. Gaddis, "Rescuing Choice from Circumstance," p. 588.

24. See Gerald Segal, "Does China Matter?" *Foreign Affairs*, vol. 78 (September-October 1999), pp. 24–36.

25. On these points, see Litwak, *Détente and the Nixon Doctrine*; Garthoff, *Détente and Confrontation*, p. 170.

26. Administration officials were particularly attuned to Watergate's effects, as Kissinger discusses at length in his memoirs. See also Hyland, *Mortal Rivals*, p. 11.

8

The United States and Vietnam: Road to Normalization

FREDERICK Z. BROWN

The road to the normalization of relations between the United States and the Socialist Republic of Vietnam has been strewn with obstacles that are as much emotional and psychological as political. Although the United States never lost a major battle, together with its South Vietnamese ally, it lost the war—and in a humiliating fashion. This unpalatable reality explains why the bitter aftermath of the war has been so difficult to overcome.

The Vietnam War had immense repercussions for winners and losers. For the losers, the war deflated the idealism of the Kennedy years, caused President Lyndon Johnson to forsake reelection, and weakened the American strategic position in Asia. It helped breed a counterculture (including the illicit drug scene) and sapped the respect of the American people for the presidency, the military, and other organs of government. It crippled congressional bipartisanship in foreign affairs and greatly strengthened congressional involvement in (some would say "interference with") the conduct of foreign affairs. As Kosovo proves, Vietnam—and its lessons, real or imagined—continues to pervade our highest councils today, limiting what the United States can do in the world. For America's South Vietnamese ally, the defeat was an unmitigated catastrophe; 2 million were forced to flee abroad, and millions more suffered retribution at home. For the winners, the war yielded a victory

of immense dimensions, expelling the vestiges of "colonialism" and unify-
ing the country under a Marxist-Leninist system. Yet the consequences of
victory were also harsh and went well beyond the horrendous physical damage inflicted and the millions of lives lost. When it came to building a new
relationship with the United States—a high priority for Hanoi once the Soviet Union collapsed—communist Vietnam, the victor, found itself all but
powerless.

This chapter examines the first attempt by the United States to normalize
relations with Vietnam after 1975 under President Jimmy Carter, compar-
ing it with the policies of the Reagan, Bush, and Clinton administrations.
The contrasts are sharp. The reasons for these dissimilarities are rooted in
the geopolitics of the cold war, the denouement of the Cambodia conflict,
and fundamental mistakes and cultural misapprehensions on both sides.[1] A
comparative analysis of the two periods provides insights into the conduct
of diplomatic negotiations seeking resolution of long-standing conflicts between bitter enemies and the role that sanctions, and the incentives posed
by their lifting, can play in this process. Moreover, it reveals the multilevel
interplay between special interests, the American business community, and
domestic politics (especially Congress) in the conduct of foreign policy by
any administration, be it Democrat or Republican.

Healing Wounds: Normalization under Carter

In the aftermath of the traumatic events of April 1975, the Ford administration addressed the question of normalization of relations with Vietnam
guardedly. In June, Secretary of State Henry Kissinger, acknowledging that
"new regimes have come to power in Asia in the last few months," said that
although the United States was "prepared to look to the future," its attitude
toward these countries would be influenced by how these regimes acted toward their neighbors as well as toward the United States.[2] This position remained substantially the same throughout the Ford administration.[3]

The Carter administration inherited this situation when it took office in
January 1977. Normalization of relations with Vietnam and "putting the
war behind us" had been a Carter campaign pledge. Early on, the administration agreed to the unconditional establishment of diplomatic relations,
after which the United States would lift the embargo, support international
financial institution loans to Vietnam, and consider granting most-favored-
nation trading status. Vietnamese and American negotiators met in Paris
three times during 1977. Although, for some Americans, there was an emotional desire "to heal the wounds of war," cold war strategy was paramount

in the minds of U.S. policymakers. In this post-1975 era, the international context was shaped by an intense U.S.-Soviet rivalry that had spread to Iran, Afghanistan, Central America, Africa, and East Asia. Soviet aircraft were flying reconnaissance over the western Pacific, and there were concerns that the Soviet Far East Navy would, in the not too distant future, challenge the U.S. Seventh Fleet. Reaching out to Vietnam was a long shot that seemed worth taking. Normalization, it was posited, might entice Vietnam away from the embrace of the Soviet Union, which had taken over American bases at Cam Ranh Bay, Danang, and elsewhere.

Personally, President Carter viewed an opening to Vietnam less as part of a new, comprehensive Asian strategy for the United States than as a symbolic conclusion to an unhappy chapter in history.[4] In an October 1976 memorandum setting out specific goals and priorities for a Carter foreign policy, Cyrus Vance emphasized normalizing relations with Vietnam as "an opportunity for a new initiative. . . . The Vietnamese are trying to find a balance between over-dependence on either the Chinese or the Soviet Union. It is also to the interest of the U.S. that Vietnam not be so dependent."[5] Although Vance put normalization in the context of promoting the future development and stability of Southeast Asia, Vietnam itself was the dominant focus; the 1976 memorandum made scant reference to the rest of the region. The Association of Southeast Asian Nations (ASEAN), which had begun to receive declaratory importance in 1977, gained genuine importance in American eyes in 1978 as normalization with Vietnam faltered and war in Cambodia loomed.[6] During the 1976 presidential campaign, the Democrats had called for the "fullest possible accounting of MIAs," and U.S. and Vietnamese representatives held several official and private meetings on this issue. Therefore, when Carter took office, the government of Vietnam was aware of American priorities, and the way had been paved for further contacts with the new administration. Nonetheless, it is doubtful that the Hanoi politburo had by then really registered the depth of American feeling on American servicemen missing in action or possibly held prisoner—the POW-MIA issue.

President Carter's first foreign policy initiative was to send Leonard Woodcock, president of the United Auto Workers Union, to Vietnam to test Hanoi's attitudes on normalization and to determine specifically what the Vietnamese were prepared to do to meet U.S. requirements regarding the MIAs. Secretary of State Cyrus Vance and his assistant secretary for East Asia and the Pacific, Richard Holbrooke, recognized that this assessment was necessary to blunt domestic opposition to normalization from veterans groups and others outspokenly hostile to the victors in Hanoi. They believed the window of opportunity for such a move would not stay open long, and if the

MIAs became a domestic political issue, normalization would be enormously complicated. Their judgment proved to be accurate.[7]

In Hanoi, Woodcock made a strong case for putting the MIA issue to rest through the Vietnamese providing full information and as many remains as possible. Then the two countries could move on to a new relationship that would alleviate the pain and antagonisms generated by the war on both sides. However, Vietnamese willingness to comply with these demands was conditional on U.S. economic assistance. The Vietnamese held fast to their demand for aid under the terms of the February 1973 Nixon letter to Pham Van Dong pledging best efforts to "contribute to postwar reconstruction in North Vietnam without any political conditions . . . in the range of $3.25 billion in grant aid over five years."[8] Woodcock rejected this demand summarily by pointing out that the 1973 Paris Agreement, the basis for Nixon's pledge, had been destroyed by North Vietnam's massive violations in 1974–75.[9] Although eventually retreating from the specifics of this pledge, the Vietnamese deputy foreign minister Phan Hien continued to express a clear expectation of eventual humanitarian assistance in return for information on the MIAs. Woodcock deemed this stance reasonable, as the demand for what would be construed as development assistance under the defunct Paris Agreement appeared to have been dropped, and announced that the talks had "started a process which will improve the prospects for normalizing U.S.-Vietnamese relations."[10]

On one level, the Woodcock mission was a remarkable success. It broke the ice on the U.S.-Vietnam relationship, gave hope of further progress on a sensitive American domestic concern, and apparently established a favorable atmosphere for formal negotiations toward diplomatic relations. Yet there was also an element of imprecision, false optimism, and perhaps undue eagerness on the American side. The seeds of miscalculation on both sides, which were to bedevil subsequent negotiations, were planted in this initial encounter and watered by the almost euphoric reaction to the meeting in Washington, including statements made by the president himself.

The first miscalculation arose because the relationship between "humanitarian aid" and "full accounting" for the MIAs was left vague as to timing and definition. Although Woodcock had tried to separate the issues, the Vietnamese clung to the notion of an inevitable quid pro quo quality to normalization. After Woodcock had adamantly rejected linkage, Phan Hien retorted, "they are separate issues but closely interrelated."[11] The Vietnamese continued to operate on the presumption that the United States owed Vietnam economic assistance legally and morally, that American public opinion would pressure the administration to pay this debt of conscience, and that humanitarian aid could meet a wide spectrum of reconstruction needs. Woodcock's response may have encouraged this thinking, as did President Carter's statement, after the delegation's return, that "if, in normalization of relationships, there evolves trade, normal aid processes, then I would respond well."[12] The president left open the question of whether aid might come as part of a normalization deal or after normalization had occurred. Whatever the definition, the Vietnamese chose to believe that the United States had not foreclosed the possibility of large-scale official aid.

In addition, there was no clear understanding about either what Vietnam would do or what Vietnam would be expected to do to resolve the MIA problem. President Carter's remarks following the commission's return seemed to send a signal to the Vietnamese: "I think this is about all they can do. I don't have any way [to] prove that they have accounted for all those about whom they have information. But I think so far as I can discern, they have acted in good faith."[13] Several months before, the report of Representative Sonny Montgomery's (Democrat of Mississippi) House Select Committee on Missing Persons in Southeast Asia had rejected the possibility of live Americans being held captive in Indochina. Moreover, it had stated flatly that a "total accounting by the Indochinese governments is not possible and should not be expected."[14] The Woodcock Commission report had reiterated this sentiment. Thus the Vietnamese had reason to believe that the MIAs, while not crossed off the American negotiating agenda, had receded in priority and could be handled satisfactorily with an unspecified minimum effort on the part of Hanoi.

Having conquered the South and humbled a superpower, Vietnamese leaders seemed blind to a central reality: Hanoi needed normalization far more than Washington, and it was Hanoi, not the United States, that was the *demandeur*, despite plaintive American insistence on Hanoi's cooperation on the MIA issue. The Vietnamese may have been encouraged by the residue of antiwar sentiment, which seemed to indicate that the American guilt complex would force Carter's hand and yield multibillion-dollar reparations.[15] In any event, Hanoi remained adamant on aid, a miscalculation that cost valuable months during the 1977 negotiations.

Following the Woodcock mission, American and Vietnamese negotiators met in Paris in May, June, and December of 1977. The United States had already pledged to support Vietnam's membership in the United Nations. During the first meeting in May, Holbrooke proposed unconditional establishment of diplomatic relations, after which the U.S. trade embargo would be lifted. Phan Hien, however, reiterated the demand for economic assistance as a precondition to normalization, linking it to cooperation on the

MIAs. Worse, he restated Vietnam's demands at a press conference after the meeting, producing immediate congressional reaction in the form of an amendment to the House of Representatives' State Department authorization bill prohibiting use of any funds "for the purpose of negotiating reparations, aid or any other form of payment."[16] Later the Senate followed suit with an amendment requiring U.S. opposition to international financial institution loans to Vietnam.[17]

Then just before the June meeting, the Vietnamese published the text of the 1973 Nixon letter and rekindled their public campaign in the United States for aid. This was another tactical blunder. Hanoi's demands only served to arouse conservative criticism of the normalization gambit, and congressional actions narrowed still further Holbrooke's room for maneuver. The possibility of even humanitarian aid after normalization became remote; the window had begun to close. The June 1977 meeting produced information on twenty MIAs as well as Phan Hien's private expressions of flexibility as to the form and amount of U.S. assistance the Vietnamese expected. "Contributions to heal the wounds of war" became the standard term of reference, but Hanoi did not publicly renounce its demand for reparations, which would have been a crucial factor in resuscitating the negotiations.

Further movement was blocked when the State Department learned that the Vietnamese permanent representative to the United Nations, Ambassador Dinh Ba Thi, had received stolen classified documents from a United States Information Agency (USIA) officer who hoped thereby to gain the release of his girlfriend from Vietnam. Consequently, the December 1977 negotiations became especially delicate from the American perspective, and they proved to be merely a repetition of the earlier meetings. When the USIA officer and his associate were arrested in January 1978, and Ambassador Thi declared persona non grata, any hope for a fourth Paris round in February or March was dashed. No negotiations were feasible during the well-publicized spy trial, which lasted until June 1978. This amateurish spying escapade was a gratuitous blunder by Ambassador Thi that cost Vietnam dearly on a vastly more important front.

During the winter of 1977–78 intelligence became available on the brutal incursions into southern Vietnamese border provinces by the Khmer Rouge regime of Pol Pot. By early summer 1978, it was evident that Vietnam was preparing to invade Cambodia with the intent of deposing Pol Pot. Given Thailand's vulnerability and presumed Vietnamese expansionist impulses, regional security alarm bells began to sound.

The pace of Washington's normalization negotiations with the People's Republic of China also quickened during this period. National Security Adviser Zbigniew Brzezinski and his Asia deputy Michel Oksenberg believed that normalization with Vietnam had become incompatible with normalization with China, a process moving toward fruition since 1972 but still uncertain. In their eyes, the China gambit was far more valuable than a relationship with Vietnam. Vance and Holbrooke had already argued that a relationship with Hanoi would benefit long-term U.S. strategic interests, including the U.S.-Soviet and U.S.-China strategic equations. Brzezinski, fixated on the China connection as a way to constrain and harass the Soviets, presented the contrary opinion that normalizing with Vietnam, an ancient enemy about to attack China's Cambodian ally, would damage and perhaps derail the establishment of full diplomatic relations with China. He was ultimately joined in this view by Leonard Woodcock, who had become U.S. Liaison Office chief in Beijing.

During this period the administration's concerns over growing Soviet-Vietnamese ties were validated. For two years after 1975, Vietnam, wary of China's reaction, had resisted Soviet pressure to join the Council for Mutual Economic Assistance (COMECON). However, in late June 1978, the Vietnamese signed up, thereby putting their economy on the road to greater reliance on trade with and economic assistance from the Soviet bloc. This move may have reflected disappointment over the course of normalization talks with the United States. Yet it also underscored Hanoi's conviction that only the Soviet Union could provide quick help to a Vietnamese economy that had gone from bad to worse since 1975, thanks to coerced collectivization and the harsh repression of South Vietnam's free market practices. The decision to join COMECON was another nail in normalization's coffin. In the long term, it would make economic and political relations with the West far more problematic.

A few days after the end of the spy trial, and with normalization prospects dim, the Vietnamese signaled that they were prepared to accept a long-standing U.S. invitation to visit the Joint Casualty Resolution Center and Central Identification Laboratory in Hawaii, the site of technical efforts to identify MIA remains. During the four-day "technical" meeting in Honolulu, the senior Vietnamese delegate made clear in private that Vietnam had dropped its aid precondition and wanted normalization on American terms "by Labor Day or at the latest Thanksgiving." No mention was made of Christmas, the day on which Vietnam was to invade Cambodia. Although this statement seemed explicit and unequivocal, it was nonetheless a trial balloon hoisted at the working level and it required high-level expression. The message was conveyed immediately to the State Department, where it became enmeshed in the bureaucratic infighting with the National Security Council staff.[18] A Vietnamese proposal shortly thereafter for another Paris meeting was rejected by the United States.

The Vietnamese did give public hints of flexibility during the summer, notably Phan Hien's July 10 statement in Tokyo that "a new, forward-looking attitude is being shown by the Vietnamese side." Phan Hien said Vietnam would not seek aid as a precondition for normalization but, when pressed for clarifications, added "if they [the Americans] come with something in their hands, they will be more welcomed than if they come with empty hands."[19] Congressional delegations visiting Hanoi received some MIA remains, but could not pry a convincing renunciation of the aid demand from the top leadership.

The impression that Hanoi was still playing fast and loose on preconditions severely handicapped the State Department in its battle with the National Security Council staff over the compatibility of the twin-track normalization efforts with Beijing and Hanoi. Only on September 27, 1978, in New York, was Holbrooke finally able to extract from Foreign Minister Nguyen Co Thach the absolute acceptance of normalization of relations without preconditions that Holbrooke had sought for eighteen months. Acceptance, however, was ad referendum to Washington, and at this point only President Carter could resolve the conflict between the competing U.S. strategies toward China and Southeast Asia. On October 1, the president accepted the Brzezinski-Woodcock recommendation to defer normalization with Vietnam. The reasons given retrospectively were concern over the implications of growing Vietnamese hostility toward Cambodia, expanding Soviet-Vietnamese ties, and the tide of refugees fleeing Vietnam ("boat people," most of whom were Vietnamese of Chinese ethnicity, or "Hoa people"). These were certainly significant factors, especially the rapidly expanding Soviet connection, but in the end the China card was primary in this decision.

On November 3, 1978, Vietnam and the Soviet Union signed a mutual security treaty, and prospects for U.S.-Vietnam normalization collapsed. With the December 1978 Vietnamese invasion of Cambodia and the overthrow of Pol Pot's regime in January 1979, followed in February by China's three-week punitive expedition into northern Vietnam, the geopolitical chessboard was frozen. The Soviets reinforced their military presence at Cam Ranh Bay and Danang, and the United States and China, which had consummated their normalization in December 1978, embarked on a multifaceted relationship that would have direct strategic impact upon both the Soviet Union and Vietnam.

Timing, of course, is all. In 1977, the time seemed ripe for Vietnam and the United States to get together. A sympathetic new American administration was in office with some latitude in foreign affairs; feelings about the POW-MIAs were strong, but had not yet coalesced; and there was adequate support on Capitol Hill for normalization as long as the POW-MIA question was handled carefully. Vietnam was clearly pro-Soviet but had not taken the plunge into COMECON or signed a security pact; there was genuine debate in the Vietnamese politburo on future multiple links with the capitalist world versus a total reliance on the socialist bloc. Even China was aware of how normalization of U.S.-Vietnam relations might help blunt Vietnam's growing dependence on the Soviets; in this respect Brzezinski may have been mistaken. ASEAN was not opposed to normalization if it would help tame the Vietnamese tiger, and indeed, its members warily pursued the same track.

Why did normalization, something both sides genuinely sought initially, fail? Several reasons stand out. Vietnam's flat demand for economic assistance as a precondition, no matter how justified in the eyes of the politburo, prevented normalization during the first six months of the Carter administration, when the window was wide open. This failure to perceive objective reality, that prized Marxist precept for political action, was the key strategic blunder of the entire period. After Hanoi's 1975 military conquest, reparations by any other name were never in the cards. The 1977 spying affair delayed negotiations at a crucial moment, when the window was still half open. The bureaucratic antagonism between the State Department and the National Security Council staff on a number of foreign policy issues, and the brittle relationship between Secretary of State Cyrus Vance and National Security Adviser Zbigniew Brzezinski, also complicated matters, particularly when normalization with China neared completion.[20]

The prevarications and coy zigzagging as Hanoi gradually modified, or appeared to modify, its position wasted valuable time. When Thach finally conceded to normalization without the precondition of aid, other factors in Asia (in particular improving relations with China) had become the dominant concern for the United States. Elsewhere, the Carter administration's foreign policy troubles were beginning to mount: the fight over the Panama Canal Treaty, rumblings in Iran, the SALT II negotiations, and Angola. It was no time for a controversial venture with a former foe.[21]

Hard Ball: Normalization under Reagan and Bush

Under the Reagan administration, talks on humanitarian concerns eventually resumed, with MIA discussions again the main vehicle for communication. Three more issues were added to the dialogue: emigration of Vietnamese children of American fathers (the "Amerasian children" program), the orderly departure program (ODP) permitting emigration of Vietnamese with connections to the United States, and the U.S. attempt to gain the exit from Vietnam of former inmates of Vietnamese "reeducation camps."

In 1985, Vietnam permitted the excavation of a B-52 crash site near Hanoi by U.S. teams. Hanoi announced that it would make a unilateral effort to resolve the POW-MIA issue within two years. About one hundred MIA remains were repatriated as a result of this fresh effort. With Vietnam still wedded to its Soviet military and economic connection, looking at Vietnam as a potential strategic asset received relatively little consideration. The Reagan administration's view of Indochina was shaped by day-to-day concerns over the POW-MIAs. Lurid publicity, stimulated by "Rambo" movies, was given to rumors that American servicemen were still being held prisoner in Indochina, and reports of "live sightings" of prisoners had inevitable political reverberations. The administration was roundly criticized by activist veteran groups for not doing more to rescue the supposed prisoners; several private soldier-of-fortune forays into Laos were launched from Thai soil.

Nonetheless, the humanitarian dialogue became the music for the U.S.-Vietnam mating dance. Vietnam found it a useful means of carrying on a discussion with the United States that would on occasion lap over to broader political issues of China, the cold war, and future bilateral relations. Moreover, this dialogue was helpful to Hanoi in keeping ASEAN on edge regarding American steadfastness; ASEAN's leaders were worried that U.S. preoccupation with the POW-MIAs might undermine their priority objective, to get Vietnam out of Cambodia. Hanoi's longer-term strategy, of course, was to play U.S. influence off against China and the Soviet Union and to seek U.S. help to revive the Vietnamese economy after normalization.

Cambodia was the limiting factor. It made no sense from Hanoi's perspective to grant the Americans concessions on humanitarian matters at a time when Cambodia was deadlocked, thereby making normalization of relations out of the question. The Vietnamese listened as congressional and executive branch visitors reiterated the same theme: although humanitarian affairs (POW-MIA, ODP) were separate from politics (Cambodia), normalization would proceed more smoothly if there were sustained progress on political issues beforehand. Hanoi came to understand this not-so-subtle linkage and saw the political value of granting better cooperation but only at an advantageous moment. It is not surprising that the pace of the U.S.-Vietnam humanitarian dialogue picked up after 1986 as the Cambodia stalemate began to break and as Hanoi, as a result of the Sixth Congress of the

Vietnamese Communist Party, initiated reform measures in the direction of free market economics.

Regarding the latter, U.S. economic sanctions—that is, the conditions under which they would be modified or lifted—were obviously a potent bargaining chip with which the Americans could influence the Vietnamese. Vietnam found itself both politically and economically isolated; during Vietnam's ten-year military occupation of Cambodia, the members of the United Nations General Assembly voted overwhelmingly in favor of ASEAN's annual resolution in the General Assembly demanding Vietnam's withdrawal. The United States saw the Cambodia conflict both as aggression by Vietnamese communism and as a proxy war between China and the Soviet Union. Simultaneously, because of Vietnam's intimate links with the Soviet Union, the conflict became one more facet of the U.S.-Soviet rivalry in the Pacific. Cambodia became a key element of the "strategic relationship" between Beijing and Washington in confronting the Soviet Union and its surrogate, Vietnam. Whatever hurt the Vietnamese hurt the Soviets.

The Reagan administration, as noted above, had reaffirmed U.S. preconditions for normalization: a complete and verified withdrawal of Vietnamese troops from Cambodia. The "pace and scope of normalization" would be influenced by Vietnamese cooperation on resolution of the POW-MIA and other humanitarian issues. In 1985, the administration amplified this condition; the Vietnamese withdrawal would have to be "in the context of a compromise political settlement in Cambodia." As Cambodia peace negotiations gained momentum and Vietnam completed its military withdrawal in September 1989, the Bush administration became even more specific about what Hanoi must do—namely, actively engage in a peace settlement and influence the "puppet regime" of Prime Minister Hun Sen in Phnom Penh to do likewise—in order to begin formal U.S.-Vietnam normalization.

In April 1991, the Bush administration announced a timetable keyed to Cambodia and POW-MIAs. This "road map" was a response to Democratic critics charging that American policy toward Indochina was adrift strategically and prevented American businessmen from taking advantage of opportunities in Vietnam. The road map attempted to codify a quid pro quo procedure whereby Vietnam knew what was expected of it and what benefits would accrue as reciprocal steps in the normalization process were taken. The road map unequivocally outlined the U.S. demands that Vietnam had to accept as a practical basis for moving incrementally toward full diplomatic relations and modification or removal of sanctions. To critics, the road map presented unilateral, inherently unfair U.S. demands levied on Vietnam. To practitioners of realpolitik, the road map stated the obvious: that the United States held the advantage. Both camps were, of course, correct in their interpretation. The road map reflected an abiding American distrust of Hanoi's commitment to honoring diplomatic agreements. It also represented a crude fact of international politics: while normalization was attractive to a Hanoi witnessing the disintegration of Soviet communism, it was a low priority in the array of Washington's global foreign policy objectives. On Capitol Hill, the reaction of some members of Congress who paid attention to Vietnam was "Let them stew in their own juices."

During this period, America was in a position to exert maximum leverage. Vietnam, already under pressure to compromise on Cambodia and suffering from sharp reductions in Soviet aid, faced economic woes at home. It had little choice but to pursue normalization under the terms set by the United States and hope that a trading relationship with the lucrative American market would eventually help rescue the failing Vietnamese "socialist market" economy.

Vietnam's actions must also be seen in the context of the global political sea changes occurring at the time. Vietnam signed the UN-sponsored Cambodia peace accords drafted by the Paris International Conference on Cambodia and backed by ASEAN.[22] Moreover, official Vietnamese cooperation on resolving POW-MIA issues improved considerably. On both issues, American sanctions were unquestionably powerful weapons. Yet sanctions alone would probably not have forced Vietnam to adopt such abrupt changes in policy had the Soviet Union and the Eastern European communist regimes not disintegrated. In the final count, the collapse of Eurocommunism and relentless pressure by China were the key factors that forced Vietnam to abandon its effort to keep Cambodia under its thumb.

Moving the Goalposts

Despite progress on Cambodia, the Bush administration indicated that all requirements of the first parts of the road map had not been completed. Specifically, insufficient progress had been made on the repatriation of MIA remains and access to all information the United States desired (for example, Vietnamese logs, maps, and provincial reports relevant to missing personnel). Recognizing some positive moves on the part of Vietnam, in March 1992 the United States pledged a $3 million humanitarian aid package in the form of scholarships to Vietnamese students coming to the United States and expanded aid in prosthetics and health care by U.S. medical teams on MIA field searches. Telephone communication between Vietnam and the

United States was restored. Commercial transactions meeting "basic human needs" criteria (for example, prosthetics and other health care, assessment of education and training needs, books) were routinely allowed. U.S. government restrictions on American nongovernmental organizations operating in Vietnam were lifted, and shipment to Vietnam of NGO humanitarian assistance was facilitated.

The influence of Japan in securing further Vietnamese compliance was significant. With an eye to the November 1992 presidential election, Tokyo informed Hanoi that it would not go against the United States in providing official development assistance or in supporting international financial institution loans to Vietnam as long as the POW-MIAs remained a highly charged political issue. The Japanese did not need another irritant in their bilateral relationship with the Americans. Thus indirect economic pressures on Hanoi by third countries bolstered U.S. policy.

The April 1992 visit to Vietnam by the U.S. Senate Select Committee on POW-MIA Affairs was designed explicitly to lay the groundwork for congressional acceptance of a normalized relationship with Vietnam. The delegation was headed by Senators John Kerry, a combat hero who had turned against the war, and Bob Smith, a conservative Republican from New Hampshire who championed the POW-MIA cause. Senator Kerry, along with Senator John McCain, the influential conservative Arizona Republican who had spent five years as a prisoner of war in the "Hanoi Hilton," were prepared to lead the effort in a positive direction. The Select Committee's report stated that "there is at this time no compelling evidence that proves that any American remains alive in captivity in Southeast Asia."[23] Nevertheless, the committee's contentious hearings and the public squabbles between factions within the U.S. government and among POW-MIA interest groups failed to put the issue to rest. While better Vietnamese cooperation had been gained, the passionate domestic discord on the American side still frustrated further movement.

The Bush administration, in its waning days, considered taking additional steps toward normalization, perhaps even contemplating lifting the embargo entirely and agreeing to embassies. But the Vietnamese, for whatever reason, had not chosen to go the last mile in providing information on the remaining one hundred or so "last known alive" MIA cases that might have precipitated a favorable U.S. response. Even had the Vietnamese done so, the National Security Council believed that it was prudent to withhold this step until the Cambodian electoral process in May 1993 had been completed.[24] Moreover, given the bitterness of the election campaign and Clinton's vulnerable position regarding Vietnam, the outgoing Republicans probably had no desire to spare the incoming Democrats the political misery of dealing with the delicate POW-MIA issue. President Clinton was left to make peace with Hanoi, perhaps to announce at some future date that the POW-MIA issue was finally resolved, and to take the political heat that would come from this declaration.

Tiptoeing toward Normalization under Clinton

In January 1993, with the advent of a Democratic administration headed by a president with weak foreign affairs credentials, particularly regarding Vietnam, normalization faced additional problems. To move forward, the administration would need to rely on proponents of normalization in the Congress, primarily Senators Kerry and McCain, to make the administration's case to the public. Kerry's vice-chair, Bob Smith, had retreated to his original negative position on Vietnamese cooperation and voiced the residual hostility toward Vietnam felt by a vocal minority of the American public.[25] Some House members with Vietnamese American constituencies echoed these views, as did Representative Benjamin A. Gilman, chairman of the International Relations Committee.

After cooperation on POW-MIAs, the road map's principal demand was continued Vietnamese cooperation on the Cambodian peace process. This condition had been satisfied by Vietnamese actions since the 1991 Paris Agreements and by Vietnam's subsequent relations with the Cambodian coalition government put in place as a result of the May 1993 Cambodian national elections.

In April 1993, however, the political impact of an unconfirmed report that Vietnam had failed to release 614 American POWs at the time of the 1973 Paris Accords delayed the administration from making good on the final step of phase 2 of the 1991 road map, that is, helping Vietnam eliminate its arrears to international financial institutions.[26] The administration vetoed Vietnam's access to such loans, which had been proposed by France and Japan for the April meeting of the International Monetary Fund and the World Bank. It was not until a congressional delegation returned from Hanoi and argued in favor of forward movement that the president was in a stronger position domestically to announce that the United States would no longer oppose such lending.

The next six months illustrated the inherent contradiction in U.S. policy that had been created by the emotions of the POW-MIA issue. Lifting the veto on international lending without lifting the embargo put American businesses at a disadvantage in competing with foreign firms for major infrastructure projects made possible through World Bank funding. Yet the administration—and certainly the vocal POW-MIA lobbying groups—were unwilling to give up what was deemed the last real leverage in negotiating for greater access to sensitive files and "tangible progress" in the hundred or so "discrepancy cases" that the Vietnamese appeared capable of resolving. Similarly, the POW-MIA lobby supported by the American Legion and several smaller veterans groups opposed any opening to Vietnam (the Veterans of Foreign Wars was divided but took a generally positive position on normalization). In contrast, an increasingly powerful proponent of normalization was the American business community. Beginning in 1992, Vietnam's economic reforms were taking hold and prospects for U.S. investment seemed bright. Dozens of leading American commercial firms seeking to participate in the Vietnamese market—such as Boeing, Caterpillar, Citibank, Mobil—lobbied Congress and the administration.

Another administration delegation visited Hanoi in July 1993 (more than a year after the Kerry-Smith Select Committee) to press once again for more progress on POW-MIAs. In a July 21 appearance before the Senate Foreign Relations Committee, the delegation stated that the embargo should not be lifted absent more concrete progress. At the same time, the delegation underscored the potential commercial advantages to improved relations and the fact that other countries were beginning to dominate the Vietnamese marketplace. Employing a stick with a few carrots, President Clinton renewed the embargo in September, but simultaneously approved $3.5 million in humanitarian aid for Vietnamese orphans and prosthetics programs. In December, the president eased the embargo by allowing U.S. companies to bid on projects financed by international financial institutions "pending a lifting of the embargo." By then, there was a sense of inevitability; the question was not if, but when, diplomatic normalization would take place.

On February 3, 1994, President Clinton ordered an end to the remaining sanctions in place under the economic embargo; on May 26, Vietnam and the United States announced their intention to open liaison offices in the other's capital.[27] On July 11, 1995, the president announced that the United States would, at long last, establish full diplomatic relations with the Socialist Republic of Vietnam. A few days later, the Association of Southeast Asian Nations (ASEAN) proclaimed that Vietnam would become its eighth member, symbolizing communist Vietnam's quarter-century journey from regional pariah to regional respectability.

With the lifting of the embargo and establishment of diplomatic relations, one important sanction against Vietnam was still in effect: the denial of nondiscriminatory trade status (most-favored-nation status, now called "normal trade relations"). The president waived the Jackson-Vanik Amendment concerning freedom of emigration in 1998 (and again in 1999) without congressional objection, thus allowing negotiations for the Bilateral Trade Agreement to proceed. Resolving the details of the agreement proved almost as difficult as the Cambodia conflict, and it was only on July 25, 1999, that an "agreement in principle" was initialed in Hanoi, with certain "technical details" to be worked out. The final agreement was scheduled for signature by President Clinton and Vietnamese Prime Minister Phan Van Khai at the Asia Pacific Economic Cooperation meeting in September in Auckland, New Zealand. At the last moment the Vietnamese side requested a postponement of the signing in order to discuss further the "technical details," thus dashing the hopes for consideration by the U.S. Congress during 1999. The Bilateral Trade Agreement's fate is consequently uncertain. The agreement cannot be presented to the Congress before January 2000, and given the vagaries of the forthcoming U.S. presidential election, it is unlikely that the agreement will move forward until 2001. Various reasons have been given for Hanoi's refusal to sign, such as anger over Secretary of State Madeleine Albright's statements on human rights during her pre-APEC visit to Vietnam and pressure from Beijing on Hanoi not to sign before China is admitted to the World Trade Organization. The most likely explanation, however, is that this refusal reflected rivalries within Vietnam's top leadership jockeying for power before the next party congress in 2001, a struggle that in turn reflected deep-seated fears regarding possible consequences of opening up the Vietnamese economy to foreign competition in ways the agreement would require.

Conclusions

In trying to negotiate a new U.S.-Vietnam relationship, why did the process founder in 1977–78 yet seem on the verge of success in 1999 with only a bilateral trade agreement to be concluded? What lessons pertinent to the general practice of American policy from year 2000 onward can be learned from this tortuous twenty-five-year process?

First, and probably most important, negotiations during the Carter and Reagan-Bush periods took place in radically different global contexts. The Carter administration faced a Vietnam that viewed itself as the wave of the future; in the words of Vietnam's Communist Party General Secretary Le Duan, Vietnam was an "impregnable outpost of the socialist system, an important factor of . . . national independence, democracy, and social progress in Southeast Asia."[28] Moreover, at the time, Vietnam enjoyed the support of a superpower, the Soviet Union. Ignorant of the workings of the American political system (Nixon's "best efforts" letter stated explicitly that reconstruction aid would be granted only in accordance with constitutional procedures, that is, congressional concurrence), the Vietnamese in 1977 felt they had a strong position from which to bargain and behaved accordingly. By contrast, the Bush and Clinton administrations faced a Vietnam whose Marxist economic system had failed miserably. The country had been abandoned by Soviet president Mikhail Gorbachev beginning in 1986 and then had later witnessed both the collapse of the Eastern European communist bloc in 1989 and the implosion of Soviet Union in 1991. Hanoi could hardly fail to notice that the United States held all the high cards, and, again, it behaved accordingly, at least up to the moment it declined to sign the Bilateral Trade Agreement, as noted above. So the first lesson is "ripeness"—that the geopolitical context of the moment must be conducive either to compromise by both parties or to a clearly superior position by one party that makes further debate by the other party moot. In light of this realization, one can conclude that the primacy that the United States enjoys today in the post–cold war era has made engagement a more feasible and viable option for pursuing American foreign policy objectives, assuming, of course, that the United States wishes to engage.

Moreover, the Carter period proved that the rhetoric of good intentions is no substitute for precision and clarity when negotiating understandings between former foes. The Woodcock mission began a process, but its results were imprecisely couched and generated inaccurate expectations, which hampered formal negotiations in 1977 and 1978. "Dizzy from success" (in Lenin's words) after beating a superpower, the Vietnamese clung to the notion of an inevitable equal quid pro quo quality to normalization. No plan of action was devised, and matters were left in the realm of imprecise Vietnamese intentions on MIAs and unclear American expectations.

Contrast this loose approach with the road map under Bush and Clinton. The road map is an example of how sanctions and the lure of their removal can be used effectively to influence the sanctioned party. The road map codified a quid pro quo procedure that was in fact unequal; the United States held the whip handle. Vietnam knew what was expected of it and what benefits would accrue as reciprocal steps in the process were taken. The road map was deliberately vague in parts, specific in others; the United States was the sole interpreter of when a given condition had been fulfilled, be it regarding Cambodia or POW-MIAs. The road map thus reflected accurately, if bluntly, the relative power positions of the two countries.

In addition, these two episodes offer important lessons about managing engagement strategies in a sensitive domestic political environment. Under Carter, there was little effort to prepare a domestic base for normalization. Announcement of the 1977 Woodcock mission was made during the very first week of the new Carter administration. Carter was making good on a pledge made during the 1976 presidential campaign. The prime movers of normalization, Vance and Holbrooke, were eager to heal the psychological wounds of the Vietnam War (as well as move Vietnam away from the Soviets). This eagerness may have led policymakers to misjudge the extent of the American public's desire to "put the war behind us." A strong hint of future domestic problems that normalization would face came in June 1977 when, in response to Vietnam's public demand for "reparations" at the first Paris meeting, Congress immediately forbade any such payments. In contrast, under Reagan, elaborate attention was paid to the precise steps needed to make progress on the POW-MIA issue, which eventually emerged as the nation's "highest priority." Similarly, under Bush and Clinton, the issue continued to be placed front and center. Congressional actions, with some exceptions, complemented administration policy. The testimony, findings, and stated positions of influential members of Congress and official delegations were generally helpful in paving the way for the president to take further incremental steps. By the same token, there is a pathetic irony in Vietnam's refusal in September 1999 to sign the Bilateral Trade Agreement, something that had been seen by the reformers as immensely beneficial to Vietnam's economy. The Vietnamese negotiators, after three years of minute haggling with their American counterparts, apparently got too far ahead of the politburo, the constituency that really counts in Vietnam.

Finally, the normalization process under Bush and Clinton not only reveals the importance of managing the momentum of an engagement process, but also offers possible tactics for doing so. Small quid pro quo maneuvers are always important in a long negotiation. Rather than simply refusing to advance to the next stage of the road map, the administrations coupled their reservations with disbursements of humanitarian aid to keep the process alive. Both administrations encouraged the creation of a consensus in the business community that favored lifting the trade embargo on the basis of enlightened self-interest, that is, to gain a future share of the Vietnamese market.[29] This constituency counterbalanced POW-MIA groups that tended to resist concessions to Vietnam. In the end, the pressure by the private sector on Congress and the administration was probably decisive.

Ultimately, every case must be understood in its own unique context. However, the lessons offered by contrasting the various efforts over the last decades to normalize relations with Vietnam are valuable for policymakers who might be considering normalization with other countries today.

Notes

1. Robert S. McNamara and others, *Argument without End: In Search of Answers to the Vietnam Tragedy* (New York: Public Affairs, 1999), explores this question from both the Vietnamese and American perspectives.

2. Henry Kissinger, "The United States and Japan in a Changing World," Japan Society speech, June 18, 1975, *Department of State Bulletin*, vol. 73 (July 7, 1975), pp. 1–8.

3. In September 1976, Assistant Secretary of State for East Asia and the Pacific Arthur Hummel reiterated that regarding Vietnam the United States still looked to the future, not the past, but specified that "for us the most serious single obstacle in proceeding toward normalization is the refusal of Hanoi to give us a full accounting of those missing in action [MIAs]." Regarding provision of postwar reconstruction assistance to Vietnam as part of the Kissinger-Le Duc Tho package, Hummel stated categorically that "the [1973] Paris Agreement was so massively violated by Hanoi that we have no obligation to provide assistance, and in any case Congress has prohibited such assistance by law [under the Foreign Assistance Appropriation Act of 1976]." U.S. Congress, House Committee on International Relations, Special Subcommittee on U.S. Policy in Southeast Asia, *Hearings*, September 1976, p. 6, cited in Frederick Z. Brown, *Second Chance: The United States and Indochina in the 1990s* (New York: Council on Foreign Relations, 1989), pp. 20–21.

4. Nayan Chanda, *Brother Enemy: The War after the War* (Harcourt Brace Jovanovich, 1986), p. 146 (interview with Richard Holbrooke).

5. Cyrus Vance, *Hard Choices: Critical Years in America's Foreign Policy* (Simon and Schuster, 1983), p. 450.

6. See Brown, *Second Chance.*

7. Woodcock's delegation included Senator Mike Mansfield, Representative G. V. (Sonny) Montgomery, Ambassador Charles Yost, and human rights advocate Marian Wright Edelman. All except Montgomery had been critical in some measure of the American involvement in the war. They met with Prime Minister Pham Van Dong, Foreign Minister Nguyen Duy Trinh, and Deputy Foreign Minister Phan Hien, later Holbrooke's counterpart in the Paris normalization talks.

8. "Text of Message from the President of the United States to the Prime Minister of the Democratic Republic of Vietnam, February 1, 1973," *Congressional Record*, June 22, 1977, p. 20290.

9. Soon after the Paris Agreements were signed, the North Vietnamese commenced massive road and pipeline construction along the Ho Chi Minh Trail leading south to the Saigon area, readily observable from the air but immune from attack under the agreements. In the Mekong Delta, by late spring 1974, communist forces had regained all the territory that had been lost to the Thieu government before the ceasefire. Preparations for what turned out to be the final North Vietnamese offensive

began in the summer of 1974. These activities are amply documented in the accounts of the ranking North Vietnamese Army and National Liberation Front commanders in the south at the time. See General Van Tien Dung, *Our Great Spring Victory: An Account of the Liberation of South Vietnam*, trans. John Sprageas Jr. (Monthly Review Press, 1977); General Tran Van Tra, *Vietnam: History of the Bulwark B2 Theatre*, vol. 5, *Concluding the 30-Years' War*, trans. Joint Publications Research Service, Arlington, Va. (Springfield, Va.: National Technical Information Service, 1983); Alan Dawson, *55 Days: The Fall of South Vietnam* (Prentice-Hall, 1977), pp. 22–25.

10. *Washington Post*, March 18, 1977, quoted in Chanda, *Brother Enemy*, p. 141.

11. Office of the White House Press Secretary, *Presidential Commission on Americans Missing and Unaccounted for in Southeast Asia: Report on Trip to Vietnam and Laos, March 16–20, 1977*, p. 11.

12. "President Carter's Press Conference, March 24, 1977," *Public Papers of the Presidents: Jimmy Carter*, vol. 1 (Government Printing Office, 1977), p. 501.

13. Ibid., p. 499.

14. House Select Committee on Missing Persons in Southeast Asia, *Americans Missing in Southeast Asia: Final Report Together with Additional and Separate Views of the Select Committee on Missing Persons in Southeast Asia*, Report 94-1764, 94 Cong. 2 sess. (December 13, 1976), p. 114.

15. This judgment is based on author's observations, July 1977–August 1978, as country director for Vietnam, Laos, and Cambodia in the Department of State's Bureau of East Asian and Pacific Affairs under Assistant Secretary Holbrooke.

16. Amendment (offered by Representative John Ashbrook) to Foreign Relations Authorization Act, Fiscal Year 1978, Sec. 113, *Congressional Record*, May 4, 1977, p. 13417.

17. Amendment (offered by Senator Robert Dole) to Omnibus Multilateral Development Institutions Act, H.R. 5262, Sec. 703, *Congressional Record*, May 19, 1977, p. 15625.

18. Vu Hoang, discussions with author, July 12, 1978, as described in Brown, *Second Chance*, chap. 3; Chanda, *Brother Enemy*, chap. 9.

19. Transcript of Phan Hien press conference, cited in Chanda, *Brother Enemy*, p. 270.

20. For a spirited account of the Vance-Brzezinski relationship, see Patrick Tyler "The (Ab)normalization of U.S.-Chinese Relations," *Foreign Affairs*, vol. 78 (September-October 1999), pp. 93–122, where the antagonism between the State Department and the National Security Council is described as an "all-out civil war." Comments by former president Carter and Mr. Brzezinski on Tyler's article are found in *Foreign Affairs*, vol. 78 (November-December 1999), pp. 164–66.

21. One can speculate how history might have been different. Hanoi could have had diplomatic normalization by mid-1977 on better terms (including prospects for humanitarian aid) than it appeared to accept in fall 1978. That said, even granting Hanoi's prevarications and ultimate intentions regarding Cambodia, the Carter administration approached the Vietnam issue narrowly, gave unwarranted weight to Deng Xiaoping's anti-Vietnam animus, and consequently may have shortchanged

U.S. strategic interests. Normalization in 1977 might have helped nudge Vietnam in the direction of moderation in internal reforms and economic relations with the West and away from COMECON. The Soviet bear hug might have been delayed or at least softened. China would have had less cause for anger over Vietnam's "ingratitude." Vietnam might have been more inclined to mobilize international opinion against Pol Pot early in 1978 rather than go it alone in December. After August 1978, however, normalization would have had little chance of positive effects. By then Hanoi had decided to remove the Khmer Rouge from power by force; and China, despite its disapproval of Pol Pot's provocative military actions against Vietnam, was unwilling to back down. This in turn served to harden Vietnam's position and drive it further toward the Soviets. By the time Thach relinquished Vietnam's preconditions to normalization with the United States in September 1978, the leading players in this Greek drama had embarked on conflicting, unalterable courses. See Stephen Morris, *Why Vietnam Invaded Cambodia: Political Culture and the Causes of War* (Stanford University Press, 1999).

22. United Nations, *Agreements on a Comprehensive Political Settlement of the Cambodia Conflict*, DP/1180-92077 (UN Department of Public Information, January 1992).

23. See text of Final Report of the U.S. Senate Select Committee on POW-MIA Affairs Committee, *Congressional Record*, February 3, 1993, p. S1089.

24. Karl D. Jackson, who served as Bush administration National Security Council senior staff member for Asia, interview by author, October 18, 1999.

25. During the Reagan administration, the National League of Families of American Prisoners and Missing in Southeast Asia became prominent in U.S. domestic political machinations on Vietnam issues. The league coordinated communication between the administration and the approximately 2,400 (as of 1980) families with relatives missing in Southeast Asia, mainly in Vietnam or areas controlled during the war by North Vietnam. Building close relations with staff members of the National Security Council and the Department of Defense, the league's executive director became a member of the official U.S. government working group on POW-MIA issues and accompanied government missions to Vietnam and Laos. Charging the Nixon, Ford, and Carter administrations with betrayal of POW-MIA families, the league used its political clout to influence members of Congress, indeed so successfully that by 1988 few members would openly challenge the almost theological assumption that Americans might still be held prisoner in Vietnam. The league's influence was diminished in the Bush administration, as countervailing pressures increased from the business community. In the league's view, whatever cooperation Hanoi had granted did not justify relaxation of the embargo. A sharp split emerged between the league and the State and Commerce Departments over how to deal with Vietnam. The league's executive director went so far as to brand General John Vessey, former U.S. Army chief of staff and President Bush's special emissary to Hanoi for POW-MIA affairs, as a traitor. In March 1995, the league refuted statements by Secretary of Defense William Perry that Vietnam was cooperating fully and accused Assistant Secretary of State for East Asia and Pacific Affairs Winston Lord of testifying "in error" before the Senate Appropriations Committee (see League newsletter, *Con-

cerned Citizens, March 24, 1995). The league remained opposed to diplomatic nor-malization when it took place in July 1995.

26. Susumu Awanohara and Murray Hiebert, "Vietnam New MIA Row Dogs Hanoi," *Far Eastern Economic Review,* April 29, 1993, p. 12.

27. The decision came following months of intense negotiations and a Senate vote on January 27 that gave the president some political cover. The Senate language was attached to House bill H.R. 2333 and signed into law as PL 103-236, April 30, 1994.

28. General Secretary of the Vietnamese Communist Party Le Duan's Political Report as recorded in *Communist Party of Vietnam, 4th National Congress: Documents* (Hanoi: Foreign Languages Publishing House, 1977), p. 39, cited in Vo Nhan Tri, *Vietnam's Ecoonomic Policy since 1975* (Singapore: Institute of Southeast Asian Studies, 1990), p. 62.

29. The U.S.-Vietnam Trade Council, an affiliate of the International Center, played a significant role during the 1990s in coordinating this effort and in educating the Vietnamese government bureaucracy on U.S. law and trade regulations.

9

Conclusion

RICHARD N. HAASS AND
MEGHAN L. O'SULLIVAN

This volume makes clear that strategies of engagement deserve
further consideration as a means of achieving foreign policy
objectives. In contrast to the substantial attention devoted to the
use of military force, economic sanctions, diplomatic endeavors,
and intelligence gathering, minimal deliberation has been given
to the use of incentives as a foreign policy instrument.[1] The schol-
arly disregard for engagement mirrors the infrequency with which
policymakers have employed this strategy. This neglect is itself in
part a reflection of the fact that engagement strategies are never
easy policy options to choose. Selecting a sanctions-dominated
strategy geared toward the isolation of a recalcitrant regime will
always be politically popular with some segments of the population and can always be justified as taking the moral high ground.
In contrast, the onus of defending a policy that some will inevitably criticize as "appeasement" or "immoral" rests with the policymakers advocating engagement. As the case of Iraq shows quite
vividly, the political costs of a failed engagement strategy can be
high. Even engagement strategies that are less than stark failures
become subject to substantial criticism. Détente with the Soviet
Union, while an overall disappointment, can claim significant successes in the arms control arena; nevertheless, Henry Kissinger is

still defending the achievements of this policy and the rationale behind it more than a quarter of a century later.[2]

As highlighted in Robert Suettinger's chapter on China, the term *engagement* has come to mean many things in the parlance of American politics. To the extent that engagement is perceived to be synonymous with interaction, globalization has promoted it by undermining strategies of isolation. However, this volume defines *engagement* in a much more specific sense to connote strategies employing a strong incentives component to shape the behavior of problem countries. In examining the use of these incentives-oriented strategies, this book endeavors to distill broader lessons from cases in which a variety of foreign policy objectives were pursued through the use of inducements. In so doing, we do not necessarily advocate the greater use of engagement in foreign policy but merely aim to promote adequate consideration of such strategies alongside the more obvious options of military force, sanctions, and the like.

Although the fair or equal consideration of engagement strategies could be anticipated to lead to their more frequent employment, we recognize that, regardless of how fitting engagement may seem in any circumstance, there is no guarantee of success. Inherent in every engagement strategy is the reality that, while the target country has the ability to cooperate and ensure success, it also holds the option to thwart, stall, deceive, and force failure. Nevertheless, past successes attest that engagement can achieve important goals where other policies and strategies fail. Moreover, globalization, by diminishing the impact of unilateral sanctions, prods us to look for suitable alternatives or accompaniments to more common foreign policy approaches.

In presenting the findings and lessons of the cases examined and in formulating guidelines for the future use of engagement, this conclusion focuses on two critical questions. First, is it possible to identify the proper or most favorable circumstances for embarking on engagement? Answering this question requires widening one's perspective to consider the larger context in which engagement would be launched. Just as successful negotiations demand a number of prerequisites that cumulatively connote a certain "ripeness" in a situation, engagement necessitates its own conditions that suggest the use of engagement over other options.[3] Second, once an engagement strategy is under way, how should it be implemented to maximize chances of achieving its goals? Unlike sanctions-dominated policies, which, for better or worse, often demand little attention once they are in place, engagement strategies are "high-calorie" efforts, requiring constant monitoring and continuous efforts from policymakers.[4]

When Should Policymakers Consider Engagement?

An accurate assessment of the larger context in which the strategy will be employed can make the difference between successful and failed engagement. However, as suggested by Johannes Reissner in the chapter on Europe's critical dialogue with Iran, the question of when to engage has often been largely determined by the domestic economic concerns of Europe or the United States.[5] While it would be naive and impractical to ignore the role that domestic factors play in determining when engagement is to be initiated, policymakers should keep the following lessons in mind when considering the option of engagement.

Equal consideration should be given to engagement as is given to other policy options.

In the past, for reasons explored throughout this book and in the opening pages of this conclusion, policymakers have preferred to deal with "rogue" regimes or other problem countries by using punitive measures. However, we strongly believe that the use of incentives—or engagement strategies— can be applicable to managing relations not only with allies but also with adversaries. The policy tools chosen and implemented should be those deemed the most appropriate in light of the costs and benefits, as well as assessments of the probabilities for success, of the range of options available. The North Korean case demonstrates clearly how incentives can be the most sensible option when considered alongside other policy choices. As Leon Sigal describes in the chapter on North Korea, policymakers turned to engagement because both economic sanctions and military force appeared unattractive. America had campaigned ardently to secure the backing of North Korea's neighbors for the imposition of multilateral sanctions but had achieved only limited success.[6] At the same time, the U.S. military was skeptical that bombing could successfully eliminate the threat of continued North Korean nuclear development. Moreover, American civilians and military personnel alike feared that the use of either punitive approach could trigger a military attack by North Korea across the thirty-eighth parallel. Against this background, the United States successfully crafted an agreement that promised economic and political incentives in return for restraints on North Korean nuclear capability.

Engagement, even when it appears to be a long shot, often makes sense as a strategy that will open opportunities for employing other types of policies further down the road.

Engagement strategies, if tried and found unsuccessful, can build support for sanctions or military force among other countries, particularly given the international reputation of the United States as biased in favor of punitive action. Given that multilateral action is almost always preferable to unilateral action, a failed engagement strategy can still be a success. This paradox is demonstrated most clearly in the case of Iraq. The Iraqi invasion of Kuwait in August 1990 revealed that previous U.S. attempts to engage Saddam Hussein had abjectly failed. The diversity and breadth of the international coalition that America forged, and the successful military campaign that followed from it, are well known. As Kenneth Juster points out, American efforts to mobilize this coalition were greatly facilitated by the fact that the United States had pursued a policy that sought cooperation with Iraq for the years preceding the invasion.[7] This earlier policy prevented Iraq's Arab neighbors, who had urged the United States to engage Saddam Hussein in the late 1980s, from justifying the invasion of Kuwait on the grounds that it was an Iraqi response to American pressure. Instead, previous engagement efforts gave the Bush administration credibility, which allowed it to garner support beyond its traditional allies for both sanctions and military force.

The best potential candidates for conditional engagement are often countries in which decisionmaking is highly concentrated.

Promising partners in engagement must not only be *willing* to commit their governments to undertake a contractual relationship, but must also be *able* to do so. This distinction—while having little relevance for engagement with U.S. allies, whose populations expect and generally support cooperation with the United States—is an important one when addressing engagement with "rogues" or other problem regimes considered in this book. The fact that some regimes may be willing but not able to cooperate with the West implies that, while no regime is necessarily beyond engagement, certain types of regimes do make better candidates for engagement than others.[8] For instance, the Agreed Framework between the United States and North Korea was negotiated under the government of Kim Il Sung and continues to be implemented under the rule of his son, Kim Jong Il. Instead of hindering efforts to craft an engagement strategy, the indisputably totalitarian nature of both these regimes facilitated talks between the North Koreans and the

Americans by allowing American negotiators to focus on the needs and preferences of the rulers of the time. This simplification was one important factor making engagement an apparently effective strategy for reducing the
nuclear threat on the Korean peninsula.[9]

Similarly, engagement proved possible to undertake with authoritarian
regimes. Rather than a source of détente's disappointments, the strong position of General Secretary Brezhnev was a key factor in delivering détente's
achievements. Having consolidated his power, Brezhnev was able to control
internal criticism and challenges to his chosen foreign policy. In short, the
strong position of the Soviet leader eliminated many uncertainties inherent
in negotiating with other types of regimes; if Nixon and Kissinger could
develop an agreement appealing to Brezhnev, they could be confident that
the agreement would not fall prey to internal squabbling during its implementation, at least on the Soviet side. As engaging with authoritarian regimes entails narrowly focusing on the preferences of relatively few actors,
political incentives are likely to be most useful. Inducements such as entry
into international associations, the extension of diplomatic recognition, or
the scheduling of summits and high-level visits appeal to a small ruling elite
by shoring up the political position of those in power. By increasing the
legitimacy of the ruling autocrats, these sorts of incentives are meaningful
to authoritarian regimes, which by nature are often insecure.

In contrast to engagement with totalitarian or authoritarian regimes, European Union efforts to engage Iran were hindered by the complex domestic
politics of Iran's volatile hybrid theocracy-democracy and the inability of the
European Union to understand how these internal Iranian politics created
constraints on domestic actors. Although it appears that the EU's critical
dialogue policy was timed to capitalize on moderating Iranian trends, in
reality, the Iranian political system had already become mired in political
conflict by the time the policy was launched in December 1992. Not only
were significant clashes occurring between individuals and factions, but also
fundamental ideological questions about the nature of the system in Iran
were being debated by many.[10] In such an environment, the more moderate
elements that Europe sought to engage risked being discredited for under-
taking a contractual relationship with the West. At the same time, few Iranian actors had sufficient domestic room to maneuver to make bargains
with Europe about human rights, terrorism, and weapons of mass destruction. These internal political dynamics—in conjunction with the failure of
Europe to appreciate them—dashed unrealistic European hopes of promoting political moderation through engagement.

This lesson contains two important corollaries that, while perhaps obvious, are worth highlighting. Although authoritarian and even totalitarian

regimes may make better partners in engagement due to their ability to commit and execute often controversial agendas, their leaders are often unattractive on many other fronts. For policymakers who need to sell their
strategies at home, qualified cooperation with dictators and violators of
human rights presents its own specific problems. Similarly, as mentioned
earlier, the very concentration of power that enables these leaders to fulfil
the obligations they make also allows them to jettison engagement with little
warning or domestic backlash.

Countries with acute economic and strategic vulnerabilities can make good engagement partners.

In the past, economic weaknesses or strategic insecurities were seen as indications that the country in question could be easily or quickly isolated; policies involving sanctions, diplomatic pressure, or military force often followed.
However, as seen in this volume, such vulnerabilities can also be interpreted
as providing important windows to engagement. Both the failures and successes examined in this book reveal that exploiting such circumstances requires a detailed and accurate understanding of the domestic realities within
the target country. Not only must policymakers be aware of economic and
strategic details or happenings, they—or the intelligence community that
advises them—also need a precise appreciation of what motivates people in
positions of power.

Accurate assessments of economic and strategic vulnerabilities have enabled American policymakers to craft promising engagement strategies with
former adversaries. For example, as Soviet support ebbed, North Korea found
itself grappling with an increasingly imperiled economy. Recognizing this, the
United States and its allies crafted a deal that would ease North Korean economic deprivation and address energy shortages if the country would forgo
its nuclear ambitions. Similarly, the Soviet collapse heightened Vietnamese
economic and strategic insecurities and assisted American negotiators in charting a mutually acceptable course to normalization of relations. During the
Carter administration, Vietnam had resisted normalization unless it would
occur under Hanoi's specified conditions; however, in the 1990s, judicious use
of American aid and other incentives (including the lifting of economic sanctions) was sufficient to entice Hanoi to comply with most American concerns
before normalization occurred.

Finally, the case of détente with the Soviet Union reveals how an accurate
appreciation of certain economic and strategic vulnerabilities is also critical in
crafting engagement between more equal powers. American desires both to
limit military expenditure in the wake of the Vietnam War and to contain

revolutionary movements in the developing world made détente attractive to the United States. Yet Kissinger and Nixon recognized that the political and economic incentives they were willing to offer Brezhnev in exchange for reductions in weapons and limitations on defense research would also appeal to a Soviet Union anxious for Western technological assistance and international political recognition.

A cautionary word is in order. While economic vulnerabilities do signal extraordinary opportunities to influence target regimes, the economic incentives that policymakers may use to engage such weak regimes can entail some notable drawbacks, particularly when pursuing nonproliferation objectives. Almost any economic incentive enhances the foreign exchange supply of unsavory regimes that, if not used directly for nefarious behavior, can free up other reserves for just that purpose. In addition, certain types of economic incentives, such as aid or the provision of material goods, have a limited ability to ensure compliance to agreements or ongoing moderated behavior. To the extent that they involve one-off transfers, such incentives can fuel a cycle of demands as the engaged regime seeks to maximize the "price" extracted for the desired changes.

Nevertheless, other economic incentives, such as the adjustment of tariff rates or investment or trade credits, are self-perpetuating in the sense that they provide enduring benefits to both sides as long as the relationship is viewed as mutually beneficial. Similarly, the provision of aid or other goods with economic value spaced out over a long period of time can also provide sufficient motivation for ongoing compliance; the regular delivery of fuel oil to North Korea from 1994 until the completion of the light-water reactor project sometime in the first years of the twenty-first century is an excellent example of how an economic incentive can be structured to encourage ongoing compliance with an agreement.[11] However, a drawback to these sorts of economic incentive is that they can create vested interests in the country formulating the engagement strategy.[12] As shown in the case of the European Union and Iran, these vested interests can cloud an objective assessment of the engagement strategy and can complicate efforts to discontinue it after its failure becomes apparent.

An engagement strategy makes the most sense when adequate domestic U.S. political support among key constituencies— or the potential for creating it—exists.

As Pauline Baker's chapter on South Africa demonstrates vividly, the viability of an engagement strategy is limited if it is inconsistent with the sentiments and interests of politically important groups of Americans at home.

Throughout the 1980s, the Reagan administration sought to continue its policy of engaging the government of President P. W. Botha. However, strident objections voiced by the U.S. Congress and influential civic groups increasingly challenged this strategy. After the South African government's brutal repression of anti-apartheid protesters in 1984, many Americans increasingly viewed the variety of engagement pursued by President Reagan and his Assistant Secretary of State for African Affairs Chester Crocker as morally repugnant. It was ultimately this domestic reaction—reflected in the U.S. Congress's overwhelming bipartisan vote to override President Reagan's veto of the Comprehensive Anti-Apartheid Act in 1986—that forced a new, more limited type of engagement strategy more consistent with American moral concerns.

From the policymaker's perspective, it would be ideal if a well-prepared domestic base in favor of engagement existed even before an engagement strategy were considered. However, as shown by the Vietnamese and Iraqi cases, the architects of engagement can craft such bases, either through political or economic means. In a bitter and hostile atmosphere, the efforts of the Carter administration to normalize relations with Vietnam stumbled in part because there was no domestic constituency supporting Carter's endeavors; in contrast, years later, the Clinton administration was able to bring this process to fruition with the backing of carefully solicited, influential congressional leaders and the support of American businesses, even in the face of organized opposition from various veterans lobbies. In the case of engagement with Iraq, both honey and vinegar were used: economic incentives were combined with political penalties to try to induce Iraq to modify its behavior. While perhaps it was not the specific intention of the architects of engagement with Saddam Hussein, the extension of U.S. government agricultural credit guarantees to Iraq—by appealing to American industrial and agricultural interests that saw Iraq as a large, promising market for their goods—created one American constituency in favor of continued engagement with Iraq.[13]

Often the generation of support for a policy of engagement is essential to counterbalance preexisting constituencies that already wield leverage in the political system. As the cases of Vietnam and Iraq demonstrate, key constituencies can be developed. However, their cultivation often requires the investment of resources, political and otherwise. Before embarking on a strategy of engagement that may have few politically influential constituencies mobilized in its favor, an administration should question whether it is committed to building sufficient support for its policy among American interest groups that will be critical to its success.

Engagement should be considered mostly as a means for achieving modest goals, although on occasion it can be a vehicle for pursuing more ambitious ones.

Modest goals, as opposed to ambitious ones, are those that are not perceived by the regime to threaten its survival.[14] Classifying objectives in this manner helps explain engagement's uneven record of success in the pursuit of what appear to be similar goals. As examined in this volume, an incentives-oriented engagement strategy was critical in reducing the threat of nuclear proliferation on the Korean peninsula. Moreover, the utility of positive inducements in achieving nonproliferation objectives is also confirmed by cases outside the breadth of this volume; in conjunction with domestic considerations, American encouragement and incentives helped Argentina, Belarus, Brazil, Kazakhstan, South Africa, South Korea, Sweden, Taiwan, and Ukraine and to choose a path of denuclearization.[15] However, at the same time, engagement strategies failed to curtail the development of weapons of mass destruction by Iran and Iraq. Presumably, unlike the majority of the countries forgoing nuclear weapons programs, Iran and Iraq believed that their development of unconventional weapons was essential to their survival. In these instances, larger issues of regional security must be addressed; any amount of incentives will be insufficient to coerce regimes to take actions that, in their views, amount to suicide.

As the underlying basis of most forms of engagement is cooperation between governments, it is sensible that engagement works best in pursuit of modest goals and often falters in pursuit of ambitious ones.[16] The difficulties of enticing a regime to make changes or concessions that it perceives as threatening to its survival are obvious. However, engagement strategies can claim some triumphs in achieving greater democratic expression or the promotion of human rights, achievements that often come at the direct expense of a regime's control. Merely within the group of cases examined here, there is a range of success stories. For instance, U.S. engagement with China has contributed to the emergence of a political system that, while still repressive, is far more moderate than it would be in the absence of engagement. In comparison with the performance of sanctions in achieving such an ambitious goal, even a qualified record of engagement is impressive.

Both the Soviet and South African cases demonstrate why engagement has succeeded in achieving ambitious goals in addition to modest ones. As pointed out by James Goldgeier, a fundamental miscalculation on the part of Soviet leaders led to one of détente's greatest achievements. Brezhnev both overestimated the ability of Nixon and Kissinger to deliver the incentives they offered and underestimated the potential impact of the human rights provisions in the Helsinki Accords. While agreeing to "basket three" of these accords in order to obtain the economic and security benefits offered in the other two baskets, the Soviets inadvertently laid the groundwork for political liberalization at home and in Soviet satellite states.

Beyond relying on the miscalculations of the target state, the success of engagement in pursuing ambitious goals is also attributable to the flexibility of engagement as a foreign policy strategy. Unlike a sanctions-only policy, engagement strategies can target a number of actors in a society and provide them each a different package of incentives, thereby creating the impetus for change from many directions. The benefits of this multitiered approach to engagement are most clearly demonstrated by the South African case. In its second and most successful stage, engagement with South Africa involved economic penalties, which sought to inflict harm on the economic interests of the elite and thereby persuade the leadership into negotiations with its political adversaries. At the same time, engagement placed a new emphasis on cultivating and supporting broader elements of South African society, especially elements of the opposition and civil society. Moreover, the amplification of a widely followed investment code gave the private sector an active role in agitating for a new South Africa. The cumulative effect of these multiple engagement strategies geared toward different tiers of society contributed to altering white attitudes and changing the South African domestic political agenda.

How Should Engagement Strategies Be Implemented?

Every bit as important as knowing *when* to use engagement as a policy instrument is knowing *how* engagement should be used once it is selected as the tool of choice. When faced with the challenge of managing a strategy of engagement, policymakers should consider the following lessons:

A key element in successful engagement is a well-delineated road map.

A road map outlines with great precision the conditions to be fulfilled for the relationship to advance and spells out the benefits that will accrue to each side as it moves forward. While the contents of a road map could be made public, in cases of particular sensitivity stemming from nationalism or anti-Americanism where publication of such a document could open a regime to severe domestic criticism, it may be sensible to keep the specifics out of the public domain. In particular, two cases examined in this volume—which each look at two phases of engagement with the United States, one successful and one unsuccessful—support the utility of such agreements. As highlighted by Frederick Brown, during attempts to normalize relations with Vietnam under the Carter administration, the relationship between humanitarian aid to Vietnam and the process of full accounting of American POW-MIAs by Vietnam was left vague. Given that each factor was the key element to unlocking domestic support for the process of normalization in each country, the respective leaderships were unwilling to move forward without receiving explicit guarantees from the other side.

The dilemma created by this ambiguity caused both countries to lose a window of opportunity to normalize their relations before cold war political considerations all but obliterated the opportunity to do so. However, the centerpiece of the successful engagement strategy adopted by the Bush administration and continued by President Clinton was a meticulously crafted road map charting movement forward toward normalization. This detailed plan enabled both sides to maintain a level of momentum that was sustainable and conducive to eventual success. Similarly, the policy of constructive engagement launched toward South Africa by President Reagan in his first term was initially imprecise, even concerning its ultimate goals. In contrast, the modified form of engagement pursued with South Africa after 1986 laid down explicit steps to be taken by the South African government to improve relations with the United States. U.S. expectations and intentions were specific, and the desired actions—such as the opening of talks with the opposition—were reasonable. As demonstrated by Pauline Baker, this structure of engagement facilitated cooperation, rather than thwarted it, once domestic and international developments forced the South African regime to reconsider its position.

Our advocacy of detailed road maps is not just due to the positive outcome of these two cases once such maps were created; certainly, the use of precise agendas was not the only factor that differed in each of the two episodes.[17] Relying on road maps also makes intellectual and psychological sense. The engagement policies we are exploring are, by nature, strategies that the United States pursues with difficult countries as it seeks to improve relations or manage problems with them. Often America has no record of interaction with these regimes; or worse, its history with them has been hostile, suspicious, or belligerent. In these situations, little or no trust exists between the United States and the target country, making engagement somewhat of a gamble for both sides. The creation of carefully calibrated agendas not only diminishes uncertainty but also, by laying out incremental steps, serves as a series of confidence-building measures to stabilize an uncertain relationship.

At the same time, these explicit agendas facilitate the implementation of engagement by minimizing the potential for misreading the actions of the other country. Particularly in countries where U.S. intelligence capabilities are limited, road maps take on even greater importance by reducing the need to determine the ultimate intentions of the target country. By delineating acceptable and unacceptable actions clearly, policymakers can better discern when belligerent rhetoric or questionable behavior indicates a departure from engagement or when it might merely be intended for domestic political purposes. The case of Iraq makes this point most clearly. Given limited U.S. intelligence about Iraqi behavior and the vague confines of U.S. engagement with Iraq, American policymakers struggled to interpret the behavior of Saddam Hussein. Had a road map been employed, it is likely that Saddam Hussein would have violated obligations specified under it, highlighting Iraq's troubling behavior and suggesting growing Iraqi radicalism well before the Iraqi invasion of Kuwait in August 1990. Instead, American policymakers had few benchmarks against which to assess Saddam Hussein's actions and tended to interpret them in a way that justified their policy, rather than challenged it.[18] Finally, Kenneth Juster suggests that the failure of engagement with Iraq offers another point in support of explicit agreements about the path to better relations. By marking out the parameters of acceptable behavior, such maps provide a form of political insurance to the implementers of engagement by diminishing the ability of later critics to misrepresent earlier political calculations.

While there are many clear benefits to road maps, their use also entails real responsibilities. First, as mentioned earlier, careful and ongoing evaluation of any engagement policy is crucial; however, a clearly articulated framework makes monitoring not just wise but indispensable, as the credibility of such an agreement is only as good as its latest step. If the target country discovers that it is possible to move to the next stage of the agenda without satisfying earlier conditions, or if the regime suspects that its compliance with commitments is not verified, much of the rationale behind the road map will be undermined. In such circumstances, a road map becomes a ruse, not a tool.

Second, the provision of a road map obligates the United States to follow certain steps as much as it binds the target country. The consequences of the relationship breaking down as a result not of the obstreperousness of the target country, but of American intransigence are grave. Not only are the potential gains of the carefully sequenced agenda forgone if U.S. noncompliance forces an end to the agreement, but any hope for crafting an alternative policy that commands both adequate domestic and international support will also be dashed by the failure of the United States to live up to its earlier responsibilities.[19] Iraq after the 1990–91 Gulf War is relevant in this regard. UN Security Council Resolution 687 in effect articulates a detailed road map, explicitly delineating the moves that must be undertaken by Iraq before sanctions are eased. To revoke these sanctions before these conditions are fulfilled would be to invalidate the road map and undermine the utility of this tool in the future with not just Iraq but also other countries. However, attempts, most notably by the United States, to supplement this road map with additional stipulations—to move the goalposts—are equally threatening to a credible process and ongoing policy. Although several influential countries have advocated the easing or lifting of UN sanctions on Iraq, the United States had been able to garner support among many nations by demanding that Iraq adhere to the original UN resolutions. However, when America openly embraces other goals, it should not be surprised to find it more difficult to enlist international support in its positions concerning Iraq at the United Nations.

Obviously, the specifics of any road map should reflect the particular insecurities and situations of the countries involved. However, general guidelines can be offered. A road map should be divided into manageable, verifiable phases, with benefits accruing to each party at the completion of each segment. Ideally, each step would be as discrete from the others as possible, so that if the process is derailed, all benefits accrued to each side would not necessarily be revoked; if a missed step were to require the unraveling of the whole process, this reality might create strong pressures to persevere with the road map, even in the absence of compliance. These rewards should be carefully composed so that they enable each side to build a domestic constituency for engagement. This is particularly important given that the establishment of an outline to better relations with the United States may, in itself, open some regimes to domestic criticism. From the target country, the United States might elicit some highly symbolic moves, such as the removal of the call to destroy Israel from the charter of the Palestine Liberation Organization. In contrast, the target country might require the provision of U.S. aid, the removal of certain sanctions, or the arrangement of meetings between heads of state or other officials. Even when a huge power discrepancy between the actors exists, some sense of equality should govern the concessions granted at each stage. A process that is perceived as reciprocal, rather than one-sided, is more likely to succeed. Finally, serious consideration should be given to the placement of the most attractive incentives along the agenda. In some cases, certain powerful incentives are necessary to launch the process; in other circumstances, holding out the most sought-after prize until the end is the best guarantor of faithful compliance.

Incentives should be used to engage a country's civil society and, where possible, its military.

Civil society engagement is often possible when the provision of political or economic incentives is precluded. For example, at times, opaque domestic politics in the target country may frustrate efforts to discern who is in a position of power and who can deliver on promises made in exchange for certain incentives. Or the overriding goal may be the change of a regime. These sorts of situation may preclude conditional engagement, when the United States seeks to establish a contractual relationship with the government of a country. However, they may be ideal times for the initiation of unconditional engagement: the offering of incentives without any expectation of reciprocal acts. While in theory, any type of incentive could be offered unconditionally, cultural incentives or inducements to civil society are the most appropriate measures because they are the least likely to shore up dubious regimes.[20] Such incentives may also be the most suitable option when the U.S. government is faced with domestic lobbies adamant on the isolation of certain regimes. In these cases, even the most strident domestic groups are unlikely to protest measures geared toward easing physical hardship and cultural isolation of the population at large in the target country.

Particularly when the economy of the target state is not state dominated, the provision of economic incentives to the private sector can be an effective mode of unconditional engagement. In more open economic climates, some of the benefits of economic interaction may accrue to the regime or to the political elites who support it; yet in all likelihood, some economic actors nourished by the exchanges made possible under economic engagement will be agents for change and natural allies in some Western causes. To the extent that economic engagement builds the private sector and other nonstate actors within the target country, it is likely to widen the base of support for engagement with America specifically and the promotion of international norms more generally. Certainly, U.S. engagement with China has nurtured pockets sympathetic, if not to American ideals per se, then at least to trade and open economic markets and the maintenance of good relations to secure them.

One relatively unexplored, but promising, mechanism for effective unconditional engagement is the use of investment codes. One such code, the Sullivan principles—by providing guidelines for corporations continuing to operate in South Africa, yet wishing to promote fair employment practices and the advancement of the nonwhite work force—provided assurance that limited economic engagement would be consistent with long-term American interests. The success of the Sullivan principles—as well as the accomplishments of the MacBride principles, which offered standards for investment in Northern Ireland—suggests that investment codes can be consistent with promoting economic growth while simultaneously encouraging interaction and nondiscrimination in severely ethnically, racially, or religiously divided societies. In this way, investment codes are likely to have wide applicability to many postconflict situations, perhaps in the Middle East as well as in Bosnia and, possibly, Kosovo. Conventions like the Arcos principles governing investment in Cuba indicate that investment codes may play a useful role in promoting human and labor rights under repressive regimes.[21] In light of such possibilities, the formulation of investment codes—and subsequent campaigns for international adherence to them—may be appropriate in shaping economic relations with Myanmar if and when current unilateral U.S. sanctions on investment there are reconsidered. American businesses, which are often accused of opposing current sanctions policies solely on mercantilist grounds, might be wise to advocate the greater use of investment codes. Such advocacy would suggest to many that these commercial interests are not simply seeking to make money, but have a broader interest in promoting American ideals abroad.

The only constraint on the scope and development of unconditional engagement is the range of available collaborators in civil society or the private sector. Admittedly, globalization—through its explosion of economic players operating on an international level—has made the economic isolation of a country more difficult to achieve. Yet, fortunately, the same proliferation of actors that makes economic isolation more problematic presents a multitude of possible partners for unconditional engagement with nonstate actors. Their existence, and their ever-increasing importance in the society and economy of most countries, widens the options open to policymakers.

As recent U.S. policy toward Cuba has indicated, such a strategy may bring about serious short-term setbacks. Castro's crackdown on Cuban civil society shortly after the American government announced measures to reach out to Cuban nonstate actors was surely no coincidence. However, when regime change is the ultimate objective, engaging such entities makes sense in the long run. As Poland's trade-union-turned-political-party Solidarity demonstrates, opposition groups and subsequent regimes often trace their roots back to civil organizations. Moreover, it is in the interest of the United States to maintain communication with segments of the society that welcome Western contact; the isolation of a regime through economic and political measures need not entail the isolation of a population. Such links can mitigate the ability of a recalcitrant regime to promote anti-Western sentiment and provide an important window into domestic developments in the country. In addition, civil actors have already proven to be important elements in helping international bodies monitor a country's compliance to international treaties and accords, particularly in the realm of nonproliferation.

This call for promoting civil society and the private sector may appear at odds with our earlier statement that the best potential candidates for conditional engagement are the ones in which decisionmaking is the most concentrated; presumably, the realization of a vibrant civil society and private sector would lead to the diffusion of power within a society. However, because each recommendation is focused on a very different time horizon, the probability that the two efforts would work at cross-purposes is, in reality, very small. The recognition that engagement may work best with authoritarian regimes is relevant for policymakers considering embarking on a conditional engagement strategy immediately or in the short term. In contrast, endorsement and encouragement of civil society and the private sector under a policy of unconditional engagement is only likely to undermine an authoritarian regime in the long run. If conditional engagement with a regime has not produced results by the time unconditional engagement bears its fruits, the United States should be willing to struggle a bit more in its engagement efforts in exchange for having a partner that is more democratic and more globally economically integrated.

Finally, limited forms of military engagement are almost always helpful in achieving foreign policy goals, whether these aims be modest or ambitious. Particularly in societies like Pakistan, where the military is a key institution in political and daily life, maximizing contact with the armed forces makes plain sense. If the transfer of arms or dual-use technology would be counterproductive, programs like International Military Educational Training (IMET) amount to sound investments and should almost never be rescinded as a sanction. Not only do they enable the United States to influence the conduct of the military today, they allow America to build connections with military leaders who may be important political figures later in their careers.

To be most effective, incentives offered in engagement strategies almost always need to be accompanied by credible penalties.

In some cases, the penalties will involve the imposition of new sanctions or military force if the target country refuses the incentives extended and continues with egregious behavior. In the view of many, both tools were important in the case of North Korea. Although, in this volume, Leon Sigal posits that the incentives offered to North Korea were enough in themselves to spur Kim Il Sung to sign the Agreed Framework, we believe it is at least as plausible that the threat of sanctions and military force were significant factors in Pyongyang's ultimate decision to accede to the agreement. Whereas Sigal believes that the North was seeking cooperation with the United States, we would argue that North Korea had to be both enticed and pressured into cooperation.

Similarly, as shown very clearly in other cases, engagement is only effective when the alternative, disengaging, is a credible alternative. For example, the European Union's critical dialogue policy with Iran stumbled because it effectively involved no "sticks." Rather than bolstering the leverage that the European Union could use in conjunction with incentives to alter Iranian behavior, extensive economic ties between Europe and Iran undermined the critical dialogue policy. As an important source of energy for European needs, as well as a market for European goods, Iran was confident that Europe would not sever its mutual economic bonds regardless of Iranian behavior. Moreover, the fact that an underlying premise of the critical dialogue strategy was to maintain contact with Iran—at least in part, if not largely, for economic reasons—confirmed this impression. As a result, European desires to settle disputes such as that over the *fatwa* on Salman Rushdie lacked urgency in Iranian eyes. Economic interdependence is not tantamount to leverage; as important as having economic influence is the other party's belief that one is willing to jeopardize it in order to meet wider objectives.[22]

In addition to the need for incentives to be coupled with penalties, the cases in this volume suggest some subtle lessons about combining honey and vinegar. In several instances, the incentives were offered by the executive branch, while the sanctions were threatened by the U.S. Congress. As the case of South Africa demonstrates, this combination can be an effective one. However, would the strategy of constructive engagement with South Africa have been superior had both the reward and punishment elements of the policy been articulated by the same branch of government? Certainly, if President Reagan had expounded a policy that incorporated both incentives and penalties, the domestic ruptures that developed in America over U.S. policy toward South Africa would have been significantly diminished. At the same time, the South African interpretation of American policy would have involved fewer calculations, and the message that the United States sent to South Africa would have been clearer. As explored in the previous section, clarity of goals as well as clarity of consequences almost always contribute to a more effective engagement strategy.

Effective implementation of engagement strategies
requires intense coordination with allies.

There is growing consensus that sanctions, when employed unilaterally, are rarely effective.[23] Certainly, American attempts to pressure Iran economically were undermined by a much more conciliatory European approach. Instead of placing enormous pressure on Iran, American sanctions—particularly secondary sanctions mandated by the Iran-Libya Sanctions Act—created friction between Europe and the United States, and between the American congressional and executive branches. Recognition of this need for coordination with key allies in implementing coercive policies was largely responsible for America's decision to jettison a sanctions strategy and, to a lesser extent, a military strategy to deal with nuclear proliferation in North Korea.

A corollary exists for the provision of incentives: engagement strategies that disregard the international environment in which they are crafted are also likely to fail. Just as a U.S. embargo of a country's oil sales is ineffective in forcing changes when Europe will buy the barrels America forgoes,[24] incentives are less able to cajole when their equivalents are being offered elsewhere unconditionally. For example, had China been willing to donate or to sell North Korea subsidized fuel oil, or to assist the DPRK in the construction of additional energy sources, the package offered under the Agreed Framework would have carried far less weight.

Unquestionably, as with sanctions, close coordination with allies can facilitate the smooth implementation of engagement strategies. However, the parallels with sanctions strategies are not perfect. Because incentives are consistent with market forces that promote ties between countries rather than obstruct them, incentives can still be influential when offered solely by the United States. In fact, as the case of South Africa demonstrates, sometimes an incentive can be most powerful when America is the only one to extend it. During the early years of the Reagan administration's constructive engagement policy toward South Africa, one of the most potent incentives at the disposal of the United States was its willingness to extend legitimacy to the regime in Pretoria through its interactions with it. This recognition was particularly important to the government of South Africa because, at the time, most European and African countries were seeking to isolate Pretoria politically.

The more complex the relationship to be managed,
the less of a role linkage should play.

Conceptually, the perfect engagement strategy would be much like the one envisioned by Kissinger and Nixon in the formulation of détente with the Soviet Union. The target country would be persuaded to moderate its behavior in a variety of realms not only because the incentive offered in each was enticing but also because the whole set of incentives was reinforcing. Ideally, by linking progress on one front with progress on the other fronts, America could maximize its leverage and move the entire relationship forward. However, this grand plan claimed only modest successes with the Soviet Union, while attempts to create such a strategy with China have failed. Why?

First, a collective lesson offered by the cases explored in this volume is that linkage is only effective when the United States is willing to hold the entire bilateral relationship hostage to one overriding concern. For instance, the United States was able to secure a North Korean commitment to terminate its nuclear program precisely because America was able to identify nuclear proliferation as the area of principal importance to it. American willingness to jettison the prospect for improved relations in any other area in the absence of progress in the nuclear realm made linkage effective. In contrast, U.S. efforts to link most-favored-nation trading status for China to the improvement of human rights there only resulted in bitter domestic battles and an embarrassing retreat by President Clinton from one of his original campaign promises. While certainly the threat to terminate special trading status for China was a grave one, Chinese calculations that the United States was unwilling to jeopardize the entire U.S.-Chinese relationship in the interest of human rights proved correct.[25]

The Chinese and Soviet experiences suggest that linkage strategies are particularly ill suited to managing complex relationships with important global powers. In these instances, in which it is often impossible to identify one overwhelming concern, the maintenance of multiple, delinked agendas, or road maps, can be a more appropriate way to manage multifaceted relations. Such an approach is consistent with the realities of the post–cold war world, in which American foreign policy is concerned with promoting a range of objectives across a wide variety of issue areas. In this way, trade issues, democratization, nonproliferation, human rights, the rule of law, intellectual property rights, and many other concerns can be pursued in tandem.

The main advantage to the use of multiple road maps is obvious and overwhelming: it allows progress to be made on some aspects of a complex relationship even while snags or serious rifts may hold back advancement on other fronts. Realistically, it is impossible to separate completely each realm from the other, although momentum gained in one area will be as useful to the overall relationship as stagnation in another sphere will be detrimental. Moreover, the creation and maintenance of multiple road maps inevitably narrows the range of incentives that can be used to spur progress in each area. However, this constraint should not be too inhibiting, partially since incentives comprise only one element of managing each part of the overall relationship, with sanctions and possibly military force rounding out the inducements.

Given that the use of multiple agendas means that fewer incentives can be employed in each arena, policymakers should strive to offer incentives closely related to the area of concern. For instance, when possible, economic incentives should be employed to shape behavior in economic matters, such as trade. We call this form of narrow linkage *germaneness* and consider it to be of great importance in the construction and maintenance of multiple agendas. Not only is germaneness warranted in order to spread the range of incentives across issue areas, but also there are good reasons to believe that incentives directly connected to the area of interest are those most likely to form the basis of successful policy.[26] First, germaneness facilitates negotiations that are an inherent part of engagement. When trying to influence a group of political actors to take specific actions, U.S. policymakers are more likely to get the desired response when they employ levers that affect these individuals most directly. Second, adopting a strategy that meets the germane criterion is easier to defend at home, as the relationship between the actions taken and the effects desired requires far less justification. Finally, as germaneness facilitates efforts to maintain multiple agendas, it is a critical part of limiting negative spillovers when setbacks occur in one realm of the overall relationship. Although we acknowledge that adherence to germaneness results in a certain loss of leverage in each discrete circumstance, we believe that, overall, the benefits of doing so in complex relationships outweigh the costs.

Engagement requires policymakers to expend at least as much energy in the U.S. domestic political realm as they do working with the target country.

Engagement strategies often fail not simply because of disagreements between the United States and the country it is engaging, but also because American domestic political considerations warp the strategy or make it untenable. Détente between the United States and the Soviet Union is the best case in point. Kissinger and Nixon carefully crafted their linkage strategy, wherein the Soviet Union would be offered political and economic incentives in return for restrained behavior in the strategic arena. This trade-off did encourage Brezhnev to negotiate and sign significant arms control agreements with the United States, and certainly some of the agreements and the summits at which they were signed accorded the Soviet Union a much-desired increase in political status. However, Kissinger's capacity to pursue détente was damaged by the inability of the Nixon administration to deliver the pledged trade concessions. Kissinger and Nixon promised the Soviet Union most-favored-nation (MFN) trading status in return for its cooperation in other global arenas, but they failed to convince the U.S. Congress of the importance of this deal. As a result, led by Senator Henry Jackson, Congress passed the Jackson-Vanik Amendment, which, in contravention of Kissinger's promises to Brezhnev, linked MFN status to the internal behavior of the Soviet regime. This move tied the hands of Kissinger and helped undermine the strategy of détente.

In demonstrating the power of domestic constituencies (in this case, those lobbying for Jewish emigration from communist countries) and their representatives, the fate of détente reveals how engagement strategies can be thwarted by rivalries between the executive and congressional branches of government. The U.S.-Soviet case reveals another challenge to those promoting engagement in democratic societies. As James Goldgeier points out, in order to build domestic support for U.S.-Soviet détente with an uncertain public, the Nixon administration was forced to oversell the policy. By talking up the peaceful benefits of engagement with the Soviet Union, Kissinger and Nixon fostered unrealistic expectations among the American people. When the Soviets continued to meddle in the developing world and resisted arms reductions in some areas, domestic support for the path Kissinger was forging with the Soviet Union plummeted, leaving détente faltering.

Although the strong backing of domestic public opinion will always be valuable to those implementing an engagement strategy, it is the support of Congress and representatives of key constituencies and businesses that is critical to the success of engagement. While the American public at large may favorably view the use of incentives in foreign policy, a general predisposition toward engagement is no substitute for the cooperation of lawmakers and organizations willing and able to devote vast amounts of political and financial resources to influence the course of a policy.

Securing support for engagement among these critical actors in democratic societies such as the United States requires intense coordination between various branches of government. As the case of North Korea aptly illustrates, too often engagement strategies are pockmarked by executive efforts to evade congressional involvement and congressional attempts to thwart executive endeavors. From the perspective of the executive branch, a strength of the Agreed Framework signed with North Korea was that it was *not* a treaty. While this technicality spared the agreement from the necessity of Senate ratification, Congress asserted itself later in the process through its reluctance to finance commitments made under the accord. While not initially standing in the way of the implementation of the framework, Congress has placed constraints and conditions on the provision of fuel offered to North Korea in return for abandonment of its nuclear ambitions.

For several reasons, the executive branch should take the lead in implementing engagement strategies. Not only is the articulation of the rationale behind the chosen foreign policy strategy best handled by the president and his principals, but clearly the executive branch is also uniquely positioned to negotiate with foreign countries and their leaders. However, rather than regard Congress as an impediment to the smooth implementation of engagement, the president and his advisers need to consider Congress as another partner in a multifaceted consultation. Ideally, these efforts would go beyond simply briefing Congress about the state of relations with candidates for engagement to include the appointment of joint executive-congressional delegations and fact-finding missions. In return for such efforts, Congress should recognize that the executive branch needs some discretion to negotiate with target countries with the reasonable expectation that it can deliver the incentives it extends.

Congress can also facilitate presidential efforts to undertake engagement in the way that it handles the process of sanctioning countries. As was the case with Vietnam, the gradual easing of sanctions can be extended as a powerful incentive for cooperation and would be part of any road map to better relations between the United States and the country in question. Using the lifting of sanctions as an effective incentive requires that the president have the power to order their removal when the engagement process warrants it. For sanctions imposed by the president himself, the executive branch maintains the ability to lift the sanctions by executive order. However, with sanctions imposed directly by Congress through legislation it enacted, Congress must provide the president with a waiver allowing him to lift or suspend sanctions. The provision of such waivers by Congress to the president has understandably been a contentious issue. Yet despite the argument that the deterrent effect of sanctions is greater when no waiver exists, the president needs the flexibility that a waiver grants him when he or his principals are negotiating strategies of engagement. Congress need not provide the president with an unqualified waiver, but could delineate circumstances under which the waiver could be employed. (Congress could also give itself the ability to override a presidential waiver through a two-thirds vote by each chamber.) The inclusion of such specifics in sanctions legislation would be useful, partially in that it could provide the executive branch domestic cover when it utilizes the waivers in sensitive situations. Perhaps even more important, such precise language would clearly map out the road to rehabilitation to any country subject to American sanctions, something sorely lacking today.

Skillful congressional-executive coordination can increase leverage in favor of successful engagement. Particularly when contrasted with efforts of the Carter administration, the successful process of normalization with Vietnam under Presidents Bush and Clinton exhibits how Congress, when working with the executive branch, can be an essential partner in preparing a domestic political base for engagement. Repeatedly, the Clinton administration was temporarily constrained from moving forward with Vietnam by the opinion of powerful domestic constituencies such as the American Legion. On more than one occasion, it was the advocacy of influential senators—or the testimony of congressional delegations that had visited Vietnam—that gave President Clinton the domestic political cover to push ahead with normalization.

Future Candidates for Engagement

These cases, and the lessons arising from them, are obviously of more than historical interest. Given the disappointments that sanctions-dominated strategies have produced, in terms of both unsatisfactory results and unexpectedly high costs, the rationale for revisiting U.S. foreign policies toward long-term problem countries is strong. Incentives-oriented engagement strategies present possible alternatives to the policies the United States has in place today toward difficult regimes, such as Cuba, Iran, and Libya. In addition, although the United States is already pursuing policies of engagement with China and North Korea, these ongoing strategies demand re-evaluation. Quite possibly, the architects and implementers of engagement with these two Northeast Asian countries can gain insight into the dilemmas they face by considering the lessons extracted above. Although we do not consider prospects for further engagement with Iraq in detail here, we make no pretensions that Iraq should not be included among the most problematic of America's state-to-state relations. Indeed, engagement is explicit in United Nations Security Council resolutions, which offer Iraq specific rewards in exchange for compliance. However, Saddam Hussein—in spurning the UN resolutions mapping the path to better relations with his country's neighbors and the West—has rejected the possibility of any mutually reciprocal engagement process.

China

When considered in light of the findings of this volume, not only does the failure to manage relations with China according to a linkage strategy seem unsurprising, the mere attempt to do so appears almost foolish. Now, and for the foreseeable future, the relationship between the United States and China will be multifaceted, encompassing a range of serious concerns in many areas. Some of these concerns will be modest; others will relate to more ambitious goals. None will take such precedence over the others that U.S. policymakers will be able or willing, with any credibility, to hold the entire U.S.-Chinese relationship hostage to it. Moreover, China's growing importance will ensure that America cannot dictate the terms of its relationship with China.

At the same time, despite alarmist projections, China and the United States are not equals in terms of strategic, military, or economic power; America maintains significant advantages, which it should use, not to try to manipulate China, but to shape the direction of Sino-American relations for the decades to come. This will require discarding empty and misleading phrases like *strategic partnerships* and *constructive engagement* in favor of a specific, well-crafted agenda, or rather, agendas. The intricacy of the relationship between the United States and China will only be realistically managed by numerous and simultaneous road maps.

The rationale for individually handling the complexity of American concerns—whether they be over Taiwan, trade, Korea, human rights, nonproliferation, cooperation in international organizations, democratization, or intellectual property rights—is sound. Regardless of what happens in one realm, progress in another would be welcome; the successful co-optation of China into a comprehensive nonproliferation regime and the development of a sound Chinese dual-use export control system would constitute a significant achievement, even if it occurred against the backdrop of deteriorating enforcement of intellectual property rights or rising friction over missile defense issues. Similarly, Chinese pressure on North Korea to scale back its militarization is crucial, quite apart from progress made on admitting China to the World Trade Organization. This multidimensional strategy also leaves room for the United States to take exception to some Chinese behavior—for example, by advancing a UN resolution censuring China for its human rights practices, as was done most recently in April 2000—without holding the entire relationship hostage to the issue. In constructing these multiple road maps, policymakers should consider the germaneness of the incentives to the issues of interest. As discussed earlier, economic incentives—by appealing to Chinese actors influential in the economic realm—are most likely to shape China's behavior in economic matters.

Cuba

Although the ultimate goal of the United States—the peaceful transition to a democratic, market-oriented Cuba—has not changed, the context in which this aim can be pursued has altered significantly. When stringent U.S. sanctions were placed on Cuba in 1962, Cuba posed a threat to the United States as an outpost of communism in the Western Hemisphere and an ardent exporter of revolution to its neighbors. However, some forty years later and in the wake of the cold war, Cuba's importance has dwindled and its ability to promote radical politics among its democratizing neighbors has almost entirely collapsed. Arguably, the greatest threat that Cuba presents to the United States today is a tide of anxious and destitute refugees. Ironically, this situation is only worsened by the embargo, not mitigated by it. Not only has much of the rationale for isolating Cuba collapsed, but U.S. policy toward the country—in particular the imposition of secondary sanctions—has created tensions with America's European allies that outweigh Cuba's importance. Finally, America's sanctions-dominated policy toward Cuba demands reevaluation because it is warping the message that the United States sends to potentially moderating "rogue" regimes elsewhere. Cuba remains on the terrorism list (a grouping of countries designated by the United States as state sponsors of terrorism), even in the absence of a Cuban-sponsored terrorist act for many years. This discrepancy signals to others on the terrorism list that their renouncement of terrorism will not necessarily free them from this designation and relieve them of the many sanctions that are a consequence of it.

Despite the many good reasons to reassess current U.S. policy toward Cuba, formidable obstacles have prevented the sort of policy overhaul that is needed. Most important, sections of the Cuban-American community have vehemently opposed any policy changes that would confer legitimacy on Castro or possibly prolong his rule. In addition to feeling passionately about isolating Castro, segments of the Cuban-American population have been well organized and politically influential, particularly given their concentrated voting strength in pivotal states like Florida and New Jersey. Nevertheless, generational changes have opened possibilities for moderates to gain prominence in this community. In addition, the growing number of American farmers and businessmen expressing interest in doing business in Cuba, and recent calls by the U.S. Chamber of Commerce for further trade with Cuba, indicate the existence of at least one influential domestic U.S. constituency favoring engagement with Cuba.

Unquestionably, the complexity of the situation has contributed to the continuation of the status quo. However, even in this rapidly changing environment, past initiatives suggest that conditional political engagement with the Cuban regime continues to be unlikely. Consultations between American and European officials occurring throughout 1995 and in the early months of 1996 led to the formulation of a less confrontational approach to dealing with Cuba.[27] In a meeting in February 1996, a European representative offered Castro a range of political and economic incentives in exchange for Castro's pledge to allow some economic and political liberalization. Instead of welcoming this proposal, Castro rebuffed it. Shortly afterward, Cuban authorities stepped up repression of Cuban dissidents; less than two weeks later, the Cuban air force shot down two U.S.-licensed airplanes. The significance of these actions is not simply that they effectively jettisoned American efforts to shape a more conciliatory Cuban policy; they also suggested to many Castro's desire to thwart U.S.-EU cooperation and to prolong U.S.-Cuban animosity, not mitigate it. Even more recently, Canada embarked on its own policy of political engagement with Castro, with equally disappointing results.[28] Collectively, these two episodes intimate that, while Castro's consolidated power would easily enable him to commit to a road map leading to better relations with the United States, Castro himself is not a willing partner in an engagement process that he views as threatening to his continued rule.

The United States should simultaneously pursue two forms of engagement with Cuba. First, it should continue to seek Castro's willingness to engage in a conditional relationship and to chart a course toward more satisfactory relations. The United States should attempt to strike a dialogue with Castro in which reasonable benefits are offered to him in return for reasonable changes. Rather than accentuating American desires for regime change or immediate democratic elections in Cuba, U.S. policymakers should make lesser goals the focus of their policy, as the more ambitious the demands, the less likely Castro is to enter into a process of engagement. For instance, the release of political prisoners and the legitimization of political parties might be offered in exchange for the selected lifting of elements of the embargo. Regardless of Castro's reaction to such an approach, benefits would accrue to the United States. If Castro accepted this dialogue, U.S. policy would be promoting meaningul political liberalization on the island; if Castro rejected these attempts at conditional engagement, America would still ease tensions with its European allies by demonstrating it was willing to take a more flexible line toward Cuba.

Second, while pursuing whatever conditional engagement is possible under Castro, unconditional engagement can be undertaken and expanded. The recent easing of certain restrictions in the hopes of building ties between the United States and Cuba at the civic level is laudable.[29] Additional air links and liberalized travel restrictions already undertaken will increase Cubans' exposure to the United States. Although such changes may require Castro's consent, they are unconditional incentives in the sense that they are not offered in an attempt to change specific aspects of the regime's behavior in the short term. Instead, these efforts are intended both to help temper the negative image of America held by many younger Cubans and to cultivate outward-looking segments of Cuban society. Both groups will be influential in determining future levels of cooperation between the United States and Cuba once Castro is gone. Regardless of Castro's leanings, these already existing American attempts to engage Cuban civil society should be even further expanded by easing all travel restrictions, a move that will encourage further contact between people and civic organizations and institutions such as the Catholic Church.

In addition to these civic measures, the United States should also expand unconditional engagement with Cuba in economic matters, for several important reasons. Particularly given that America has few serious concerns about Cuban behavior abroad, no worries exist that foreign exchange that accrues to Cuba through economic engagement will fuel dangerous activities; in fact, the large volume of remittances that cross the Florida Straits to Cuba has already made America the second largest source of external capital for Cuba. In this situation, limited economic engagement is a low-risk strategy that can gradually promote internal changes as Cubans benefit from new economic opportunities with America. The Clinton administration has already authorized increased levels of allowable remittances and expanded trade with nongovernment entities. However, these changes do not go far enough. There should be no ceiling on the amount of remittances that Cuban families can receive from relatives living in the United States. Moreover, even if Castro resists conditional engagement that could be linked to the gradual easing of the embargo, U.S. policymakers should consider ways in which investment codes could replace elements of the embargo. The possibility of employing investment codes that allow for American trade with and investment in Cuban entities meeting specific conditions concerning ownership structure and labor rights should be explored.[30] Given the paucity of privately owned businesses in Cuba today, the instant effects of such codes in boosting trade and investment would probably be minimal. However, the employment of investment codes, in place of more blanket restrictions, would offer immediate psychological support as well as tangible incentives for growth to Cuba's struggling private sector.

Iran

Before the February 2000 parliamentary elections in Iran, the notion of embarking on a conditional engagement strategy with Iran seemed almost naive and certainly implausible. Unquestionably, the severe economic difficulties faced by Iran as a result of its large debt and fluctuating oil prices throughout much of the past decade would make potential American economic incentives particularly powerful. However, while Iranian economic vulnerabilities might have suggested it was an opportune moment for conditional engagement, most other factors advised caution.

In particular, the volatile domestic political situation—with internal power struggles exploding into violence on the streets of Iran in the summer of 1999—underlined the difficulties architects of engagement would face in crafting a successful strategy. Not only did mantras denouncing America remind policymakers that certain factions would be opposed to closer contact with the United States, but it also strongly suggested that such association would be a political flashpoint and potential liability for those eager to engage.[31] In short, although President Khatami might have been willing to strike a deal with the West, there was little evidence to suggest that he had adequate power to ensure its execution. At the same time, American and Israeli intelligence reports revealed continued Iranian financial support to groups such as Hezbollah and Hamas that oppose Middle East peace;[32] this backing boded badly for conditional engagement with Iran, both by disclosing that those in charge of security and foreign affairs maintained a hard-line orientation and by shoring up American domestic opposition to engagement with Iran.

Nevertheless, the overwhelming success of relatively moderate candidates in the 2000 parliamentary election has changed the political landscape in Iran. Although the campaign and the electorate focused primarily on domestic issues, the comments of some leading politicians have suggested a willingness to consider improved ties with the United States. Most importantly, the new face of the Iranian parliament has strengthened President Khatami's power base in his long-standing struggle with more conservative elements in Iranian society and the regime itself. Although these developments far from ensure a successful dialogue between Washington and Tehran, they do make the arguments for exploring the possibility of conditional engagement with Iran stronger.

In this context, steps taken by the Clinton administration in March 2000 to lessen hostility between Iran and the United States are most welcome. Relaxing sanctions on U.S. imports of Iranian carpets, pistachios, and caviar—Iran's most important non-oil exports—promises to help address Iran's ongoing, pressing economic need to secure foreign exchange.[33] Secretary of State Madeleine Albright's acknowledgment of U.S. involvement in domestic Iranian affairs in the past could well ease Iranian resentment.[34] These actions, in combination with renewed U.S. commitment to resolve the issue of outstanding claims between both countries, signal the seriousness of the United States in changing its relationship with Iran—much more so than did the lifting of earlier restrictions on U.S. agricultural sales to Iran.[35]

However, these steps are not without their risks. Those Iranians desirous for a more amicable relationship with the West are far from triumphing over their more conservative and inward-looking counterparts; in fact, hardliners continue to dominate the national security apparatus, where the decisions made are of greatest concern to the United States. Quite apart from Iranian politics, these gestures are likely to intensify the already heated debate in the United States about maintaining strict sanctions on Iran. Businesses and commercial interests eager to become involved in Iran will be heartened by the easing of the import sanctions. A tacit—if unintended—recognition that unilateral efforts to deny foreign exchange to state supporters of terrorism are largely futile, the limited easing of imports from Iran will prompt U.S. energy companies to argue that oil sanctions should be lifted under the same logic. Similarly, any resumption in lending by international financial institutions to Iran will further fuel global competition to bring technology, services, and private capital into Iran, only heightening the relative sense of deprivation felt by many U.S. companies.[36] In contrast, if these conciliatory U.S. actions are not met with a favorable Iranian response, Americans wary of engagement with Iran will clamor for a return to a more uncompromising policy. These pressures from both sides are likely to further circumscribe the U.S. president's latitude to act.

Regardless of Iran's response to American initiatives, the United States should strive to maintain momentum that will be critical for improved U.S.-Iranian relations, if not soon, then sometime in the future. The United States should go beyond speeches by Secretary Albright and other State Department officials in which the United States offers to construct a road map with Iran, to actually propose the specifics of such a road map as the United States envisions it.[37] Such a road map would start with very modest steps. Most likely, in the opening stages, U.S.-Iranian contacts would be limited to non-governmental envoys and agencies; only further in the process would government-to-government meetings be introduced. Much of the initial phases would include confidence building measures, such as business-to-business exchanges and visits to Iran from high-profile individuals beyond the circle of Middle East policy and academic experts. Only later in the road map would agendas be set for moving forward in the areas of greatest concern to the United States: terrorism, Iran's weapons program, and peace in the region. In order to encourage the moderation of Iran's position in these three areas, the United States should delineate the gradual easing of sanctions that Iran could expect. Calculated movements toward the full lifting of U.S. sanctions might involve U.S. support for international financial institutions in Iran, oil swaps, resumed U.S. agricultural credits, and the allowance of American investment in Iran under a certain threshold, including expanded opportunity for investment in the oil and gas sectors.[38] On the Iranian side, possible interim steps toward normalization of relations could entail cooperation with the United States on investigations into the Khobar Towers bombing, willingness to meet U.S. officials in international forums, and a public statement disavowing support for radical groups like Hezbollah.[39]

Formulating a road map along these lines would allow policymakers to test Iran's willingness to thaw American-Iranian relations. While it is possible that Khatami could surprise the United States by seizing such an initiative, merely the extension of a road map could help shift in the domestic political debate in Iran more in his favor. Often, an abstract offer of undefined benefits is easier to resist than a concrete extension of specific incentives. At the same time that the United States is pursuing these avenues, it should continue to expand its unconditional engagement with Iranian civil society. Not only is this type of engagement likely to have long-range benefits, but it will also allow America to stay more closely attuned to the intricate Iranian domestic politics that will shape any future form of engagement.

Finally, the Clinton administration, as well as future administrations, should strive to reformulate how both policymakers and the average American think about Iran. For decades now, Iran has been demonized. It has been castigated as a "rogue" state and held up as an embodiment of the threats facing America in the world.[40] Iran's likely continued support for terrorism ensures that it will not join the ranks of American allies anytime in the foreseeable future. However, while it is right for Americans to regard U.S. relations with Iran as problematic, it is counterproductive to perceive them as hostile by definition. American policymakers have already begun to retreat from confrontational rhetoric, jettisoning the policy of "dual containment" which suggested that Iran is as much an outlaw as Iraq. This welcome trend should be supplemented by the clear articulation of realistic expectations for future U.S.-Iranian relations: although perhaps not a friend, Iran need not be an enemy. American policy and public opinion has accepted this middle ground for many other countries since the end of the cold war. It is time to do the same for Iran.

These developments—the proposal of a road map, unconditional engagement with civil society, and a reconceptualization of relations with Iran—have the added advantage of enabling the United States to better manage its relationship with Europe. Particularly since the passage of the Iran-Libya Sanctions Act—legislation that mandated secondary sanctions on foreign companies investing in Iranian or Libyan petroleum industries—American policy toward Iran has lacked virtually all credibility in European eyes. Evidence of a new U.S. willingness to tailor its policy more toward Iranian subtleties than domestic American constituencies would facilitate a European-American dialogue on Iran. U.S.-EU consultations on Iran would help smooth an irritant in transatlantic relations while at the same time providing the United States a mechanism for ensuring that Europe does not maintain an unqualified relationship with Iran.[41]

Libya

Libya has struggled under the full gamut of U.S. unilateral sanctions since 1986. These sanctions were imposed in an effort to coerce the Qaddafi regime to change its behavior in three specific areas: its attitude toward the state of Israel, its support for international terrorism and extremist movements, and its desire to obtain weapons of mass destruction. Recent developments suggest that some progress has been achieved on these fronts. American intelligence reveals that Libyan progress in acquiring nuclear or chemical weapons has been stunted (although thwarted progress should not be construed as a change in Libyan ambitions). Similarly, the years when Libya actively promoted radical movements and engaged in expansionist forays into Chad appear to be in the past. Perhaps most important, Libyan support for terrorism seems to have waned while—as indicated by the surrender of two Libyan suspects implicated in the Pan Am 103 bombing—Libya appears willing to bear at least some responsibility for past terrorist acts. These changes in Libyan behavior, in conjunction with pressures from American commercial entities eager to do business with Libya now that UN sanctions have been suspended, provide both a rationale and an impetus for the reassessment of U.S. policy.

However, as articulated by the Clinton administration, these positive developments and U.S. commercial pressures are far from sufficient to warrant a full American embrace of Qaddafi. Moreover, the strength of certain U.S. domestic constituencies, particularly the families of the victims of Pan Am 103, prohibits rapprochement with Qaddafi and Libya at least until Libya's willingness to cooperate fully with the trial in the Netherlands is proven. Finally, a great deal of uncertainty continues to surround Libyan domestic politics. How strong is Qaddafi's position as the supreme, if unofficial, leader of Libya? To what extent does discontent in the military and Islamic opposition pose a threat to Qaddafi's leadership? Until these questions are answered, crafting engagement with Libya will remain a huge challenge.

The United States faces a dilemma posed by the desire to encourage positive developments in Libya and the inability to remove sanctions currently in place absent further progress. Here the Vietnamese case offers relevant lessons about how the complex use of various incentives and penalties can allow subtle messages to be conveyed. During the Bush administration, the United States felt that Vietnam had shown insufficient progress in reaching the markers set out to move the bilateral relationship forward to phase two of the road map. However, the declaration of such a blunt evaluation risked derailing the process, which, overall, was promising. To maintain the momentum achieved without catapulting to the next stage of the road map before all the conditions were fulfilled, the United States pursued a more nuanced approach. While recognizing some positive moves on the part of Vietnam, the Bush administration delineated the areas in which it desired further progress. This statement was accompanied by an aid package that included monetary aid, country-to-country student exchanges, telephone links, and the lifting of restrictions on the operation of American nongovernmental organizations in Vietnam. Cumulatively, these actions kept the normalization process alive, encouraging Vietnam without rewarding it for moves yet to be taken.

Such a creative approach should be considered regarding U.S. policy toward Libya. A specific road map should be fashioned, detailing the conditions and circumstances under which U.S.-Libya relations can improve. Ideally, such a road map would have been articulated in the very legislation that placed sanctions on Libya; in general, any instrument—whether it be legislation or an executive order—that imposes sanctions should also delineate the specific actions that the country in question must undertake to be freed of the sanctions. However, a road map for Libya still remains to be crafted. It would include a series of Libyan steps desired by the United States: Libyan cooperation during the trial of the two Pan Am 103 suspects, Libyan renunciation of terrorism, and a reaffirmation of Libya's commitment to the Nuclear Nonproliferation Treaty and the Comprehensive Test Ban Treaty. In exchange for these actions, or as explicit enticements to force them, Libya could look forward to the gradual easing of U.S. economic sanctions, its eventual removal from the terrorism list, possible normalization of diplomatic relations, entry into international associations, and economic cooperation. While Libya has recently experienced a slackening of American sanctions in agricultural trade, these modifications were the product of pressure from domestic U.S. agricultural interests.[42] To date, although sorely needed, there has been no clearly articulated path for countries wishing to orchestrate their honest removal from the terrorism list or to trigger a process of desanctioning. Given the long history of animosity between America and Libya, the United States should consider launching the road map with public statements welcoming Libya's recent positive moves and extending token gestures, such as those taken with Vietnam, like lifting the ban on travel by U.S. citizens to Libya.[43]

North Korea

Engagement with North Korea continues to be both promising and frustrating. Despite fits and starts, the United States and its allies and North Korea have maintained their commitment to the Agreed Framework into the fifth year after its signing. However, throughout the summer of 1999, there were strong indicators that North Korea was preparing to test a long-range ballistic missile, the Taepodong II, which could have the capability of reaching Alaska as well as North Korea's closer neighbors. As North Korea rightly pointed out, such a test would not be a violation of any agreement signed by the country; moreover, the North Koreans maintain that it is their sovereign right to test missiles. While these claims might be technically true, a North Korean test of the Taepodong II would have changed regional security dynamics in important ways. Indeed, the mere threat of such a test catalyzed concerted discussions among the United States, Japan, and South Korea about missile defense systems, which China strongly opposes; Japanese public opinion began to debate the possibility of changing its "peace" constitution; South Korea and Japan started to plot further military spending in the event of a North Korean missile test.

The immediate crisis was allayed when talks in Berlin in September 1999 led to an understanding between North Korea and the United States and its allies: North Korea would place a moratorium on all missile testing as long as talks on the normalization of relations between America and North Korea continued. The United States began this new phase in its relationship with North Korea by easing some of the sanctions that had been in place on the communist country for decades. In former Defense Secretary William Perry's report on the findings and recommendations to emerge from his review of U.S. policy toward North Korea, Perry specifies a "two-path strategy" for conducting relations with North Korea. The first path is preferable: a path of step-by-step engagement in which North Korea terminates all nuclear or missile activity (including the manufacture and export of missiles) in return for the eventual resumption of economic and political relations between the communist country, its neighbors, and the United States. However, as pointed out by Perry, successful continuation along this path "depends on the willingness of the DPRK to traverse it with us."[44] In the absence of full cooperation by North Korea, America and its allies can opt for the second path, one of containment of the threat that North Korea poses through whatever means necessary.

These efforts deserve support. Perry's team labored to bring about the high levels of coordination and consensus between the United States and its allies in South Korea and Japan that a successful engagement strategy demands. Moreover, the current review of policy, in recognizing the multiplicity of concerns that the United States holds in North Korea, is right not to link all areas of concern in North Korea to one another. Although the Perry Report clearly prioritizes nuclear and missile issues above other concerns—such as Republic of Korea family reunification and the implementation of the North-South Basic Agreement—it does not make progress on one front contingent on advancement on the others. In fact, the new policy even acknowledges that barring progress on the missile talks, the United States and its allies should still endeavor to keep the Agreed Framework intact. Finally, this stage of engagement with North Korea warrants a reiteration of an earlier lesson explored in this conclusion: *engagement—even when it appears to be a long shot—often makes sense as a strategy that will open opportunities for employing other types of policies further down the road.* As William Perry and Secretary Albright have stated, if these tentative steps of cooperation with North Korea falter, the United States maintains its ability to employ other policy tools. If America finds itself in this position one day, as was the case with Iraq, this period of attempted cooperation with North Korea will likely facilitate U.S. attempts to organize a coalition for punitive action against the North.

While the United States should maintain multiple road maps to deal with the various issues of concern in North Korea, policymakers should also be careful to consider the variety of incentives available to the United States and how they may be best distributed. As the case of South Africa demonstrated clearly, when pursuing a variety of objectives, the same incentives cannot be utilized to spur action on a multitude of unconnected agendas; if America hopes to address a range of issues with North Korea over the next year or even decade, it should be reluctant to promise too much for each step without adequate forethought about what incentives or other instruments it maintains for pursuing future objectives or stemming future threats.

Despite our cautious optimism about current U.S. policy, we recognize that the fate of engagement with North Korea is by no means certain, not simply because of the North's own volatility, but also due to significant U.S. domestic opposition among important constituencies. The report by the House of Representatives' North Korea Advisory Group—in which the group's members criticize U.S. policy toward North Korea as one that does not address the principal threats the country poses to American interests— is just one of many indications that congressional opinion is, at best, wary of engagement with North Korea.[45] As suggested throughout the pages of this conclusion, the administration needs to cultivate the backing of other key constituencies to provide a counterweight to interests that clearly oppose current policy. Just as the Clinton administration needs to consult intensively with American allies over current policy toward North Korea, it needs to involve the U.S. Congress as an important, and sometimes reluctant, partner in its endeavors to encourage moderation and nonproliferation in North Korea. A clearer public articulation of the rationale for pursuing engagement with North Korea would go a long way toward this end. The risks that the Clinton administration is taking with North Korea are real, but they are also justified and based on sound calculations. A better explanation of both sides of this reality is in the interest of all and would be likely to increase support for current engagement efforts.

Russia

As with China, the United States faces an immense challenge in maintaining and advancing U.S.-Russian relations, due to both the complexity of the relationship and its vociferous critics. Yet well-reasoned engagement with Russia is crucial; with an aging nuclear arsenal, a constantly lurching economy, volatile domestic politics that include strong nationalist and revisionist elements, and territory that spans eleven time zones, Russia maintains the ability to destabilize Europe, Asia, and indeed the world as no other country does. While the importance of engaging Russia cannot be overestimated, the difficulties of doing so are no less apparent. No longer ruled by a tightly controlled authoritarian regime, Russia today is a fragile, partial democracy. While a most welcome development, the democratization of Russia presents the practitioners of engagement with many associated problems: ascertaining who is best positioned to make commitments on a range of internal and strategic issues, assessing to what extent domestic forces hinder Russian leaders from making or keeping promises, and fearing that engagement with the West may become a liability to the forces the United States wishes to promote within Russia. The election of Vladimir Putin as president does suggest that the United States will have a stronger partner in engagement than former president Boris Yeltsin proved to be. However, American leaders should be wary of too closely linking their interests with Putin's rule, particularly while his intentions for governing remain unclear.

Although Russia's fledgling democracy is likely to make engagement with it even more complex than similar efforts to engage China, some obvious parallels and important policy prescriptions are applicable to the management of relations with both powers. U.S. policymakers should adopt and create numerous road maps for dealing with the various areas of concern in Russia. In particular, issues of economic reform, corruption, and weapons proliferation will loom large. While the temptation to link largely unrelated areas will be at times hard to resist, policymakers should strive to maintain the principle of germaneness wherever possible. For instance, rather than terminating lending by international financial institutions in an attempt to curb Russian excesses in Chechnya, policymakers should search for levers in the political realm that more directly affect the motives and aspirations of those ordering and carrying out the carnage.

At the same time, America should expand its efforts at unconditional engagement through highly focused, incentives-oriented strategies such as the Nunn-Lugar program (formerly the Cooperative Threat Reduction Program) initiated in 1991. Through this carefully crafted initiative, American funding has been used to help safeguard and demilitarize the former Soviet nuclear arsenal.[46] This program is not only a good example of a discrete agenda that has been followed despite glitches in the overall U.S.-Russian relationship, but it is also a fine instance of narrow linkage or germaneness. In part, the extension of monetary and other incentives to scientific institutions has been linked to altering the agenda of these organizations from weapons-related research to other civilian needs.[47] Yet where these focused incentives are unsuccessful in curbing the involvement of a specific institution in weapons proliferation, the United States should continue to use targeted sanctions to penalize the institution.

Syria

Although initial hopes for a rapid peace between Syria and Israel after the 1999 election of Israeli Prime Minister Ehud Barak were overly optimistic, the achievement of a lasting peace between Israel and Syria is still within the realm of possibility. In the interest of this peace, the United States should continue to stand ready to engage Syria—a country long-sanctioned by America for its support of groups that use terrorism to advance their causes— if the Assad regime or its successor demonstrates the desire and flexibility needed to realize a mutually satisfying resolution to its longstanding conflict with Israel. While the role that the United States will play in achieving any such peace will be only peripheral, the creative use of American incentives can undoubtedly make the road to peace a bit smoother.

The prospects of better relations between Syria and the United States will continue to be one significant incentive that can be used to entice Syria to make peace with Israel. Any peace between the two Middle Eastern neighbors would definitely require an end to Syrian support for radical groups carrying out violent acts against Israel. The United States should both declare its desire to remove Syria from the terrorism list and specify clearly what steps need to be taken by Syria—including the closing of training camps and the banning of activities by certain groups such as the Islamic Jihad— before America takes such action. Once Syria is no longer designated a supporter of terrorism, the path will be clear for increased investment and trade. While the removal of American sanctions is perhaps the largest carrot the United States has to offer, its placement near the beginning of negotiations may be essential to maintain momentum, or to jumpstart flagging Israeli-Syrian peace talks.[48] At the same time, such moves will also further the interest of peace by helping President Assad consolidate constituencies for peace in his country.

While it is important for the United States to demonstrate its willingness to engage Syria in the interest of peace in the Middle East, there are no assurances that Syria will choose to accept this invitation. Indeed, developments in the first few months of 2000 appeared to suggest diminished Syrian readiness to conclude a formal peace with Israel. As mentioned earlier, one of the risks inherent in an engagement strategy is that the target country will choose not to seek a better relationship with the United States and refuse to cooperate with American efforts to forge a path to more stable relations. Syria should understand that if the United States judges that Israeli-Syrian peace efforts are stalled largely due to Syrian obstreperousness, or if an Israeli withdrawal from Lebanon results in increased Hezbullah-sponsored violence that is facilitated by Syria, then Syria should expect continued economic penalties and political isolation at the official level. The power of any such message would obviously be increased to the extent the United States was speaking not only for itself, but for others as well.

Conclusion

The briskly globalizing post–cold war world of today is arguably more complicated than the world of a decade or so ago. At the same time, the countries that the United States has uniformly labeled as "rogues" have proven to be more varied than such a classification suggests. Given these complexities, and others that are likely to arise, it is no surprise that policies such as containment and tools such as sanctions have been insufficiently nuanced to deal with the multitude of challenges facing the United States. This reality demands that policymakers explore, and where appropriate, use, a greater variety of foreign policy tools and strategies. Engagement, although often overlooked in favor of punitive policies, has the potential to significantly widen the spectrum of serious policy options.

Engagement, however, is clearly not a panacea. Not only are such strategies often difficult to implement domestically, but even with perfectly crafted, managed, and executed engagement strategies, there are no guarantees of success. Because engagement relies so heavily on the politics and inclinations of the target country and its willingness to work with the United States, the very nature of engagement is more precarious and volatile than other foreign policy strategies. Nevertheless, a place for engagement strategies exists in the foreign policy tool kit. In some cases, conditional engagement is an appropriate vehicle for change; in most others, unconditional engagement can be pursued.

Despite all these caveats, engagement offers a promising alternative to policies of punishment that have either not achieved their objectives or have done so only at extremely high costs to the United States and the target country. The posture and policies currently taken by the United States in some of its most problematic relationships—such as those with Cuba, Iran, Libya, and, to a lesser extent, Syria—demand re-evaluation. Quite possibly, these relationships could be substantially improved if they incorporated varying degrees of engagement. Where the United States is already involved in engaging difficult regimes—as with China, North Korea, and Russia—policymakers would benefit from a more systematic understanding of engagement strategies in order to ensure the better management of many of these still uncertain relationships. For all these reasons, we urge that engagement strategies be accorded equal deliberation—if not necessarily adoption—alongside the options of military force, sanctions, covert action, and diplomacy.

Notes

1. As mentioned in the introduction, notable exceptions to this generalization are David Cortright, *The Price of Peace: Incentives and International Conflict Prevention* (Lanham, Md.: Rowman and Littlefield, 1997); William J. Long, *Economic Incentives and Bilateral Cooperation* (University of Michigan Press, 1996); Alexander George, *Bridging the Gap: Theory and Practice in Foreign Policy* (Washington, D.C.: United States Institute of Peace Press, 1993).

2. See Henry A Kissinger, "Between the Old Left and the New Right," *Foreign Affairs*, vol. 78 (May-June 1999), pp. 99–116.

3. Ripeness in negotiations implies that four conditions are satisfied: a mutual desire to reach an agreement, the existence of a leadership on both sides able to commit itself to an accord, the formula of an agreement that enables each party to claim that it protected the national interests of its side, and the existence of a mutually acceptable process to the negotiations. See Richard N. Haass, *Conflicts Unending: The United States and Regional Disputes* (Yale University Press, 1990), esp. pp. 27–29, 138–50. Also see I. William Zartman, *Ripe for Resolution: Conflict and Intervention in Africa*, 2d ed. (Oxford University Press, 1989). Zartman describes "ripe moments" as ones that have a mutually hurting stalemate, the presence of valid spokespersons, and a formula for a way out.

4. While in practice sanctions-dominated strategies have received little ongoing evaluation once they are imposed, more constant appraisal of their effects and their ability to meet their objectives would make them more effective policy tools.

5. According to the chapter by Johannes Reissner in this volume, the European policy of critical dialogue would have been most effective had it been launched directly after the end of the Iran-Iraq War. At that time, Iranian enthusiasm for reconstruction and a desire for international recognition after the death of Khomeini created real openings in the Iranian political system. The policy of critical dialogue was initiated several years later, in the early 1990s, in response to Europe's desire to forge a common foreign policy, with human rights as a centerpiece, as well as to its wish to maintain its newly positive trade balance with Iran. Similarly, the growing anxiety of American businesses over the increasing involvement of European firms in Vietnam was a substantial factor in determining the timing of normalization with Vietnam.

6. At the time, the United States already had wide-ranging unilateral sanctions in place against North Korea.

7. In contrast, others argue that this engagement policy hampered efforts of the Bush administration to cobble together this coalition as the former policy opened the administration to charges that it had appeased Saddam Hussein or contributed

to his militarization. See Zachary Karabell, "Backfire: U.S. Policy toward Iraq, 1988–2 August 1990," *Middle East Journal*, vol. 49 (Winter 1995), pp. 28–47.

8. David Cortright suggests that the use of (economic) incentives is only effective if there is a coherent regime in power. Cortright, *The Price of Peace*.

9. However, the extremely closed nature of the North Korean regime has posed some difficulties in evaluating progress along the lines of the Agreed Framework.

10. See Shireen Hunter, "Is Iranian Perestroika Possible without Fundamental Change?" *Washington Quarterly*, vol. 21 (Autumn 1998), pp. 23–41.

11. See Richard N. Haass, Kyung Won Kim, and Nicholas Platt, *Success or Sellout? The U.S.–North Korea Nuclear Accord* (New York: Council on Foreign Relations, 1995).

12. At the same time, these incentives also create vested interests in continued engagement among segments of the target country's population that benefit from the policy. This phenomenon can be seen in a number of the cases explored in this volume, perhaps most notably in China.

13. However, as discussed subsequently, these vested interests also created difficulties, as they pushed for the continuation of engagement even in the face of failure.

14. The important factor in distinguishing between modest or ambitious goals is the perception of the target state, not the opinion of the United States or Europe. In many cases, the target country's perception of what constitutes a threat to itself will differ substantially from how people in the West view a particular goal.

15. See Mitchell Reiss, *Bridled Ambition: Why Countries Constrain Their Nuclear Capabilities* (Washington, D.C.: Woodrow Wilson Center Press, 1995). As mentioned by Leon Sigal in his chapter in this volume, domestic political considerations also played a major role in these countries' decisions to disarm or refrain from developing nuclear weapons.

16. An exception to government-to-government cooperation is civil society engagement, which obviously circumvents the regime.

17. In each case, the end of the cold war changed the parameters for interaction with the United States considerably.

18. George, *Bridging the Gap*, discusses this phenomenon, both in the Iraqi case and in general.

19. See Haass, Kyung Won Kim, and Platt, *Success or Sellout?*, esp. p. 15.

20. As mentioned elsewhere, some of these forms of engagement—programs for democratization and institution building, for instance—actually work against the rule of recalcitrant regimes.

21. See Rolando H. Castañeda and George Plinio Montalván, "The Arcos Principles," in George Plinio Montalván, ed., *Cuba in Transition*, vol. 4 (Florida International University Press, 1994), pp. 360–67.

22. Although a less extreme example, the case of U.S. engagement with Iraq makes the same point. The policy of economic engagement generated vested interests in the perpetuation of this strategy, regardless of its political achievements or failures. The enthusiasm of these industrial and agricultural lobbies for maintaining engagement with Iraq may have contributed to Saddam Hussein's calculations that his questionable behavior would not lead to an immediate termination of engagement with America.

23. See the introductory chapter for references to relevant sanctions literature.

24. For instance, after the U.S. imposition of a unilateral ban on oil imports from Libya, the United States turned to North Sea oil to make up for sources lost under the embargo; in turn, the United Kingdom increased its imports from Libya by 350 percent over the first thirteen months of the American import ban.

25. See Robert S. Ross, "China," in Richard N. Haass, ed., *Economic Sanctions and American Diplomacy* (New York: Council on Foreign Relations Press, 1998), pp. 10–34.

26. Ibid.

27. See Richard Nuccio, "Cuba: A U.S. Perspective," in Richard N. Haass, ed., *Transatlantic Tensions: The United States, Europe, and Problem Countries* (Brookings, 1999), esp. pp. 14–17.

28. Canada recently scaled back political efforts to engage Cuba, citing lack of progress in the realm of human rights. Canada had sought closer political and commercial ties and had promised to lobby on behalf of Cuba for its admittance into regional organizations such as the Organization of American States in the hopes of securing political liberalization.

29. On June 30, 1999, Senator Christopher Dodd, a longtime advocate of stabilizing relations with Cuba, offered an amendment to the Foreign Operations bill that would have eased all travel restrictions to Cuba; however, it was voted down by a vote of 55 to 43.

30. The Arcos principles, formulated for investment in Cuba, could offer a starting template. See Castañeda and Montalván, "The Arcos Principles."

31. For example, in a speech marking the twentieth anniversary of the seizure of the American Embassy in Tehran, Ayatollah Ali Khamenei warned Iranian reformers that any efforts to seek closer ties to the United States would be perceived as un-Islamic and treasonable. See John F. Burns, "Ayatollah Rebukes Iran Liberals and U.S.," *New York Times*, November 4, 1999, p. A10.

32. See John Lancaster, "U.S.: Iran's Terrorism Role Grows; Increased Aid Seen as Effort to Derail Mideast Peace Bid," *Washington Post*, December 4, 1999, p. A1.

33. Of course, high oil prices mean a foreign-exchange boon to Iran that far outweighs the benefits of changes in the U.S. sanctions regime. However, as oil prices during 1999–2000 demonstrate, volatility in the price of oil means that such boons cannot be guaranteed to address long-term problems or shortages of foreign exchange.

34. Madeleine K. Albright, "American-Iranian Relations," speech to the American-Iranian Council, Washington, D.C., March 17, 2000 (www.secretary.state.gov/www/statements/2000/000317.html [April 2000]).

35. In April 1999, President Clinton issued an executive order that enabled American companies to export agricultural commodities and medical supplies to Iran, Sudan, and Libya. In Iran, this move was seen as more of an effort to appease U.S. commercial interests than as an effort to initiate a process of reconciliation with Tehran.

36. As long as Iran continues to be designated by the U.S. government as a state sponsor of terrorism, Washington will be obligated to vote against international fi-

nancial institutions–lending to Iran. However, in the absence of intense American lobbying, American opposition is insufficient to block loans to Iran. Although in the past, the United States threatened to cut back on its payments to the World Bank if it approved loans for Iran, it seems unlikely Washington will continue this hardline approach.

37. Assistant Secretary of State Martin Indyk concluded his speech to the Asia Society in October 1999 by saying: "We believe the best way to achieve these changes is through a parallel process that can only be developed through an authoritative government-to-government dialogue, without preconditions. We should move beyond the stage of gestures and symbols. Indeed, it is time for the United States of America and the Islamic Republic of Iran to engage each other as two great nations: face-to-face, and on the basis of equality and mutual respect. When the Government of Iran is ready to engage, we will be too." Martin Indyk, "Iran and the United States: Prospects for a New Relationship," Speech to the Asia Society, Washington, D.C., October 14, 1999 (www.state.gov/www/policy_remarks/1999/991014_indyk_iran.html ([April 2000]).

38. Some of these actions are currently banned as long as Iran remains on America's list of state sponsors of terrorism—or until changes are made that allow policymakers to make a distinction between the designation of a sponsor of terrorism and the penalties that such a designation brings today.

39. For an expansive discussion of road maps in the context of Iran, see Geoffrey Kemp, *America and Iran: Road Maps and Realism* (Washington, D.C.: The Nixon Center, 1998).

40. For discussion of the problematic "rogue" concept, see Robert S. Litwak, *Rogue States and U.S. Foreign Policy: Containment after the Cold War* (Washington, D.C.: Woodrow Wilson Center Press, 2000), Meghan L. O'Sullivan, "Rogue States: Les Dilemmes de la politique américaine," *Politique Etrangère*, no. 1/2000 (Spring 2000), pp. 67–80.

41. See Haass, *Transatlantic Tensions*.

42. While the strength of American agricultural interests and the severity of the recent American farm crisis in large part explains the April 1999 easing of sanctions on agricultural goods, humanitarian concerns also played a role in modifying the policy. As rightly articulated both by figures in the administration and Congress, the purchase of agricultural goods from America does not help a country obtain weapons of mass destruction or support terrorism; rather, such a sale addresses the daily humanitarian needs of the citizens of that country.

43. Technically, the ban is not on Americans traveling to Libya (which would be unconstitutional), but a ban on the use of U.S. passports or the expenditure of U.S. currency in traveling to Libya. See Jeffery P. Bialos and Kenneth I. Juster, "The Libyan Sanctions: A Rational Response to State-Sponsored Terrorism?" *Virginia Journal of International Law*, vol. 26 (1986), pp. 829–31. The possibilities for engaging Libya today are more constricted than those for engaging Vietnam in the last decade, as Libya is currently on the U.S. State Department's list of state supporters of terrorism, whereas Vietnam was not during the process of normalization.

44. William J. Perry, *Review of United States Policy toward North Korea: Findings and Recommendations* (Department of State, October 1999) (www.state.gov/www/regions/eap/991012_northkorea_rpt.html [February 2000]).

45. Other indications are the October 1999 hearings by the House International Relations Committee, "U.S. Policy toward North Korea: Misuse of U.S. Aid to North Korea," and frequent passionate statements on how North Korea is blackmailing America or on how U.S. policy toward North Korea amounts to appeasement. See North Korea Advisory Group, *Report to the Speaker, U.S. House of Representatives,* House Committee on International Relations, 106 Cong. 1 sess. (November 1999) (www.house.gov/international_relations/nkag/report.htm [February 2000]).

46. See Richard S. Soll, "The Nunn-Lugar Program: Separating Fiction from Fact," *C4I News,* January 15, 1998, p. 1.

47. The criticism of these types of programs—most recently voiced in a report by the Department of Energy—points more to the need to monitor their implementation closely than to fundamental flaws in their conceptualization. See Office of Inspector General, *Nuclear Material Protection, Control, and Accounting Program* (U.S. Department of Energy, September 1999) (www.ig.doc.gov/pdf/ig0452.pdf [February 2000]).

48. Some argue that the provision of aid to Syria, or the organization of an international consortium to provide aid, is the greatest carrot at America's disposal. However, the removal of Syria from the terrorism list—and hence, the removal of the prohibition on aid to Syria—must legally precede any aid commitments.

Contributors

PAULINE H. BAKER is president of the Fund for Peace, a non-profit organization based in Washington, D.C. that is dedicated to preventing war and alleviating the conditions that cause war. Dr. Baker also is an adjunct professor in the Graduate School of Foreign Service at Georgetown University. Dr. Baker's latest publications are *An Analytical Model of Internal Conflict and State Collapse* (Fund for Peace, 1998) and *South Africa and the World Economy in the 1990s* (Brookings, 1993).

FREDERICK Z. BROWN is the associate director of the Southeast Asia Studies Program at the Paul H. Nitze School of Advanced International Studies of the Johns Hopkins University. A former Department of State foreign service officer who served in France, Thailand, the Soviet Union, Vietnam, and Cyprus, Mr. Brown was a professional staff member for East Asia and the Pacific on the U.S. Senate Foreign Relations Committee, 1984–87. He is the author of *Second Chance: The United States and Indochina in the 1990s* (Council on Foreign Relations, 1989).

JAMES M. GOLDGEIER is an associate professor of political science and international affairs at George Washington University, where he serves as acting director of the Institute for European,

Russian, and Eurasian Studies. He is also a nonresident senior fellow in the Foreign Policy Studies Program at the Brookings Institution. Dr. Goldgeier is the author of *Not Whether But When: The U.S. Decision to Enlarge NATO* (Brookings, 1999) and *Leadership Style and Soviet Foreign Policy* (Johns Hopkins University Press, 1994).

RICHARD N. HAASS, formerly a senior aide to President George Bush, is now vice president and director of the Foreign Policy Studies Program at the Brookings Institution. Dr. Haass's previous books include *Intervention: The Use of American Military Force in the Post Cold War World* (Brookings, 1999), *Economic Sanctions and American Diplomacy* (Council on Foreign Relations, 1998), *The Reluctant Sheriff: The United States after the Cold War* (Council on Foreign Relations, 1997), and *Conflicts Unending: The United States and Regional Disputes* (Yale University Press, 1990).

KENNETH I. JUSTER is a senior partner in the Washington, D.C. office of the law firm Arnold and Porter, where he practices international law and general litigation. He served as the counselor (acting) of the U.S. Department of State from 1992 to 1993 and as the deputy and senior adviser to the deputy secretary of state from 1989 to 1992. Mr. Juster is the co-author of *Making Economic Policy: An Assessment of the National Economic Council* (Brookings, 1997).

MEGHAN L. O'SULLIVAN is a fellow in the Foreign Policy Studies Program at the Brookings Institution, where she is working on a forthcoming study on economic sanctions. Dr. O'Sullivan has consulted for the World Bank, served in the American Embassy in Sri Lanka, and worked on foreign affairs in the office of Senator Daniel Patrick Moynihan.

JOHANNES REISSNER is a research assistant at the Research Institute for International Affairs (Stiftung Wissenschaft und Politik–SWP) in Ebenhausen, Germany. Previously, Dr. Reissner was a research assistant at the University of Tübingen. In 1995, he served as an observer at the Organization for Security and Cooperation in Europe mission in Dushanbe, Tajikistan. Among his publications is "Europe, the United States, and the Persian Gulf," in Robert D. Blackwill and Michael Stürmer, eds., *Allies Divided: Transatlantic Policies for the Greater Middle East* (MIT Press, 1997).

LEON V. SIGAL is currently completing a study of cooperation with Russia at the Social Science Research Council in New York. An adjunct professor at

Columbia University's School of International and Public Affairs and at Princeton University's Woodrow Wilson School, he was a member of the editorial board of the *New York Times* from 1989 until 1995. Dr. Sigal's latest book is *Disarming Strangers: Nuclear Diplomacy with North Korea* (Princeton University Press, 1998).

ROBERT L. SUETTINGER is a visiting fellow in the Foreign Policy Studies Program at the Brookings Institution, where he is working on a book-length comparative study of the domestic politics of U.S.-China relations since 1989. A retired intelligence officer, he served as national intelligence officer for East Asia on the National Intelligence Council and as director of analysis for East Asia and the Pacific in the State Department Bureau of Intelligence and Research. From 1994 until 1997, he was director of Asian affairs on the staff of the National Security Council.

Index

Printed in the United States
153307LV00006B/23/A

9 780815 733553